STL Tutorial and Reference Guide

Addison-Wesley Professional Computing Series

Brian W. Kernighan, Consulting Editor

Ken Arnold/John Peyton, *A C User's Guide to ANSI C*

Tom Cargill, *C++ Programming Style*

William R. Cheswick/Steven M. Bellovin, *Firewalls and Internet Security: Repelling the Wily Hacker*

David A. Curry, *UNIX® System Security: A Guide for Users and System Administrators*

Erich Gamma/Richard Helm/Ralph Johnson/John Vlissides, *Design Patterns: Elements of Reusable Object-Oriented Software*

David R. Hanson, *C Interfaces and Implementations: Techniques for Creating Reusable Software*

John Lakos, *Large-Scale C++ Software Design*

Scott Meyers, *Effective C++: 50 Specific Ways to Improve Your Programs and Designs*

Scott Meyers, *More Effective C++: 35 New Ways to Improve Your Programs and Designs*

Robert B. Murray, *C++ Strategies and Tactics*

David R. Musser/Atul Saini, *STL Tutorial and Reference Guide: C++ Programming with the Standard Template Library*

John K. Ousterhout, *Tcl and the Tk Toolkit*

Craig Partridge, *Gigabit Networking*

J. Stephen Pendergrast Jr., *Desktop KornShell Graphical Programming*

Radia Perlman, *Interconnections: Bridges and Routers*

David M. Piscitello/A. Lyman Chapin, *Open Systems Networking: TCP/IP and OSI*

Stephen A. Rago, *UNIX® System V Network Programming*

Curt Schimmel, *UNIX® Systems for Modern Architectures: Symmetric Multiprocessing and Caching for Kernel Programmers*

W. Richard Stevens, *Advanced Programming in the UNIX® Environment*

W. Richard Stevens, *TCP/IP Illustrated, Volume 1: The Protocols*

W. Richard Stevens, *TCP/IP Illustrated, Volume 3: TCP for Transactions, HTTP, NNTP, and the UNIX Domain Protocols*

Gary R. Wright/W. Richard Stevens, *TCP/IP Illustrated, Volume 2: The Implementation*

STL Tutorial and Reference Guide

C++ Programming with the Standard Template Library

David R. Musser
Atul Saini

Foreword by Alexander Stepanov

ADDISON-WESLEY
An imprint of Addison Wesley Longman, Inc.
Reading, Massachusetts • Harlow, England • Menlo Park, California
Berkeley, California • Don Mills, Ontario • Sydney
Bonn • Amsterdam • Tokyo • Mexico City

Many of the designations used by manufacturers and sellers to distinguish their products are claimed as trademarks. Where those designations appear in this book and Addison-Wesley was aware of a trademark claim, the designations have been printed in initial caps or all caps.

The authors and publishers have taken care in the preparation of this book, but make no expressed or implied warranty of any kind and assume no responsibility for errors or omissions. No liability is assumed for incidental or consequential damages in connection with or arising out of the use of the information or programs contained herein.

The publisher offers discounts on this book when ordered in quantity for special sales. For more information, please contact:

Corporate & Professional Publishing Group
Addison-Wesley Publishing Company
One Jacob Way
Reading, Massachusetts 01867

Library of Congress Cataloging-in-Publication Data

Musser, David R.
    STL tutorial & reference guide : C++ programming with the standard template library/ David R. Musser, Atul Saini.
        p.   cm. -- (Addison-Wesley professional computing series)
    Includes bibliographical references and index.
    ISBN 0-201-63398-1 (alk. paper)
    1. C++ (Computer program language)   I. Saini, Atul, 1963-   .
II. Title.   III. Series.
QA76.73.C153M87   1996
005.13'3--dc20   95-45004
                                                                       CIP

Text printed on recycled and acid-free paper

ISBN 0-201-63398-1
3 4 5 6 7 8 9 10 11-MA-99989796
Third printing, October 1996

To Paul, Eric, and Martha
—David R. Musser

For Ayrton Senna (1960-1994)
—Atul Saini

CHAPTER 5

Generic Algorithms **71**

CHAPTER 6

Sequence Containers **117**

CHAPTER 7

Sorted Associative Containers **151**

CHAPTER 20

*Generic Algorithm
Reference Guide* 323

CHAPTER 21   *Function Object and Function Adaptor Reference Guide*   361

CHAPTER 22   *Allocator Reference Guide*   367

Foreword

What is STL? STL, or the Standard Template Library, is a general-purpose library of generic algorithms and data structures. It makes a programmer more productive in two ways: first, it contains a lot of different components that can be plugged together and used in an application, and more importantly, it provides a framework into which different programming problems can be decomposed.

The framework defined by STL is quite simple: two of its most fundamental dimensions are algorithms and data structures. The reason that data structures and algorithms can work together seamlessly is, paradoxically enough, the fact that they do not know anything about each other. Algorithms are written in terms of iterator categories: abstract data-accessing methods. To enable different algorithms to work in terms of these conceptual categories, STL establishes rigid rules that govern the behavior of iterators. For example, if any two iterators are equal then the results of dereferencing them must be equal. It is only because in STL all such rules are stated explicitly that it is possible to write code that knows nothing about a particular implementation of a data structure.

While it is my experience that using STL can dramatically improve programming productivity, such an improvement is possible only if a programmer is fully cognizant of the structure of the library and is familiar with a style of programming that it advocates. How can a programmer learn this style? The only way is to use it and extend it. To do this, however, one needs a place to start. This book is such a place.

The authors bring special qualifications to the writing of this book. Dave Musser has been doing research that led to STL for over fifteen years. Quoting from the original STL manual: "Dave Musser . . . contributed to all aspects of the STL work: design of the overall structure, semantic requirements, algorithm design, complexity analysis, and performance measurements." Atul Saini was the first person to recognize the commercial potential of STL and committed his company to selling its production version even before it was accepted by the C++ standards committee.

I hope that this book's publication will help programmers enjoy using STL as much as I do.

Alexander Stepanov
October 1995

Preface

In 1968 Doug McIlroy presented his famous paper, "Mass Produced Software Components" (Ref. 6). Now, more than a quarter of a century later, we still have not fully realized his vision of standard libraries of reusable components (which today are also known as "software building blocks" or "software ICs"). In some areas such as numerical and statistical computation, there is a long tradition of heavy use of standard libraries, rather than writing source code entirely from scratch, but in many other areas, standardization hasn't occurred. Even in the area of fundamental data structures and data-processing algorithms, where there is perhaps the greatest potential benefit from component standardization and wide-spread component use, no set of components has emerged and been embraced by large numbers of programmers or software development managers.

In the absence of a standard set of such data structure and algorithm components, programmers have been forced either to program everything from scratch or to adopt one of several commercial packages. While writing everything from scratch often gives programmers a sense of control, it is also a source of frustration, since there is rarely time to implement the best techniques, even assuming they are already known to the programmer. And the available commercial libraries have suffered from several drawbacks. In the C++ realm, for example, the problems include

- *Incompatibility:* The interfaces of classes supplied by various vendors are invariably different, making it difficult to write portable code.

- *Inefficiency:* The implementations of most commercially available components libraries typically involve complex class hierarchies with extensive use of inheritance and virtual functions. As a result, using these components results in significantly less-efficient programs than could be written in C.

- *Unwieldy interfaces:* In most component libraries, all operations to be performed on a data structure are part of the interface of the class defining it. Besides making it difficult for programmers to add new operations without recompiling the code, this makes the interfaces needlessly large.

These problems have been widely recognized for many years, but few solutions have been proposed and none has been widely embraced—not, that is, until now. The *Standard Template Library* is both a remarkable advance in programming methodology *and* a fully accepted part of the C++ Standard Library. It does not seem overly optimistic to expect that STL components will become some of the most widely used software in existence. The reasons are fivefold:

- C++ is becoming one of the most widely used programming languages (which is in large part due to the support it provides for building and using component libraries).

- Since STL has been incorporated into the ANSI/ISO standard for C++ and its libraries, compiler vendors are making it part of their standard distributions.

- All components in STL are *generic*, meaning that they are adaptable (by language-supported, compile-time techniques) to many different uses.

- The generality of STL components has been achieved without sacrificing efficiency.

- The design of STL components as fine-grained, interchangeable building blocks makes them a suitable basis for further development of components for specialized areas such as databases, user interfaces, and so forth.

Virtually all C++ programmers know that the origin of this language is due to one person, Bjarne Stroustrup, who began thinking of how to extend the C language to support definition of classes and objects as early as 1979. So too it is the case that the architecture of STL is largely the creation of one person, Alexander Stepanov.

It is interesting that it was also in 1979, at about the same time as Stroustrup's initial research, that Alex began working out his initial ideas of generic programming and exploring their potential for revolutionizing software development. Although one of this book's authors (D.R.M.) had developed and advocated some aspects of generic programming as early as 1971, it was limited to a rather specialized area of software development (computer algebra). It was Alex who recognized the full potential for generic programming and persuaded his then-colleagues at General Electric Research and Development (including, primarily, D.R.M. and Deepak Kapur) that generic programming should be pursued as a comprehensive basis for software development. But at that time there was no real support in any programming language for generic programming. The first major language to provide such support was Ada, with its generic units feature, and by 1987 Alex and D.R.M. had developed and published an Ada library for list processing that embodied the results of much of their research on generic programming. However, Ada had not achieved much acceptance outside of the defense industry, and C++ seemed like a better bet for both becoming widely used and providing good support for generic programming, even though the language was relatively immature (it did not even have templates, which were added only later). Another reason for turning to C++, which Alex recognized early on, was that the C/C++ model of computation, which allows very flexible access to storage (via pointers), is crucial to achieving generality without losing efficiency.

Still, much research and experimentation were needed, not just to develop individual components, but more importantly to develop an overall architecture for a component library based on generic programming. First at AT&T Bell Laboratories and later at Hewlett-Packard Research Labs, Alex experimented with many architectural and algorithm formulations, first in C and later in C++. D.R.M. collaborated in this research, and in 1992 Meng Lee joined Alex's project at HP and became a major contributor.

This work likely would have continued for some time just as a research project, or at best would have resulted in an HP-proprietary library, if Andrew Koenig of Bell Labs had not become aware of the work and asked Alex to present the main ideas at a November 1993 meeting of the ANSI/ISO committee for C++ standardization.[1] The committee's response was overwhelmingly favorable and led to a request from Koenig for a formal proposal in time for the March 1994 meeting. Despite the tremendous time-pressure, Alex and Meng were able to produce a draft proposal that received preliminary approval at that meeting.

The committee had several requests for changes and extensions (some of them major), and a small group of committee members met with Alex and Meng to help work out the details. The requirements for the most significant extension (associative containers) had to be shown to be consistent by fully implementing them, a task Alex delegated to D.R.M. It would have been quite easy for the whole enterprise to spin out of control at this point, but again Alex and Meng met the challenge and produced a proposal that received final approval at the July 1994 ANSI/ISO committee meeting. (Additional details of this history can be found in an interview Alex gave in the March 1995 issue of *Dr. Dobbs Journal*.)

Subsequently, the Stepanov and Lee document (Ref. 10) has been incorporated almost intact into the ANSI/ISO C++ draft standard (Ref. 1, parts of clauses 17 through 27). It also has influenced other parts of the C++ Standard Library, such as the string facilities, and some of the previously adopted standards in those areas have been revised accordingly.

In spite of STL's success with the committee, there remained the question of how STL would make its way into actual availability and use. With the STL requirements part of the publicly available draft standard, compiler vendors and independent software library vendors could of course develop their own implementations and market them as separate products or as selling points for their other wares. One of this book's authors (A.S.) was among the first to recog-

---

1. ANSI is the American National Standards Institute and ISO is the International Standards Organization. A joint committee of the two organizations produced the X3J16 document, a standard for both C++ and its libraries. Andrew Koenig served as editor of X3J16.

nize the commercial potential and began exploring it as a line of business for his company, Modena Software Incorporated, even before STL had been fully accepted by the committee.

The prospects for early widespread dissemination of STL were considerably improved with Hewlett-Packard's decision to make its implementation freely available on the Internet in August 1994. This implementation, developed by Stepanov, Lee, and D.R.M. during the standardization process, is the basis of Modena's STL++ product and several other vendors' offerings; it is referred to in this book as the "HP reference implementation."

The Stepanov and Lee document, while precise and complete, was aimed more at the committee than at the wide audience of C++ programmers. Along with modifying the HP reference implementation to work well with several compilers and providing several additional classes, Modena developed the *STL++ Manual*, the first comprehensive user-level documentation of STL. (D.R.M. served as an advisor to Modena and was the principal author of the Tutorial section of the *STL++ Manual*.) We recognized, though, that an even more comprehensive treatment of STL was needed, one that would have better and more complete coverage of all aspects of the library. With much encouragement and assistance from our editor, Mike Hendrickson, we have attempted to meet this goal with the present book.

With the publication of this book, Modena and Addison-Wesley are also making available on the Internet all of the source code for examples used in this book, so that readers who want to try them do not have to type them. Instructions for finding and retrieving all of this material can be found in Appendix B.

We do not want to give the impression that we believe STL is the solution to all programming problems. There are potentially still some bumps in the road to its acceptance by the broad programming community, such as compiler weaknesses and the usual opportunities for misunderstanding of a radically new approach. We hope this book will make the road for STL itself as smooth as possible, but of course there are still many fundamental data structures and algorithms that are not covered. Beyond this realm, there are many more specialized areas of computation that also cry out for component standardization. References 3 and 7 discuss the larger view in some detail. We hope that among our readers will be some who have the vision and resources to continue in the direction that STL has opened up, carrying on its ideas to other component libraries, not only in C++ but also in other programming languages.

Although in the larger scheme of things it is just a small step toward realizing McIlroy's original vision (Ref. 6), STL is a remarkable achievement and has the potential for revolutionizing the way a large number of people program. We hope this book helps you become a full participant in that revolution.

We gratefully acknowledge the encouragement and assistance of many people. First and foremost, Alex Stepanov and Meng Lee offered continuous encouragement and were always available to help straighten out any misconceptions we had about the design of the library. Invaluable assistance with code development and testing was provided by several Modena staff members, including Atul Gupta, Kolachala Kalyan, and Narasimhan Rampalli. Several reviewers of earlier drafts gave us much valuable feedback and helped us find ways to present the most crucial ideas more clearly. They include Mike Ballantyne, Tom Cargill, Edgar Chrisostomo, Brian Kernighan, Scott Meyers, Larry Podmolik, Kathy Stark, Steve Vinoski, and John Vlissides. Others who also made valuable suggestions include Dan Benanav, Bob Cook, Bob Ingalls, Nathan Schimke, Kedar Tupil, and Rick Wilhelm. We are also greatly indebted to the following people who brought to our attention errors in previous printings and suggested other improvements: Franz-Dieter Berger, Joseph Bergin, David C. Browne, Bart De Meyere, Stephen D. Evans, Mike Gursky, Roger House, Rex Jaeschke, Russell Johnston, Mehdi Jazayeri, Bruce Jolliffe, Cathy Kimmel Joly, Alexander Konstantinou, Gabor Liptak, Jonathan Miller, John I. Moore, Jr., Saul J. Rosenberg, Andrew Savige, Shankar N. Swamy, Chris Uzdavinis, Steve Vinoski, and Pavel P. Zeldin. Finally, we thank the team at Addison-Wesley for their expert editorial and production assistance: Kim Dawley, Katie Duffy, Rosa Gonzalez, Mike Hendrickson, Simone Payment, Avanda Peters, John Wait, and Pamela Yee.

D.R.M.
Loudonville, NY

A.S.
Los Gatos, CA

PART I A Tutorial Introduction to STL

In Part I, we introduce the key ideas and principles of the Standard Template Library and describe most of its components. In most cases the components are illustrated with small example programs.

CHAPTER 1   *Introduction*

The Standard Template Library—STL—provides a set of C++ container classes and template algorithms designed to work together to produce a wide range of useful functionality. Though only a small number of container classes are provided, they include the most widely useful containers, such as vectors, lists, sets, and maps. The template algorithm components include a broad range of fundamental algorithms for the most common kinds of data manipulations, such as searching, sorting, and merging.

The critical difference between STL and all other C++ container class libraries is that STL algorithms are *generic*: every algorithm works on a variety of containers, *including built-in types,* and many work on *all* containers. In Part I of this book we look at the why and how of generic algorithms and other key concepts that give STL many advantages over other software libraries. One of the most important concepts of STL is the way generic algorithms are defined in terms of *iterators,* which generalize C/C++ pointers, together with the way different kinds of iterators are defined for traversing the different kinds of containers. Besides containers, generic algorithms, and iterators, STL also provides *function objects,* which generalize ordinary C/C++ functions and allow other components to be efficiently adapted to a variety of tasks. The library also includes various other kinds of *adaptors,* for changing the interfaces of containers, iterators, or function objects, and *allocators,* for controlling storage management. All of these components are discussed in the STL overview in Chapter 2 and in more detail in later chapters of Part I.

Just reading about STL may be interesting, but to become really proficient in *using* the library, you'll have to get some actual programming experience with it. Our descriptions in Part I include many small examples that show how individual components work, and Part II presents and explains a series of more substantial programs. Though still small, these examples perform some nontrivial and useful tasks, displaying some of the power that a good software library makes available. Part III contains a complete reference guide to the library.

STL is only one part of a larger software library, the C++ (Draft) Standard Library approved by the ANSI/ISO C++ committee in its X3J16 report (Ref. 1).[1] Nevertheless, STL remains a coherent framework of fine-grained, interchangeable components that deserve treatment separate from the rest of the C++ (Draft) Standard Library. In this book we attempt to provide a complete and precise *user-level* description of STL. (For a thorough description of how STL is implemented, see Ref. 10.)

1.1 Who Should Read This Book

If you are not already familiar with any other software libraries, that shouldn't stop you from reading this book. Although comparisons to other libraries are made in a few places, the main points should be understandable without that background. All that's assumed is that you have some experience with the major C++ concepts: functions, classes, objects, pointers, templates, and stream input/output. Many books on C++ provide the needed background; one we particularly recommend is Stan Lippman's *C++ Primer*. Crucial features of templates with which some readers might not be familiar (and which might not be covered yet in some books, as these features have only recently been added to the draft language standard) are described in Section 1.3.

1.2 What Generic Programming Is and Why It's Important

STL is the embodiment of years of research on generic programming. The purpose of this research has been to explore methods of developing and organizing libraries of generic—or reusable—software components. Here the meaning of "reusable" is, roughly, "widely adaptable, but still efficient," where the adaptation is done by preprocessor or programming-language mechanisms rather than manual text editing. There has been a substantial amount of other work in software reuse (other terms often used in this connection are "software building blocks" or "software ICs"), but two distinguishing characteristics of the work that led to STL are the high degree of *adaptability* and *efficiency* of the components.

The essential ideas of the generic component construction approach are shown in the depiction in **Figure 1-1** of library components and the way they "plug together." On the right are components called *generic algorithms*, for operations such as sequence merging, sorting, copying, etc. But these algorithms are not self-contained; they are written in terms of *container access* operations, which are assumed to be provided externally. Providing these container access operations is the role of the components called *iterators* (which are depicted in **Figure 1-1** as "ribbon cables"). Each kind of iterator defines container access operations for a particular data representation, such as a linked-list representation of sequences, or an array representation.

---

1. See the Preface for more information on the background of STL and how it came to be included in the C++ (Draft) Standard.

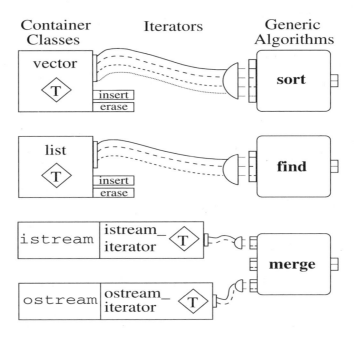

FIGURE 1-1. Connecting Containers and Algorithms with Iterators.

For this fine-grained component approach to work well, there must be a certain minimal level of support from the base programming language. Fortunately, C++ provides such support, especially with its *template* mechanism. Programmers who want to use one of the generic algorithms need only select the algorithm and the container with which it is to be used. The C++ compiler takes care of the final step of plugging together the algorithm, which is expressed as a template function, with the iterators, which are classes that are associated with the container class.

Programmers can write their own iterator class definitions, perhaps in terms of some particular list node structure already in use in existing code. An important point is that it's generally a lot easier to program such an iterator definition than it would be to recode all the generic algorithms to work with that existing data structure.

Not every generic algorithm and iterator pair can be plugged together; you could say that they must be "plug-compatible." (The enforcement of this in C++ is by means of the normal type-checking C++ compilers do when templates are instantiated. Attempts to combine incompatible components result in compile-time errors.) While it would be *possible* to make all pairs interface together, it turns out to be better not to, because some algorithms are efficient only when using a particular data representation. For example, a sort algorithm may be efficient only for a random access data structure like an array, not for a linked list. In such a case the library should provide a separate algorithm that is suitable for use with lists.

The software library designs that have resulted from this generic programming approach are markedly different from other software libraries:

- The precisely-organized, interchangeable building blocks that result from this approach permit many more useful combinations than are possible with more traditional component designs.

- The design is also a suitable basis for further development of components for specialized areas such as databases, user interfaces, and so on.

- By employing compile-time mechanisms and paying due regard to algorithm issues, component generality can be achieved without sacrificing efficiency. This is in sharp contrast to the inefficiencies often introduced by other C++ library structures involving complex inheritance hierarchies and extensive use of virtual functions.

The bottom-line result of these differences is that generic components are far more *useful* to programmers, and therefore far more likely to be *used,* in preference to programming every algorithmic or data structure operation from scratch.

These are tall promises, and you may well be skeptical that STL, or any library, can fully live up to them. As you read on, though, and start putting this remarkable library to use in your own programming, we believe you will agree that STL truly does fulfill the promise of generic programming.

1.3   *How C++ Templates Enable Generic Programming*

Adaptability of components is essential to generic programming, so now let's look at how C++ templates enable it. There are two kinds of templates in C++: *template classes* and *template functions.*

1.3.1   Template Classes

Template classes have many uses, but the most obvious one is to provide adaptable storage containers. To take a very simple example, suppose we want to create objects that can store two values, an integer and a character. For this purpose we could define

```
class pair_int_char {
 public:
   int first;
```

```
  char second;
  pair_int_char(int x, char y) : first(x), second(y) { }
};
```

We could then write, for example,

```
pair_int_char pair1(13, 'a');
cout << pair1.first << endl;
cout << pair1.second << endl;
```

If we also want objects that can store, say, a boolean value and a double-precision floating-point number, we could define[2]

```
class pair_bool_double {
 public:
   bool first;
   double second;
   pair_bool_double(bool x, double y) : first(x), second(y){}
};
```

and write, for example,

```
pair_bool_double pair2(true, 0.1);
cout << pair2.first << endl;
cout << pair2.second << endl;
```

The same could be repeated for any of the other infinitely many pairs of types, but a template class permits them all to be expressed with a single definition:

```
template <class T1, class T2>
class pair {
 public:
   T1 first;
   T2 second;
```

---

2. Type `bool` is defined in (Draft) Standard C++ as having two values, `true` and `false`. If your compiler does not support type `bool`, the following definitions can be used instead:

```
#define bool int
#define true 1
#define false 0
```

In this book we assume these definitions are contained in a header file named `<bool.h>`.

```
    pair(T1 x, T2 y)  :  first(x), second(y) { }
};
```

Here we've written the class definition in terms of two arbitrary type names, T1 and T2, which are *type parameters*. The names are introduced into the definition as type parameters by the clause

```
template <class T1, class T2>
```

which means that we can substitute *actual types* for T1 and T2 to obtain a particular *instance* of the pair template class. For example, writing

```
pair<int, char> pair3(13, 'a');
pair<bool, double> pair4(true, 0.1);
```

declares pair3 and pair4 with structure equivalent to pair1 and pair2, respectively. But now we can also use pair in countless other ways with other combinations of actual types, such as

```
pair<double, long> pair5(3.1415, 999);
pair<bool, bool> pair6(false, true);
```

Types defined by other classes can be used as the actual types; for instance,

```
pair<pair_int_char, float> pair7(pair1, 1.23);
```

or, equivalently,

```
pair<pair<int, char>, float> pair8(pair3, 1.23);
```

As illustrated here, we can use types produced as template class instances anywhere that ordinary types can be used.

   The template class definition of pair is a very simple example of a generic container class since it is adaptable to many different uses. However, there is usually more to making an ordinary class into a generic one (in the sense of being truly useful in the widest range of applications) than just adding the template keyword and type parameter list. Some modifications may be necessary to ensure that the resulting instances are as efficient as ones defined by ordinary means, no matter what actual types are substituted. Even in the case of a template class definition as simple as pair, an improvement can be made. In defining the template class, we wrote the constructor definition a little too simply:

```
    pair(T1 x, T2 y);
```

The problem with this is that x and y are passed *by value*, which means that if they are large objects, an expensive extra copy will be made when the constructor is called. Instead, x and y should be passed as *constant reference parameters*, so that only an address is passed. And this is, in fact, the way that `pair` is defined as an STL component:

```
template <class T1, class T2>
class pair {
 public:
   T1 first;
   T2 second;
   pair(const T1& x, const T2& y) : first(x), second(y) { }
};
```

In the case of more-complex class definitions, there are usually many other factors involved in making them widely adaptable and efficient. In this book we will not examine in depth the way STL is implemented, but STL's originators gave careful consideration to maintaining efficiency while making components general.

1.3.2   Template Functions

Template functions can be used to define generic algorithms. A simple example is a function for computing the maximum of two integers:

```
int intmax(int x, int y)
{
   return x < y ? y : x;
}
```

This can be used only to compute the maximum of two `int`s, but we can easily generalize it by making it a template function:

```
template <class T>
T max(T x, T y)
{
   return x < y ? y : x;
}
```

A big difference from template classes is that you do not have to tell the compiler which types you are using; the compiler is able to infer them from the types of the arguments.

```
int u = 3, v = 4;
```

```
double d = 4.7;
cout << max(u, v) << endl;    // type int is inferred
cout << max(d, 9.3) << endl; // type double is inferred
cout << max(u, d) << endl;    // error: types do not match
```

The compiler requires that values of the same type be passed for x and y since the same template type parameter, T, is used for both in the declaration. It also requires there to be a definition of the < operator on parameter lists of the form (T, T). For example, recalling one of the uses of the pair template class definitions given in the previous section

```
pair<double, long> pair5(3.1415, 999);
```

the following will not compile because there is no definition of operator< on pair<double, long> objects:

```
max(pair5, pair5);
```

But it *would* compile if we first defined some meaning for operator< on objects of this type, such as

```
bool operator<(const pair<double, long>& x,
               const pair<double, long>& y)
  // Compare x and y on their first members:
{
  return x.first < y.first;
}
```

The way the compiler is able to infer types and match up operator or function calls with the proper overloaded definitions makes template functions an extremely useful feature for generic programming. We'll see more evidence of this later, especially in Section 2.2 when we examine how STL generic algorithms are defined by template functions.

Before we leave the max example, though, we should note that the definition of this template function can be improved just as we discussed for the constructor in the pair template class definition, by using constant reference parameters:

```
template <class T>
const T& max(const T& x, const T& y) {
  return x < y ? y : x;
}
```

This is the definition used in STL.

1.3.3   Template Member Functions

In ordinary class definitions or template class definitions, member functions may have template parameters (in addition to any template parameters at the class level). This relatively new C++ feature is used in the template classes defining STL containers. For example, each STL container class has an `insert` member function that has a template parameter to specify the type of iterators to be used:

```
template <class T>
class vector {
  ...
  template <class Iterator>
  insert(iterator position, Iterator first, Iterator last);
  ...
};
```

As we'll see in Section 6.1, this `insert` member function can be used to insert elements copied from some other container (such as a `list`), using iterators supplied by the other container. Defining such a function as a template member function, with the iterator type as a template parameter, makes it much more useful than if the iterator type were a fixed type.

Unfortunately though, at the time of this writing, most C++ compilers have yet to support template member functions. Versions of STL for such compilers thus can only provide a modified and more limited form of member functions such as `insert`. In Chapter 6 we discuss this limitation and the alternatives provided.

1.3.4   Default Template Parameters

Another relatively new C++ template feature is default template parameters. For example, the actual form of the STL `vector` template class definition is

```
template <class T, class Allocator = allocator>
class vector {
  ...
};
```

The second template parameter, `Allocator`, has a default value, given by `allocator`. All STL container classes use storage management facilities as provided by `Allocator`, and `allocator` is a type (defined by a class) that provides a standard form of these facilities. Since `Allocator` has a default value, we do not have to pass any allocator when we create an instance of `vector`; that is, `vector<int>` is equivalent to `vector<int, allocator>`.

Again, however, most C++ compilers do not support default template parameters yet. As a work-around, present implementations of STL may omit the

`Allocator` parameter from the class declaration and substitute different allocators using preprocessor macros instead. For most common uses of STL, though, the standard `allocator` is sufficient, and the problem is invisible. Allocators are discussed again briefly in Section 2.6 (on page 43) and are covered in detail in Chapter 22.

1.3.5   The "Code Bloat" Problem with Templates

When different instances of template classes or template functions are used in the same program, the compiler in effect creates different versions of the source code and compiles each one into executable code (actually, different versions aren't usually produced at the source-code level but rather at some intermediate level of code representation). The main benefit is that each copy is specialized for the types used in the instance and thus can be just as efficient as if the specialized code had been written directly. But there is also a potentially severe drawback: if many different instances are used, the many copies can make the executable file huge. This "code bloat" problem is exacerbated by the generality of template classes and functions in a library such as STL, since they are *intended* to have many useful instances and since programmers are encouraged to use them as frequently as possible.

Fortunately, there are techniques for avoiding the most severe consequences of the code bloat problem, at some (usually minor) cost in efficiency. We discuss these techniques in Sections 11.3 (on page 187) and 17.2 (on page 242).

1.4 *Understanding STL's Performance Guarantees*

STL is unusual among software libraries in that performance guarantees are included in the interface requirements of all its components. Such guarantees are in fact crucial to making wise choices among components, such as choosing whether to use a list, vector, or deque to represent a sequence in a particular application. The component performance characteristics are stated using "big-Oh" notation.

1.4.1   The Big-Oh Notation and Related Definitions

In most cases, talking about the computing time of an algorithm is simplified by classifying all inputs to the algorithm into subsets characterized by some simple parameter(s). For algorithms that work on containers, usually the size n of the container is a convenient choice of parameter. For inputs of size n, we then consider the *maximum time*, $T(n)$, the algorithm takes. (This function $T(n)$ is also called the *worst-case* time for inputs of size n.)

To simplify matters further, we focus on how $T(n)$ behaves for large n, and instead of trying to write a precise formula for $T(n)$, we just look for a simple function that provides an *upper bound* on the function. For example, we might have

$$T(n) \leq cn$$

for some constant c and all sufficiently large n. We say in this case that "the time grows at worst linearly with the size of the input." The constant c might have to be chosen differently when the algorithm is compiled and run on different machines, so one last simplification that is frequently made is to express such bounds in a way that hides the constant.

This is done using *big-Oh* notation; for example, the above relation is written

$$T(n) = O(n)$$

In general, if there is some function f such that

$$T(n) \leq cf(n)$$

for some constant c and all sufficiently large n, we write

$$T(n) = O(f(n))$$

In this book the five main cases of this notation are as follows:

1. $T(n) = O(n)$

This is the case just mentioned. The algorithm is said to have a *linear time bound* or, more simply, to be *linear time* or just *linear*.

2. $T(n) = O(n^2)$

The algorithm is said to have a *quadratic time bound*, or to be *quadratic time* or just *quadratic*.

3. $T(n) = O(\log n)$

The algorithm is said to have a *logarithmic time bound*, or to be *logarithmic time* or just *logarithmic*.

4. $T(n) = O(n \log n)$

The algorithm is said to have an *n log n time bound*.

5. $T(n) = O(1)$

The algorithm is said to have an *O(1) time bound* or *a constant time bound* or to be *constant time*. Note that in this case the big-Oh notation is shorthand for $T(n) \leq c$ for some constant c and all sufficiently large n.

In each of these cases, it is important to keep in mind that we are characterizing computing times with upper bounds on *worst-case computing times*. This can be misleading if the worst case occurs extremely rarely, as is the case, for example, with the STL `sort` algorithm. The worst-case time for this algorithm is quadratic, which is much slower than two other STL sorting algorithms, `partial_sort` and `stable_sort`.

Yet for most situations the `sort` algorithm is the best choice, since it is faster *on the average* than the other algorithms. The inputs that cause worst case for `sort` are in fact so rare that in most situations they can be ignored. In a few cases such as `sort`, the descriptions we give of computing times go beyond the simple big-Oh bounds on worst-case times to discuss the average times.

The average time for an algorithm on inputs of size n is usually calculated by assuming all inputs of size n occur with equal probability. However, other probability distributions might be more appropriate in some situations.

1.4.2 Amortized Time Complexity

In several cases, the most useful characterization of an algorithm's computing time is neither worst-case time nor average time, but *amortized time*. This notion is similar to the manufacturing accounting practice of amortization, in which a one-time cost (such as design cost) is divided by the number of units produced and then attributed to each unit. Amortized time can be a useful way to describe the time an operation on some container takes in cases *where the time can vary widely* as a sequence of the operations is done, but the total time for a sequence of N operations has a *better bound* than just N times the worst-case time.

For example, the worst-case time for inserting at the end of an STL vector is $O(n)$, where n is the size of the container, because if there is no extra room the insert operation must allocate new storage and move all the existing elements into the new storage. However, whenever a vector of length n needs to be expanded, $2n$ spaces are allocated, so no such reallocation and copying are necessary for the next $n-1$ insertions.

Each of these next $n-1$ insertions can be done in constant time, for a total of $O(n)$ time for the n insertions, which is $O(1)$ time for the insertion operation when averaged over the n operations. Thus, we say that the *amortized time* for insertion is constant, or that the time is *amortized constant*.

Thus, for the above example, the amortized constant time bound for insertion more accurately reflects the true cost than does the linear time bound for the worst case.

In general, the amortized time for an operation is the total time for a sequence of N operations divided by N. Note that although amortized time is an average, there is no notion of probability involved, as there is with average computing time.

1.4.3 Limitations of the Big-Oh Notation

The big-Oh notation itself has well-known limitations. The time for an $O(n)$ algorithm might grow at a rate slower than linear growth since it is only an upper bound, or it might grow faster than a linear rate for small n, since the bound only holds for large n. Two $O(n)$ algorithms can differ dramatically in their computing times. One could be uniformly 2, or 10, or 100 times faster than the other, but the big-Oh notation suppresses all such differences. As one moves from one compiler or hardware architecture to another, the hidden constants can change, perhaps enough to alter the case for choosing one algorithm over another.

For these and many other reasons, it is advisable to do empirical performance testing of programs under situations that approximate, to the extent possible, the environment and data that are likely to be encountered in production runs.

1.5 *STL Header Files*

In order to use STL components in your programs, you must use the preprocessor `#include` directive to include one or more header files. In all of the example programs in this book, we assume that the STL header files are organized and named as in the HP reference implementation (see the Preface for background on this implementation and Appendix B for information on how to obtain it):

1. The STL container class named c is in `<c.h>`; e.g., `vector` is in `<vector.h>`, `list` in `<list.h>`, and so forth.

2. STL container adaptors (`stack`, `queue`, and `priority_queue`) are in `<stack.h>`.

3. All STL generic algorithms are in `<algo.h>`.

4. STL stream iterator classes and iterator adaptors are in `<iterator.h>`.

5. STL function objects and function adaptors are in `<function.h>`.

A somewhat different organization is specified in the ANSI/ISO (Draft) C++ Standard. Headers in the Standard do not use the `.h` extension for C++ library headers, except for those that are also C library headers. Other differences from the organization described above are the following:

1. Both `set` and `multiset` are in `<set>`, and both `map` and `multimap` are in `<map>`.

2. The `stack` adaptor is in `<stack>`, and the `queue` and `priority_queue` adaptors are in `<queue>`.

3. All STL generic algorithms are in `<algorithm>`, except generalized numeric algorithms, which are in `<numeric>`.

4. STL function objects and function adaptors are in `<functional>`.

   Other STL providers may currently organize the headers differently from either the Draft Standard or the HP reference implementation, pending finalization of the Standard. In the short term these differences may require programmers to make minor adjustments to their `#include` directives when porting code from one compiler to another. The need for such adjustments should disappear as the Standard Library is finalized and all compilers are brought into conformity.

1.6 *Conventions Used in Examples*

In this book all major and most minor points are illustrated with actual code examples. These examples are designed to be readable and understandable by sight, without being run, but many are structured so that they can be compiled and run with different parameter settings to provide a wider variety of examples and tests of STL capabilities. To make it clear to the reader what example code is supposed to do, we make extensive use of the standard C/C++ `assert` macro, from header `assert.h`. This macro takes a boolean-valued expression as its single argument and does nothing if that expression evaluates to true, but prints an informative message and terminates the program if the expression evaluates to false. First let's look at an example that doesn't use STL at all.

Example 1-1 Illustrating the `assert` macro.

```
#include <iostream.h>
#include <assert.h>
#include <string.h>

int main()
{
  cout << "Illustrating the assert macro." << endl;

  char string1[] = "mark twain";
  char string2[20];

  strcpy(string2, string1);

  int N1 = strlen(string1);
  int N2 = strlen(string2);

  assert(N1 == N2);
```

```
    // Put the reverse of string1 in string2:
    for (int k = 0; k != N1; ++k)
       string2[k] = string1[N1-1-k];

    assert(strcmp(string2, "niawt kram") == 0);
}
```

In this example, the first use of `assert` checks that the lengths of `string1` and `string2`, as computed by the standard `strlen` function, are the same. The second use of `assert` checks that `string2` contains the same sequence of characters as the string `"niawt kram"`, as determined by the standard `strcmp` function. If this little program is compiled and run,[3] it merely prints

```
Illustrating the assert macro.
```

But if there is some mistake—either in the computations being illustrated or in how the assertions are written—the execution will be terminated with a message identifying which assertion failed. For example, we might have written the reversal code erroneously as

```
    for (int k = 0; k != N1; ++k)
       string2[k] = string1[N1-k];
```

(the error is in writing `string1[N1-k]` instead of `string1[N1-1-k]`). Then the execution would produce something like[4]

```
Illustrating the assert macro.
Assertion failed: strcmp(string2, "niawt kram") == 0,
    file: c:\stl\examples\ex01-01a.cpp, line: 24
```

We would get a similar message if we wrote the reversal code correctly but wrote the assertion incorrectly; for example,

---

3. If you want to try compiling and running this or any other example in this book, it is not necessary to type it. Source files for all the examples are available via the Internet (see Appendix B). The file for Example 1-1 is named `ex01-01.cpp`, that for Example 16-2 is `ex16-02.cpp`, and so on.

4. In some cases we discuss an example in terms of modifications to a previous example without presenting it in full, as we do here with a modification to Example 1-1. The files available on the Internet include complete source files for the modified versions. Two modifications of Example 1-1 are discussed in this section; they are named `ex01-01a.cpp` and `ex01-01b.cpp`.

```
for (int k = 0; k != N1; ++k)
    string2[k] = string1[N1-1-k];

assert(strcmp(string2, "naiwt kram") == 0);
```

where the error is in writing `"naiwt"` instead of `"niawt"`. Of course, there's one other possibility: that we wrote both the code and the assertion incorrectly, but so that they agree. There's no foolproof way to avoid this problem entirely, but one can guard against it to a degree by writing more than one assertion about a computation, with the hope that at least one will catch any errors in the code. That's what we've done in many cases in this book.

1.6.1   An STL Example Written Using the `assert` Macro

We just saw an example of code that reverses a string with a for loop. STL provides a generic algorithm called `reverse` that can reverse many kinds of sequences, including character strings. Here is an example of its use:

Example 1-2   Using the STL generic `reverse` algorithm with an array.
```
#include <iostream.h>
#include <algo.h> // for reverse algorithm
#include <assert.h>
#include <string.h>

int main()
{
    cout << "Using reverse algorithm with an array" << endl;

    char string1[] = "mark twain";

    int N1 = strlen(string1);

    reverse(&string1[0], &string1[N1]);

    assert(strcmp(string1, "niawt kram") == 0);
}
```

The arguments to `reverse` are pointers to the beginning and end of the string, where by "end" we mean the first position past the actual string contents. This function reverses the order of the characters in this range in place (unlike our previous piece of code, which put the result in another string).

1.6.2   Examples Using STL Vectors of Characters

In the example above we used simple char* strings, which are just arrays of characters. All STL generic algorithms have the nice property that they do work with arrays, but since arrays are a rather weak feature of C/C++, we'll construct most of our examples using one of the sequence containers provided by STL, such as vectors. Vectors provide all the standard features of arrays but are also expandable and have many other useful features, as will be discussed in Sections 2.1.1 and 6.1. Thus, to illustrate reverse, a more typical kind of example is the following:

Example 1-3   Using the STL generic reverse algorithm with a vector.

```
#include <iostream.h>
#include <algo.h>
#include <vector.h>
#include <assert.h>

vector<char> vec(char* s)
  // Return vector<char> containing the characters of s
  // (not including the terminating null).
{
  vector<char> x;
  while (*s != '\0')
    x.push_back(*s++);
  return x;
}

int main()
{
  cout << "Using reverse algorithm with a vector" << endl;

  vector<char> vector1 = vec("mark twain");

  reverse(vector1.begin(), vector1.end());

  assert(vector1 == vec("niawt kram"));
}
```

This program defines an auxiliary function, vec, which makes a character array into a vector<char>. The function does this using a member function, push_back, to append one character of the string at a time to the vector, which starts out empty. The amount of storage allocated to the vector is expanded as necessary as the characters are appended; this automatic storage allocation is one of the advantages of vectors (and all STL containers) over arrays. The program uses this `vec` function to construct the string to which `reverse` is applied and the string to which to compare the result. In the call of `reverse`, the program uses vector member functions `begin` and `end`, which return the beginning and ending positions of a vector object. Again the convention is that the ending position is the first position past the end of the actual contents.

For the comparison of the result of `reverse` with `vec("niawt kram")`, we use the `==` operator, since STL defines this operator as an equality test for vectors. In general, STL defines the `==` operator for all of its container classes. Already we can see one of the advantages of using a vector rather than a bare array: we can write an equality test on character sequences more naturally than with `strcmp`. (The ANSI/ISO (Draft) Standard C++ library also provides a string class that makes many operations like equality tests more convenient than they are with character arrays. We'll use this string class in later examples.)

1.6.3   Examples Involving User-Defined Types

We use vectors of characters to illustrate STL's generic algorithms mainly because we can easily and concisely construct examples using literal character strings, like `"mark twain"`, by converting them to vectors with simple functions like `vec`. We make similar use of lists of characters, deques of characters, and so on, when we need to illustrate features of these STL containers.

It's important to keep in mind, though, that STL containers can be used to hold objects of any type, not just characters. Any user-defined type `U` defined by a class or struct will also do, although not all container operations will be available unless certain operators are defined on `U`. In particular, many container operations and generic algorithms require the type to have `==` defined as an equality operator. In order to convey to the reader the essential properties of a type to be used with a particular container operation or generic algorithm, we sometimes construct examples in terms of a class with a minimal definition. For example:

Example 1-4   Using the STL generic `reverse` algorithm with a vector of objects of a minimal type.

```
#include <iostream.h>
#include <vector.h>
#include <algo.h>
#include <assert.h>

class U {
 public:
   unsigned long id;
   U() : id(0) { }
   U(unsigned long x) : id(x) { }
};
```

```
// Define == on U objects (needed for vector ==).
bool operator==(const U& x, const U& y)
{
    return x.id == y.id;
}

int main()
{
  vector<U> vector1, vector2;
  const int N = 1000;

  for (int k = 0; k != N; ++k) vector1.push_back(U(k));

  for (k = 0; k != N; ++k) vector2.push_back(U(N-1-k));

  cout << "Using generic reverse algorithm with a vector "
       << "of user-defined objects" << endl;

  reverse(vector1.begin(), vector1.end());

  assert(vector1 == vector2);
}
```

Here the class U is defined to have a data member id. The constructors make it easy to produce an object with a particular id. Having such an identifier member isn't necessary to the operation of any of the vector operations or generic algorithms, but it is used here as a convenient way to identify or distinguish objects of the class.

The reverse algorithm doesn't use the == operator for type U, but we define it on pairs of U objects, in terms of the equality of their id members, in order to be able to check the equality of two vectors. The == operator is defined on vector objects as long as == is defined on the objects stored in the vectors.

For some member functions or generic algorithms, primarily for merging or sorting, we need one other operator, <, defined on objects to be stored in a container. In that case we add a definition similar to that for ==, as follows:

```
bool operator<(const U& x, const U& y)
{
    return x.id < y.id;
}
```

If operator < is defined on the type of objects stored in a container, it is also defined on container objects, in a way described in Chapter 6.

In some cases we may also add

```
ostream& operator<<(ostream& o, const U& x)
{
  o << x.id; return o;
}
```

to output the `id` number of a U object.

1.6.4   Examples Involving Nested Containers

By giving examples constructed with character sequences or with sequences of objects of a user-defined type like U, we show *some* of the generality of STL container operations and generic algorithms, but certainly not all. Another kind of example is sequences in which the objects are other sequences, such as vectors in which the objects are lists of integers:

```
vector<list<int> > vector1, vector2;
```

An example program using container nesting is given in Chapter 14. One important point about such nesting is that if equality is defined on the innermost type parameter, it is defined on the outermost sequences, since each STL container extends its parameter's definition to one for itself. In the preceding example, equality is defined on `int` and is therefore also defined on both `list<int>` and `vector<list<int> >`. Thus, we can write

```
  vector1 == vector2
```

to check the equality of `vector1` and `vector2`. The consistent way in which STL provides crucial operations like equality is an important element of its design, as will become apparent as we study STL in more detail.

CHAPTER 2 — *Overview of STL Components*

STL contains six major kinds of components: *containers, generic algorithms, iterators, function objects, adaptors,* and *allocators*. In this chapter we will cover just the high-lights of each kind of component, saving the details for later chapters.

2.1 Containers

In STL, containers are objects that store collections of other objects. There are two categories of STL container types: *sequence containers* and *sorted associative containers*.

2.1.1 Sequence Containers

Sequence containers organize a collection of objects, all of the same type T, into a strictly linear arrangement. The STL sequence container types are as follows:

- T a[n], that is, ordinary C++ array types, which provide random access to a sequence of fixed length n (*random access* means that the time to reach the ith element of the sequence is constant; that is, the time doesn't depend on i);

- vector<T>, providing random access to a sequence of varying length, with constant time insertions and deletions at the end;

- deque<T>, also providing random access to a sequence of varying length, with constant time insertions and deletions at both the beginning and the end;

- list<T>, providing only linear-time access to a sequence of varying length ($O(n)$, where n is the current length), but with constant time insertions and deletions at *any* position in the sequence.

It may seem surprising that arrays are included in this list, but that's because *all STL generic algorithms are designed to work with arrays in the same way they work with other sequence types*. One example, using STL's generic reverse algorithm with strings (character arrays), was given in Section 1.6.1, and we'll see other examples in Section 2.2. Another case in which many STL algorithms work with standard

C++ types is *streams,* as defined by the standard C++ `iostream` library. That is, many algorithms can read from input streams and write their results to output streams.

A container also provides one or more means of stepping through the objects in the collection via other objects called *iterators,* which we'll discuss at length later. For now, let's note that for *all* STL containers—both sequence containers and sorted associative containers—it is possible to step through the objects in the container as though they were arranged in a linear sequence.

Section 1.6.2 gave an example using vectors. The same example can be written using lists instead:

Example 2-1   Demonstrating generic `reverse` **algorithm on a list.**

```
#include <iostream.h>
#include <algo.h>
#include <list.h>
#include <assert.h>

list<char> lst(char* s)
  // Return list<char> containing the characters of s
  // (not including the terminating null).
{
  list<char> x;
  while (*s != '\0')
    x.push_back(*s++);
  return x;
}

int main()
{
  cout << "Demonstrating generic reverse algorithm on a list"
       << endl;

  list<char> list1 = lst("mark twain");

  reverse(list1.begin(), list1.end());

  assert(list1 == lst("niawt kram"));
}
```

The example could also be written equally well using deques. As we'll see, vectors, lists, and deques are not completely interchangeable, but in this case each one works as well as the other. That's because each defines `push_back`, `begin`, and `end` member functions with the same abstract meaning, though the implementations are quite different: vectors are represented using arrays; lists are represented using doubly linked nodes; and deques are implemented with a two-level array structure. The only difference that might be apparent to the user in the above example of using the generic `reverse` function would be in *performance*. In this simple case there wouldn't be a noticeable difference in performance, but in other cases, using different algorithms and larger sequences, there can be a tremendous performance advantage of using one kind of sequence over another. (But none is a winner in all cases, which is why more than one is provided in the library.)

2.1.2 Sorted Associative Containers

Sorted associative containers provide an ability for fast retrieval of objects from the collection based on keys. The size of the collection can vary at run time. STL has four sorted associative container types:

- `set<Key>`, which supports unique keys (contains at most one of each key value) and provides for fast retrieval of the keys themselves;[1]

- `multiset<Key>`, which supports duplicate keys (possibly contains multiple copies of the same key value) and provides for fast retrieval of the keys themselves;

- `map<Key, T>`, which supports unique keys (of type `Key`) and provides for fast retrieval of another type `T` based on the keys;

- `multimap<Key, T>`, which supports duplicate keys (of type `Key`) and provides for fast retrieval of another type `T` based on the keys.

A simple example of a sorted associative container is `map<string, long>`, which might be used to hold associations between names and telephone numbers, for example, to represent a telephone directory. Given a name, such a map would provide for fast retrieval of a phone number, as in the following example program.

---

1. The `set` class actually has a default template parameter:

   `template <class Key, class Compare = less<Key> > class set.`

   In all example programs in this book, we will show this parameter explicitly so that the code works with compilers that do not yet implement default template parameters. The meaning of the `Compare` parameter is discussed following Example 2-2. The `multiset`, `map`, and `multimap` classes also have a default parameter `Compare` with the same default value, `less<Key>`.

Example 2-2   Demonstrating an STL map.

```
#include <iostream.h>
#include <map.h>
#include <bstring.h>

int main()
{
  map<string, long, less<string> > directory;
  directory["Bogart"] = 1234567;
  directory["Bacall"] = 9876543;
  directory["Cagney"] = 3459876;
  // etc.

  // Read some names and look up their numbers.
  string name;
  while (cin >> name)
    if (directory.find(name) != directory.end())
      cout << "The phone number for " << name
           << " is " << directory[name] << "\n";
    else
      cout << "Sorry, no listing for " << name << "\n";
}
```

In this program, we use the C++ standard library `string` class from the header file `bstring.h`.[2] We declare `directory` as a map with `string` as the Key type and `long` as the associated type T. The third template parameter to the map container is `less<string>`, which is a function object used to compare two keys. This particular function object compares strings according to the usual alphabetical ordering (we will discuss such function objects in Section 2.4 and in Chapter 8).

We next insert some names and numbers in the directory with array-like assignments such as `directory["Bogart"] = 1234567`. This notation is possible because the map type defines `operator[]` analogously to the corresponding operator on arrays. If we know `name` is in the directory, we can retrieve the associated number with `directory[name]`. In this program we first check to see if `name` is a key stored in directory using `find`, a member function of the map container (and all of the sorted associative containers). The `find` function returns an iterator that refers to the entry in the table with `name` as its key if there is such an entry; otherwise it returns an "off-the-end" iterator, which is the same iterator returned by the

---

2. This `string` header is available on the Internet along with the STL source code; see Appendix B.

end member function. Thus, by comparing the iterator returned by find with that returned by end, we are able to determine whether there is an entry in the table with key name.

The STL approach to containers differs in a major way from other C++ container class libraries: STL containers do *not* provide many operations on the data objects they contain. Instead, in STL that's done mainly with *generic algorithms*, the next topic.

2.2 *Generic Algorithms*

Two of the simplest generic algorithms in STL are find and merge.

2.2.1   The Generic find Algorithm

As a simple example of the flexibility of STL algorithms, consider the find algorithm, used to search a sequence for a particular value. It's possible to use find with *any* of the STL containers. With arrays, we might write

Example 2-3   Demonstrating generic find algorithm with an array.

```
#include <iostream.h>
#include <string.h>
#include <assert.h>
#include <algo.h>

int main()
{
  cout << "Demonstrating generic find algorithm with "
       << "an array." << endl;
  char* s = "C++ is a better C";
  int len = strlen(s);

  // Search for the first occurrence of the letter e.
  char* where = find(&s[0], &s[len], 'e');

  assert (*where == 'e' && *(where+1) == 't');
}
```

This program uses find to search the elements in s[0],...,s[len-1] to see if any is equal to e. If e does occur in the array s, the pointer where is assigned the first position where it occurs, so that *where == 'e'. In this case it does occur in the array, but if it didn't, then find would return &s[len]. This return value is the location one position past the end of the array.

Now, instead of an array, we might have our data stored in a vector, a type of container that provides fast random access like arrays but also can grow and shrink dynamically. To find an element in a vector, we can use the *same* find algorithm as we used for arrays:

Example 2-4 Demonstrating the generic find algorithm with a vector.

```
#include <iostream.h>
#include <string.h>
#include <assert.h>
#include <vector.h>
#include <algo.h>

int main()
{
   cout << "Demonstrating generic find algorithm with "
        << "a vector." << endl;
   char* s = "C++ is a better C";
   int len = strlen(s);

   // Initialize vector1 with the contents of string s.
   vector<char> vector1(&s[0], &s[len]);

   // Search for the first occurrence of the letter e.
   vector<char>::iterator
     where = find(vector1.begin(), vector1.end(), 'e');
   assert(*where == 'e' && *(where + 1) == 't');
}
```

This time we construct a vector containing the same characters as array s, using a constructor member of class vector that initializes the vector using the sequence of values in an array. Instead of char*, the type of where is vector<char>::iterator. *Iterators* are pointer-like objects that can be used to traverse a sequence of objects. When a sequence is stored in a char array, the iterators *are* C++ pointers (of type char*), but when a sequence is stored in a container such as vector, we obtain an appropriate iterator type from the container class. Each STL container type C defines C::iterator as an iterator type that can be used with type C containers.

In either case, when the find algorithm is called as in

```
where = find(first, last, value)
```

it assumes that

- iterator first marks the position in a sequence where it should *start* processing, and

- `last` marks the position where it can *stop* processing.

Such starting and ending positions are exactly what the `begin` and `end` member functions of the `vector` class (and all other STL classes that define containers) supply.

If the data elements are in a list, once again we can use the same `find` algorithm:

Example 2-5   Demonstrating the generic `find` algorithm with a list.

```
#include <iostream.h>
#include <string.h>
#include <assert.h>
#include <list.h>
#include <algo.h>

int main()
{
  cout << "Demonstrating generic find algorithm with "
       << "a list." << endl;
  char* s = "C++ is a better C";
  int len = strlen(s);

  // Initialize list1 with the contents of string s.
  list<char> list1(&s[0], &s[len]);

  // Search for the first occurrence of the letter e.
  list<char>::iterator
    where = find(list1.begin(), list1.end(), 'e');
  assert (*where == 'e' && *(++where) == 't');
}
```

There is one subtle difference between this program and the previous one using a vector, due to the fact that the iterators associated with list containers do not support the operator + used in the expression `*(where + 1)`. The reason is explained in Chapter 4. All STL iterators are required to support ++, however, and that is what we use in the expression `*(++where)`.[3]

If we have our data in a `deque`, which is a random-access container similar to arrays and vectors but allowing even more flexibility in the way it can grow and shrink, we can once again use `find`:

---

3. In analogy to ++ on built-in types, STL defines ++ on iterators to change the value of the iterator as a side-effect, so `++where` is not exactly equivalent to `where + 1`. It doesn't matter in this case since the program makes no further use of `where`.

Example 2-6 Demonstrating the generic `find` algorithm with a deque.

```
#include <iostream.h>
#include <string.h>
#include <assert.h>
#include <deque.h>
#include <algo.h>

int main()
{
    cout << "Demonstrating generic find algorithm with "
         << "a deque." << endl;
    char* s = "C++ is a better C";
    int len = strlen(s);

    // Initialize deque1 with the contents of string s.
    deque<char> deque1(&s[0], &s[len]);

    // Search for the first occurrence of the letter e.
    deque<char>::iterator
      where = find(deque1.begin(), deque1.end(), 'e');
    assert (*where == 'e' && *(where+1) == 't');
}
```

This program is identical to the vector version except for the substitution of "deque" for "vector" throughout (deque iterators, unlike list iterators, do support the + operator).

In fact, the `find` algorithm can be used to find values in *all* STL containers. The key point with `find` and all other STL generic algorithms is that since they can be used by many or all containers, individual containers do *not* have to define as many separate member functions, resulting in reduced code size and simplified container interfaces.

2.2.2 The Generic `merge` Algorithm

The flexibility of STL generic algorithms is even greater than the examples involving `find` have indicated. Consider an algorithm such as `merge`, which combines the elements of two sorted sequences into a single sorted sequence. In general, if `merge` is called as

```
merge(first1, last1, first2, last2, result)
```

it assumes that

- `first1` and `last1` are iterators marking the beginning and end of one input sequence whose elements are of some type `T`;

- `first2` and `last2` are iterators delimiting another input sequence, whose elements are also of type `T`;

- the two input sequences are in ascending order according to the < operator for type `T`; and

- `result` marks the beginning of the sequence where the result should be stored.

Under these conditions the result contains all elements of the two input sequences and is also in ascending order. *This interface is flexible enough that the two input sequences and the result sequence can be in different kinds of containers,* as the next example shows.

Example 2-7 Demonstrating the generic `merge` algorithm with an array, a list, and a deque.

```
#include <iostream.h>
#include <string.h>
#include <assert.h>
#include <list.h>
#include <deque.h>
#include <algo.h>

list<char> lst(char* s)
    // Return list<char> containing the characters of s
    // (not including the terminating null).
{
  list<char> x;
  while (*s != '\0')
    x.push_back(*s++);
  return x;
}

deque<char> deq(char* s)
    // Return deque<char> containing the characters of s
    // (not including the terminating null).
{
  deque<char> x;
  while (*s != '\0')
    x.push_back(*s++);
  return x;
}
```

```
int main()
{
   cout << "Demonstrating generic merge algorithm with "
        << "an array, a list, and a deque." << endl;
   char* s = "acegikm";
   int len = strlen(s);

   list<char> list1 = lst("bdfhjlnopqrstuvwxyz");

   // Initialize deque1 with 26 copies of the letter x:
   deque<char> deque1(26, 'x');

   // Merge array s and list1, putting result in deque1:
   merge(&s[0], &s[len], list1.begin(), list1.end(),
        deque1.begin());

   assert(deque1 == deq("abcdefghijklmnopqrstuvwxyz"));
}
```

In this program we create a deque to hold the result of merging array s and list1. Note that the character sequences in both s and list1 are in ascending order, as is the result produced by merge in deque1.

We can even merge portions of one sequence with portions of another. For example, we can modify the above program to merge the first 5 characters of s with the first 10 characters of deque1, putting the result into list1 (note that we reverse the roles of list1 and deque1 from the previous program).

Example 2-8 Demonstrating the generic merge **algorithm, merging parts of an array and a deque, putting the result into a list.**

```
#include <iostream.h>
#include <string.h>
#include <assert.h>
#include <list.h>
#include <deque.h>
#include <algo.h>

// Functions lst and deq defined as in the previous
// program ...

int main()
{
   cout << "Demonstrating generic merge algorithm,\n"
        << "merging parts of an array and a deque, putting\n"
```

```
                 << "the result into a list." << endl;
    char* s = "acegikm";

    deque<char> deque1 = deq("bdfhjlnopqrstuvwxyz");

    // Initialize list1 with 26 copies of the letter x:
    list<char> list1(26, 'x');

    // Merge first 5 letters in array s with first 10 in
    // deque1, putting result in list1:
    merge(&s[0], &s[5], deque1.begin(), deque1.begin() + 10,
          list1.begin());

    assert(list1 == lst("abcdefghijlnopqxxxxxxxxxxx"));
}
```

These are simple examples, but they already hint at the immense range of possible uses of such generic algorithms.

2.3 *Iterators*

Understanding iterators is the key to understanding fully the STL framework and learning how to best make use of the library. STL generic algorithms are written in terms of iterator parameters, and STL containers provide iterators that can be plugged into the algorithms, as we saw in **Figure 1-1** in Chapter 1. **Figure 2-1** again depicts this relationship, together with relationships between other major categories of STL components. These very general components are designed to "plug together" in a myriad of different useful ways to produce the kind of larger and more specialized components found in other libraries. The main kind of "wiring" for connecting components together is the category called iterators (drawn as "ribbon cables" in **Figure 2-1** and **Figure 2-2**, which depicts the hierarchical relationship among different iterator categories). One kind of iterator is an ordinary C++ pointer, but iterators other than pointers may exist. These other kinds of iterators are required, however, to behave like pointers in the sense that one can perform operations like ++ and * on them and expect them to behave similarly to pointers: for instance, ++i advances an iterator i to the next location, and *i returns the location so that it can be stored into, as in *i = x, or its value can be used in an expression, as in x = *i.

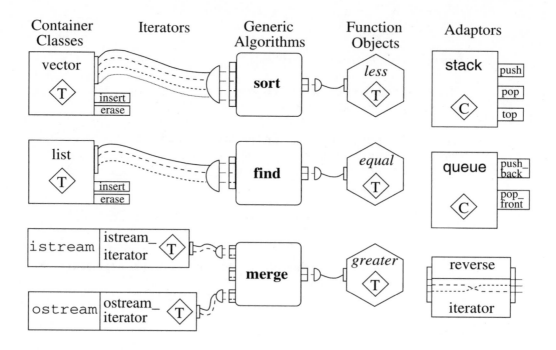

FIGURE 2-1. Five of the Six Major Categories of STL Components (Not Shown Are Allocators).

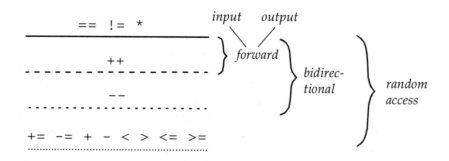

FIGURE 2-2. Hierarchical Relationship among STL Iterator Categories.

Consider the STL generic function `accumulate`. When called with iterators `first` and `beyond` and a value `init`,

```
accumulate(first, beyond, init)
```

it adds up `init` plus the values in positions `first` up to, but not including, `beyond`, and returns the sum. For example, we could write the following program to compute and print the sum of the values in a vector.

Example 2-9   Demonstrating the generic accumulate function.

```
#include <vector.h>
#include <algo.h>
#include <assert.h>

int main()
{
  cout << "Demonstrating the accumulate function." << endl;
  int x[5] = {2, 3, 5, 7, 11};
  // Initialize vector1 to x[0] through x[4]:
  vector<int> vector1(&x[0], &x[5]);

  int sum = accumulate(vector1.begin(), vector1.end(), 0);

  assert(sum == 28);
}
```

This program uses `accumulate` to add up the integers in `vector1`, which is traversed using iterators `vector1.begin()` and `vector1.end()`. We could also use `accumulate` with the array x, by writing

```
sum = accumulate(&x[0], &x[5], 0);
```

or, say, with a list of `doubles`, as in

```
double y[5] = {2.0, 3.0, 5.0, 7.0, 11.0};
list<double> list1(&y[0], &y[5]);
sum = accumulate(list1.begin(), list1.end(), 0.0);
```

In each case, the abstract meaning is the same—adding to the initial value the values in the range indicated by the iterators—but the *type* of iterators and the *type* of the initial value determine how `accumulate` is adapted to the specific task.

Let's look more closely at the way `accumulate` uses iterators. It can be defined as follows:

```
template <class InputIterator, class T>
T accumulate(InputIterator first, InputIterator beyond,
             T init)
{
  while (first != beyond)
    init = init + *first++;
  return init;
}
```

The only operations it performs on iterators are incrementing with postfix ++, dereferencing with *, and inequality checking with !=. These operations, together with prefix ++ and equality checking, ==, are the only operations required by the category of iterators called *input iterators*. One other characteristic of input iterators, from which they get their name, is that the * operation is only required to be able to read from positions in a container, not to write into them. *Output iterators*, on the other hand, require the same operations except that * is required only to be able to write, but not to read.

STL defines three other categories of iterators: *forward* iterators, *bidirectional* iterators, and *random access* iterators. Except for input and output iterators, the relationship between these categories is hierarchical, as shown in **Figure 2-2**. That is, each category adds new requirements to those imposed by the previous category, which means that iterators in a later category are also members of earlier ones. For example, a bidirectional iterator is also a forward iterator, and a random access iterator is also a bidirectional and a forward iterator.

Algorithms that are written to work with input iterators, such as accumulate find, and merge, are more generic than those that require more powerful iterators, such as sort, which requires random access iterators. For example, sort cannot be used with STL list containers, because list iterators are only bidirectional and not random access. Instead, STL provides a list member function for sorting that works efficiently with its bidirectional iterators. As we will see in Chapter 4, STL's goal of *efficiency* motivates placing limitations on the generality of some generic algorithms, and the organization of iterators into categories is the chief means of achieving this goal.

2.4 *Function Objects*

The accumulate function discussed in the previous section is very general in terms of its use of iterators, but not as general as it might be in terms of the assumptions it makes about the type of values to which the iterators refer (called the *value type* of the iterators). The accumulate definition assumes there is a + operator defined on the value type, by its use of + in the expression

```
init = init + *first++;
```

This allows the function to be used with any of the C++ built-in numeric types, or with any user-defined type T in which such an operator is defined, to add up the values in a sequence. But the abstract notion of accumulation applies to more than just addition; one can equally well accumulate a product of a sequence of values, for example. Thus STL provides another, more general, version of accumulate:

```
template <class InputIterator, class T,
          class BinaryOperation>
T accumulate(InputIterator first, InputIterator last,
             T init, BinaryOperation binary_op)
{
  while (first != last)
    init = binary_op(init, *first++);
  return init;
}
```

Instead of being written in terms of +, this definition introduces another parameter, binary_op, as the binary operation used to combine values.

How can this more general version of accumulate be used to compute a product? If we define a function mult as in the following program, we can use it as the binary_op parameter to accumulate:

Example 2-10 Using the generic accumulate **algorithm to compute a product.**

```
#include <vector.h>
#include <algo.h>
#include <assert.h>

int mult(int x, int y) { return x * y; }

int main()
{
  cout << "Using generic accumulate algorithm to "
       << "compute a product." << endl;

  int x[5] = {2, 3, 5, 7, 11};

  // Initialize vector1 to x[0] through x[4]:
  vector<int> vector1(x, x+5);

  int product = accumulate(vector1.begin(), vector1.end(),
                           1, mult);
```

```
        assert(product == 2310);
}
```

(Note that we also changed the initial value from 0 to 1, which is the proper "identity element" for multiplication.) Here we are passing to `accumulate` an ordinary function, but C++ also supports another possibility: passing a *function object*, by which we mean *an object of a type defined by a class or struct in which the function call operator is defined.* Here's how it can be done, in one of the simplest forms possible:

Example 2-11   Using the generic `accumulate` **algorithm to compute a product, using a function object.**

```
#include <vector.h>
#include <algo.h>
#include <assert.h>

class multiply {
 public:
   int operator()(int x, int y) const { return x * y; }
};

int main()
{
   cout << "Using generic accumulate algorithm to "
        << "compute a product." << endl;

   int x[5] = {2, 3, 5, 7, 11};

   // Initialize vector1 to x[0] through x[4]:
   vector<int> vector1(x, x+5);

   int product = accumulate(vector1.begin(), vector1.end(),
                            1, multiply());
   assert(product == 2310);
}
```

By defining the function call operator, `operator()`, in class `multiply`, we define a type of object that can be applied to an argument list, just as a function can. Note that the object passed to `accumulate` is obtained by calling the (default) constructor of the class, `multiply()`. Note also that this object has no storage associated with it, just a function definition (in some cases, though, it is useful to store data in function objects).

What's the advantage, if any, of using function objects rather than ordinary functions? We'll answer this question in detail in Chapter 8, but the main idea is that function objects can carry with them additional information that an ordinary function cannot, and this information can be used by generic algorithms or containers that need more complex knowledge about a function than `accumulate` does. Another important reason to prefer function objects is efficiency, since the compiler can *inline* the definitions of functions given as member functions of classes, like the `operator()` member given in class `multiply`, so that there is no overhead of function calling. When an ordinary function is used, one adds calling overhead to the computation the function body does.

Before leaving this topic, we should mention that in Example 2-11 it wasn't really necessary to define class `multiply`, since STL includes such a definition, although in a more general form:

```
template <class T>
class times : public binary_function<T, T, T> {
 public:
   T operator()(const T& x, const T& y) const {
     return x * y;
   }
};
```

This class inherits from another STL component, `binary_function`, whose purpose is to hold extra information about the function, as will be discussed in Chapter 8. Using this definition, the program can be written as follows:

Example 2-12 Using the generic `accumulate` algorithm to compute a product, using a function object.
```
#include <vector.h>
#include <algo.h>
#include <assert.h>

int main()
{
   cout << "Using generic accumulate algorithm to "
        << "compute a product." << endl;

   int x[5] = {2, 3, 5, 7, 11};

   // Initialize vector1 to x[0] through x[4]:
   vector<int> vector1(x, x+5);

   int product = accumulate(vector1.begin(), vector1.end(),
                            1, times<int>());
```

```
    assert(product == 2310);
}
```

The class `times` is defined in the header `function.h`, which is already included by `algo.h`, so we do not need any additional header files. With `times<int>()`, we just call the default constructor of class `times` instantiated with type int. A few of the other STL-provided function objects are shown in the fourth column of **Figure 2-1** in Section 2.3.

2.5 *Adaptors*

A component that modifies the interface of another component is called an *adaptor*. Adaptors are depicted in the last column of **Figure 2-1** in Section 2.3. For example, `reverse_iterator` is a component that adapts an iterator type into a new type of iterator with all the capabilities of the original but with the direction of traversal reversed. This is useful because sometimes the standard traversal order is not what's needed in a particular computation. For example, `find` returns an iterator referring to the *first* occurrence of a value in a sequence, but we might want the *last* occurrence instead. We could use `reverse` to reverse the order of the elements in the sequence and then use `find`, but we can do it without disturbing or copying the sequence by using reverse iterators. In **Figure 2-1**, a reverse iterator component is depicted as having the "wires" for ++ and -- crossed.

Continuing with `accumulate` as an example, it might not appear too useful to traverse a sequence in reverse order to accumulate its values, since the sum should be the same as with a forward traversal. That's true of a sequence of integers, with + as the combining function, since on integers + obeys the laws $(x + y) + z = x + (y + z)$ (associativity) and $x + y = y + x$ (commutativity), but these properties can fail for floating-point numbers because of round-off and overflow errors (associativity can fail even with `ints` because of overflow). With floating-point numbers, round-off errors are usually smaller if the numbers are added in order of increasing size; otherwise, values that are very small relative to the running sum may have no effect at all on the sum. Suppose we have a vector of values in descending order and we want to accumulate their sum. In order to add them in ascending order, we can use `accumulate` with reverse iterators:

Example 2-13   Demonstrating generic `accumulate` algorithm with a reverse iterator.

```
#include <vector.h>
#include <algo.h>
#include <assert.h>

int main()
```

```
{
   cout << "Demonstrating generic accumulate algorithm with "
        << "a reverse iterator." << endl;

   float small = 1.0F/(1 << 26);
   float x[5] = {1.0F, 3*small, 2*small, small, small};

   // Initialize vector1 to x[0] through x[4]:
   vector<float> vector1(&x[0], &x[5]);

   cout << "Values to be added: " << endl;

   vector<float>::iterator i;
   cout.precision(10);
   for (i = vector1.begin(); i != vector1.end(); ++i)
     cout << *i << endl;
   cout << endl;

   float sum = accumulate(vector1.begin(), vector1.end(),
                          0.0F);

   cout << "Sum accumulated from left = " <<  sum << endl;

   float sum1 = accumulate(vector1.rbegin(), vector1.rend(),
                           0.0F);
   cout << "Sum accumulated from right = "
        << (double)sum1 << endl;
}
```

In computing sum1, we use vector member functions rbegin and rend to obtain iterators of type vector<float>::reverse_iterator, which, like vector<float>::iterator, is defined as part of the vector interface. The output of this program will vary depending on the precision used in type float, but the value of small was chosen to make a difference between sum and sum1 for a precision of about 8 decimal places.[4] In this case, the output is as follows:

```
Demonstrating accumulate function with a reverse iterator.
Values to be added:
1
4.470348358e-08
```

---

4. The output shows 10 significant digits, but that is an artifact of the output routine.

```
2.980232239e-08
1.490116119e-08
1.490116119e-08
Sum accumulated from left = 1
Sum accumulated from right = 1.000000119
```

The sum accumulated from the right, using the smaller values first, is the more accurate one.

The type `vector<float>::reverse_iterator` is actually defined using an iterator adaptor. We could have used this adaptor directly in our program by writing

```
reverse_iterator<vector<float>::iterator, float,
              float&, ptrdiff_t>
   first(vector1.end()), last(vector1.begin());

 float sum1 = accumulate(first, last, (float)0.0);
```

Here `first` and `last` are declared as variables of type

```
reverse_iterator<vector<float>::iterator, float,
              float&, ptrdiff_t>
```

in which the first template parameter, `vector<float>::iterator`, is an iterator type and the second, `float`, is the corresponding value type. The third parameter, `float&`, is a reference type for the value type, and the last parameter, `ptrdiff_t`, is a distance type for the iterator type (a type capable of representing differences between iterator values). This `reverse_iterator` type provides ++ and -- operators, just as `vector<float>::iterator` does, but with their meanings exchanged. As a convenience, each of the container types that STL defines provides a `reverse_iterator` type already defined in this way, along with `rbegin` and `rend` member functions that return iterators of this type.

Besides reverse iterators, STL also has another kind of iterator adaptor. *Insert iterators* are provided to allow generic algorithms to operate in an "insert mode" rather than in their ordinary overwrite mode; they are applied to containers and produce output iterators. Insert iterators are especially useful for transferring a data sequence from an input stream or container to another container without having to know in advance the length of the sequence. Iterator adaptors are described more fully in Chapter 10.

STL also defines several kinds of container adaptors and function adaptors. A *stack adaptor* transforms a sequence container into a container with the more restricted interface of a last-in, first-out stack. A *queue adaptor* transforms a sequence container into a first-in, first-out queue, and a *priority queue* adaptor produces a queue in which values are accessible in an order controlled by a comparison parameter. These container adaptors are described more fully in Chapter 9.

The function adaptors STL provides include negators, binders, and adaptors for pointers to functions. A *negator* is a kind of function adaptor used to reverse the sense of predicate function objects, which are function objects that return a `bool` value. A *binder* is used to convert binary function objects into unary function objects by binding an argument to some particular value. A pointer-to-function adaptor transforms a pointer to a function into a function object; it can be used to give compiled code more flexibility than one can obtain using standard function objects (which helps to avoid the "code bloat" that can result from using too many compiled combinations of algorithms and function objects in the same program). These function adaptors are described in more detail in Chapter 11.

2.6 Allocators

Every STL container class uses an `Allocator` class to encapsulate information about the memory model the program is using. Different memory models have different requirements for pointers, references, integer sizes, and so forth. The `Allocator` class encapsulates information about pointers, constant pointers, references, constant references, sizes of objects, difference types between pointers, allocation and deallocation functions, as well as some other functions. All operations on allocators are expected to be amortized constant time.

Since memory model information can be encapsulated in an allocator, STL containers can work with different memory models simply by providing different allocators.

We do not cover allocators in detail in this book, since the default allocator class supplied with STL implementations is sufficient for most programmers' needs. For programmers who do need to define new allocators, Chapter 22 describes the information that an allocator must provide.

For further insight on the motivation for allocators being a part of STL, see Ref. 13 (although it should be noted that the details of the way allocators are provided have changed since that paper was written).

CHAPTER 3   *How STL Differs from Other Libraries*

Before going on to the more detailed discussion of STL components in the following chapters, let's briefly examine some of the major differences between STL and other C++ libraries.

In traditional container class libraries, all algorithms are associated with particular classes and are implemented as member functions. If a list class in such a library has a search algorithm like `find`, it is *distinct* from the search algorithm of the vector class.

This kind of organization has several problems:

- Each class in the library must contain a huge amount of source code and documentation.

- Otherwise, the library classes will simply not have many of the operations we may need to perform. In this case, we are forced either to abandon one class for another, or to convert back and forth between two data representations to do certain operations. Such conversions not only increase the number of classes we have to understand (and in some cases maintain), but are often the cause of serious run-time performance problems.

The STL approach goes a long way toward solving these problems. With STL, we have a much greater range of flexibility in choosing algorithms and containers than with traditional class libraries, yet the number of interfaces to be understood, and the total amount of source code to be maintained in the library, remains small.

3.1 Extensibility

No software library does everything, and no one claims that STL is an exception. But in comparison with traditional class libraries, it is relatively easy to *extend* STL when necessary.

In traditional libraries, where algorithms are associated with particular classes, it may be possible to add an algorithm by deriving a new class from a library class. This approach has some drawbacks:

- It only works if the original designer of the class anticipated such extensions and carefully provided hooks for them (e.g., making certain data members protected rather than private, or certain functions virtual rather than nonvirtual).

- More often than not, one must modify the source code of the classes—assuming the source is even available—possibly introducing subtle bugs or causing other problems in testing, maintenance, and version control.

STL, on the other hand, has an *open and orthogonal structure* that allows programmers to design their own algorithms to work with the library's containers or even their own containers to work with the library's algorithms, *without touching (or even reading) the source code.*

3.2   *Component Interchangeability*

How is this openness and orthogonality of STL components achieved? Basically, the solution is one with which we are already familiar in many manufacturing industries: *component interchangeability,* achieved by making the component interfaces as simple and uniform as possible.

We're all familiar with the benefits of such interchangeability in tools and parts industries, and many attempts at it have been made even in the software industry. Beginning with some of the current STL's ancestors several years ago, the push toward software component interchangeability has been greater than in any other library design.

We've already seen some aspects of the interchangeability of STL components in the STL `find` and `merge` algorithms (Sections 2.2.1 and 2.2.2). These algorithms work with such a wide variety of containers because their interfaces are designed to access the sequences involved in the computation only in very limited ways, through the pointer-like objects called iterators.

The key point to be made here is that algorithms in STL are not specified directly in terms of the data structures on which they operate. Rather, algorithms and containers in STL are combined as follows:

- For each container, we specify which category of iterators it provides.

- For each algorithm, we state with which category of iterators it works.

By specifying algorithms in terms of iterators rather than in terms of the data structures directly, data structure independence becomes possible. This is what allows the algorithms to be so "generic," allowing each algorithm to operate on a variety of data structures.

Furthermore, conventions about how iterators mark the beginning and end of the data are uniformly observed. Consider the `sort` algorithm, which, like `find`, works with the data in a single sequence (it stores the sorted result in the same sequence). Like `find`, `sort` gets access to the sequence through two iterators, marking the beginning and stopping points:

```
long a[10000];
vector<int> v;
deque<double> d;
... code to insert values in a, v, and d

// Sort all the elements in array a:
sort(&a[0], &a[10000]);

// Sort all the elements in vector v:
sort(v.begin(), v.end());

// Sort all the elements in deque d:
sort(d.begin(), d.end());

// Sort the first 100 elements in deque d:
sort(d.begin(), d.begin() + 100);
```

In short, the algorithms are uniform in the assumptions they make about how to access data, and the way containers provide access to the data is entirely consistent with the algorithms' assumptions.

The iterator concept is explained in much more detail in Chapter 4.

3.3   *Algorithm/Container Compatibility*

Now we come to one of the most crucial points in understanding STL:

> Although some STL algorithms, like `find` and `merge`, are completely generic—that is, they work with any kind of container—it is *not* possible to plug together *every* algorithm with *every* container in the library.

In theory, all STL algorithm and container components *could* be made to interface together, but it was deliberately decided not to do so simply because some algorithms would not be *efficient* when used with some containers.

The `sort` algorithm is a good example. The algorithm that's used (a variation of quicksort) is efficient only when random access to the data is possible. Such random access is provided by arrays, vectors, and deques, but not by lists or other STL containers. So it is not possible to say

```
list<int> list1;
... code to insert values in list1
sort(list1.begin(), list1.end());  // incorrect
```

The list class provides a member function sort that sorts lists efficiently. For example, in the above code one can efficiently sort list1 by calling list1.sort().

At this point, you may be getting suspicious that STL may not be that different from traditional class libraries after all—maybe it has its own proliferation of separate algorithms in different classes. That's not really the case, for the following reasons:

- First, many STL algorithms (like find and merge) are completely generic. There are only a few algorithms in STL, like list's sort member function, that are specific to a single container class. Many, like the generic sort, work with several kinds of containers, though not all.

- Second, for those algorithms that do work only with certain kinds of containers, it is not difficult to tell with which containers they can be used. We just have to look at how algorithms and containers are combined with each other using iterators, which is the topic of the next chapter.

CHAPTER 4   *Iterators*

Iterators are pointer-like objects STL algorithms use to traverse the sequence of objects stored in a container. Iterators are of central importance in the design of STL because of their role as *intermediaries* between containers and generic algorithms. They enable generic algorithms to be written without concern for how data sequences are stored, and containers to be written without having to code a large number of algorithms on them. However, as discussed in the preceding chapter, for reasons of efficiency it is not possible to have every generic algorithm work with every container. But then how do we know which combinations are possible? For the answer to this question, we have to examine one of the key technical ideas behind STL, the classification of iterators into five categories: *input, output, forward, bidirectional,* and *random access* (recall Figure 2-1). We begin this chapter by defining precisely what these categories are, and then we show how they are used in specifying which algorithms can be used with which containers.

Before we get to the categories, there is another particularly useful concept and notation related to the way STL algorithms use iterators, namely *iterator ranges*. All STL algorithms gain access to a sequence via iterators, usually through a pair of iterators `first` and `last` that mark the beginning and end of the sequence. To capture concisely the way in which such an iterator pair determines a sequence, the concept of an iterator *range* is used. The range from `first` to `last` consists of the iterators obtained by starting with `first` and applying `operator++` until `last` is reached, but does not include `last`. This range is written[1]

```
[first, last)
```

and is said to be *valid* if and only if `last` is in fact reachable from `first`. All STL algorithms assume the ranges they work with are valid; the result of application to invalid ranges is undefined.

An important special case, an *empty* range, occurs when `first == last`. An empty range is valid, but includes no iterators.

---

1. The notation is based on a similar usage in mathematics of $[a, b)$, where a and b are real numbers, to denote the set of all real numbers x such that $a \leq x < b$. This set is called a "half-open interval."

4.1 *Input Iterators*

The definitions of STL iterator categories are motivated by considering the needs of certain algorithms. As shown in Chapter 2, the STL generic `find` algorithm can be used to find values in a variety of data structures, including arrays, vectors, and lists. It can even be used to search an input stream with the aid of special iterators called istream iterators, which are discussed later in this chapter. The `find` algorithm has a simple definition as a template function:

```
template <class InputIterator, class T>
InputIterator find(InputIterator first, InputIterator last,
                   const T& value)
{
  while (first != last && *first != value)
    ++first;
  return first;
}
```

Note the expressions in this code in which `InputIterator` objects appear:

- `first != last,`

- `++first,`

- `*first.`

In order for `find` to work correctly, these expressions should be defined and have the following meanings:

- `first != last` should return true if `first` is not equal to `last`, false otherwise;

- `++first` should increment `first` and return the incremented value;

- `*first` should return the value referred to by `first`.

Furthermore, in order for `find` to work *efficiently*, each of these operations should work in *constant time*.

These requirements are almost exactly the requirements given in the definition of the input iterator category. The main additional requirements are that `==` also be defined with the meaning of an equality test and that postfix `++` also be defined, with the same meaning as prefix `++`, except that it returns the value the iterator had before incrementing (as is the case with built-in pointer types).

These requirements are, of course, met by built-in pointer types. Note, however, that built-in pointer types have many other properties that are not required by the definition of input iterators. In particular, input iterators are *not* required to support *writing* into a position with *first = ... A particular input iterator *may* support this operation, but it's not required. (As we'll see in the next section, *output iterators* have the opposite requirement, that is, it must be possible to write with operator* but not necessarily to be able to read with it.)

Note that the term "input iterator" does not refer to a type. Instead, it refers to a family of types, all of which satisfy the basic requirements outlined above. To see that several different types satisfy input iterator requirements simultaneously, consider the following example program:

Example 4-1   Demonstrating the generic find **algorithm with input iterators associated with arrays, lists, and iostreams.**

```
#include <iostream.h>
#include <assert.h>
#include <algo.h>
#include <list.h>

int main()
{
  // Initialize array a with 10 integers:
  int a[10] = {12, 3, 25, 7, 11, 213, 7, 123, 29, -31};

  // Find the first element equal to 7 in the array:
  int* ptr = find(&a[0], &a[10], 7);

  assert(*ptr == 7 && *(ptr+1) == 11);

  // Initialize list1 with the same integers as in array a:
  list<int> list1(&a[0], &a[10]);

  // Find the first element equal to 7 in list1:
  list<int>::iterator i = find(list1.begin(),
                                list1.end(),7);

  assert(*i == 7 && *(++i) == 11);

  cout << "Type some characters, including an 'x' followed\n"
    << "by at least one nonwhite-space character: " << flush;

  istream_iterator<char, ptrdiff_t> in(cin);
  istream_iterator<char, ptrdiff_t> eos;
  find(in, eos, 'x');
```

```
cout << "The first nonwhite-space character following\n"
     << "the first 'x' was '" << *(++in) << "'." << endl;
}
```

In the first part of this program, we use the `find` algorithm with ordinary pointers, which behave as input iterators for C++ arrays. The second part uses `find` with list iterators, which also satisfy the conditions outlined above. Finally, STL provides special input iterators called *istream* iterators, which are used to read values from an input stream. The last part of the program fragment keeps reading the standard `cin` input stream until the character `x` is found, or the end of the stream is reached. It then increments the istream iterator to the next nonwhite-space character and outputs that character.

In the cases of array and list iterators, other operations besides input iterator operations are supported, such as storing into positions to which an iterator refers. With istream iterators, however, the only operations supported are those of input iterators. Istream iterators are explained in greater detail later, in Section 4.7.

4.2 *Output Iterators*

In the previous section, we saw that input iterator objects can be used to read values from a sequence, but we are not necessarily able to write into it. Output iterators have the opposite functionality: they allow us to write values into a sequence, but they do not guarantee that we can read from it. That is, if `first` is an output iterator, we can say `*first = ...`, but it not guaranteed that we can use `*first` in an expression to obtain the value it refers to. One other difference from the requirements for input iterators is that there is no requirement that `==` or `!=` be defined on output iterators. Output iterators have the same requirements as input iterators for prefix and postfix `++` operations. As with input iterators, the term *output iterator* does not in itself represent a type. Instead, it can be applied to any type that satisfies the above requirements.

For example, consider the STL `copy` algorithm, which copies from one sequence to another:

```
template <class InputIterator, class OutputIterator>
OutputIterator copy(InputIterator first, InputIterator last,
        OutputIterator result)
{
  while (first != last)
    *result++ = *first++;
  return result;
}
```

Once again, ordinary pointers can be used as output iterators for built-in C++ arrays:

```
int a[100], b[100];
... code to store values in a[0], ..., a[99]

copy(&a[0], &a[100], &b[0]);
```

This copies the values in a[0],...,a[99] into b[0],...,b[99].

STL provides special output iterators called *ostream* iterators, which are used to write values to an output stream. For example, the following code fragment writes the elements of a list to the cout output stream:

```
list<int> list1;
... code to insert values in list1

// Declare an ostream iterator object, out:
ostream_iterator<int> out(cout, "\n");

copy(list1.begin(), list1.end(), out);
```

The arguments to the ostream_iterator constructor are an output stream object and a string to be written between values on the output stream; in this case a newline is used so that each value appears on a separate line. Ostream iterators are explained in greater detail later, in Section 4.7.

The array pointers used in the first example of copy do allow reading from the positions they refer to, but ostream iterators do not, so we could not have used ostream iterators in the first two argument positions of copy.

4.3 *Forward Iterators*

We have seen that input iterators can be used to read values from a sequence and that output iterators can be used to write to them. A *forward* iterator is one that is both an input iterator and an output iterator, and it thus allows both reading and writing and traversal in one direction. Forward iterators also have a property that input and output iterators are not required to have: it is possible to save a forward iterator and use it to start traversing again from the same position. This property allows forward iterators to be used in *multipass* algorithms, as opposed to *single-pass* algorithms (like find and merge).

As an example of an algorithm that does both reading from and writing to positions in a sequence, consider the STL replace algorithm, for replacing all occurrences of a value x in a range [first, last) by another value y:

```
template <class T>
void replace(ForwardIterator first, ForwardIterator last,
             const T& x, const T& y)
{
  while (first != last) {
    if (*first == x)
      *first = y;
    ++first;
  }
}
```

This algorithm can be used to replace values in a variety of data structures provided the type used to instantiate `ForwardIterator` satisfies the requirements of the forward iterator category.

Built-in pointer types, used with arrays, satisfy these requirements:

```
int a[100];
... code to store values in a[0], ..., a[99]

// Replace all values in the array equal to 5 by 6:
replace(&a[0], &a[100], 5, 6);
```

Since the type `deque<T>::iterator` also satisfies all forward iterator requirements, we can also use the above algorithm to replace elements in a deque:

```
deque<char> deque1;
... code to insert characters in deque1;

// Replace all occurrences of 'e' by 'o' in deque1:
replace(deque1.begin(), deque1.end(), 'e', 'o');
```

4.4 *Bidirectional Iterators*

In the last section we saw that forward iterators allow us to read values from and write values into a data structure while traversing it in a single direction. A *bidirectional* iterator is similar to a forward iterator, except that it allows traversal in either direction. That is, bidirectional iterators must support

- all forward iterator operations, plus

- the -- operation, making it possible to reverse direction in a sequence.

Both prefix and postfix versions of `operator--` are required, where the prefix version decrements the iterator and returns the new value, and the postfix version decrements the iterator but returns the old value. Both the prefix and the postfix `operator--` must be constant time operations.

The ability to traverse a data structure in the reverse direction is important because it would not otherwise be possible for certain algorithms to work efficiently. For example, the STL `reverse` algorithm can be used to reverse the order of elements in a sequence, provided bidirectional iterators are available. For example, built-in pointer types used with arrays satisfy all of the requirements of bidirectional iterators, and we can write

```
int a[100];
... code to store values in a[0], ..., a[99]

// Reverse the order of the values in the array:
reverse(&a[0], &a[100]);
```

But STL's `list` containers are also required to provide bidirectional iterators, and we can use them with `reverse`:

```
list<int> list1;
... code to store values in list1

// Reverse the order of the values in the list:
reverse(list1.begin(), list1.end());
```

As you might expect, the requirement that the `list` class supports bidirectional iterators implies that the list representation must be doubly linked. With singly linked lists, it would not be possible to implement `operator--` efficiently (in constant time).

Thus, the requirements for bidirectional iterators allow us to ensure that certain algorithms, such as `reverse`, which need to traverse a sequence in either direction, will operate efficiently.

4.5   Random Access Iterators

In the previous sections, we have seen four different categories of iterators, which allow us to express varying constraints that different algorithms impose on the data structures they work with, in order to operate efficiently. We have seen examples of algorithms that require data structures that can *at least* be

- read and traversed in one direction (expressed by saying that the algorithm accepts *input* iterators),

- written and traversed in one direction (expressed by saying that the algorithm accepts *output* iterators),

- read and written and traversed in one direction, with the additional ability to save iterators and resume scanning from saved positions (expressed by saying that the algorithm accepts *forward* iterators),

- read and written and traversed in either direction (expressed by saying that the algorithm accepts *bidirectional* iterators).

It turns out that these four different categories of data structures are not enough to account for all algorithms. There are some algorithms that impose even stronger requirements on iterators. To operate efficiently, these algorithms require that any position in a sequence be reachable from any other in *constant time*.

For example, consider the STL generic `binary_search` algorithm. When called as

```
binary_search(first, last, value)
```

where `first` and `last` delimit a sequence that is sorted into ascending order, the algorithm returns true if there is a position in the sequence where `value` occurs, false otherwise. This is similar to the specification of `find`, but `binary_search` takes advantage of the ordering of the sequence to produce its answer in $O(\log N)$ time rather than $O(N)$, where N is the length of the sequence. It is able to do this by comparing the value in the *middle* of the sequence with `value`, and confining its search to the first half if the middle value is larger than `value` or to the second half if the middle value is smaller. That is, the search space is cut in half with each comparison, so at most $\log_2 N$ comparisons are required. But for the overall computing time to be $O(\log N)$, *getting to the middle element* must be a constant time operation.

Clearly, lists do not have this property. Given pointers to the beginning and end of a list, the only way to get to the middle element is to traverse elements one by one. This takes time proportional to the length of the list.

On the other hand, vectors and arrays allow constant time access to an arbitrary element in the container. Thus, the `binary_search` algorithm will work efficiently for vectors and arrays:

```
vector<int> vector1;
... code to insert values in vector1

// Search vector1 for the value 5; if found,
// return true; otherwise, return false:
bool found =
    binary_search(vector1.begin(), vector1.end(), 5);
```

From this example, we see the need for yet another iterator category—a *random access* iterator category.

Random access iterators are required to support all operations supported by bidirectional iterators, plus

   a. additions and subtractions of an integer, expressed with r + n, n + r, and r - n (where r is a random access iterator and n is an integer expression),

   b. bidirectional "big jumps," expressed with r += n and r -= n (where r is a random access iterator and n is an integer expression),

   c. iterator subtraction, expressed as r - s (where s is another random access iterator), producing an integer value,

   d. comparisons, expressed as r < s, r > s, r <= s, and r >= s, producing `bool` values.

STL random access data structures, such as vectors and deques, require their iterators to satisfy the above requirements, so that any location in the data structure may be reached in constant time.

4.6 *The STL Iterator Hierarchy: Combining Algorithms and Containers Efficiently*

The key to understanding iterators and their role in STL is understanding why it is useful to classify iterators into the categories of input/output, forward, bidirectional, and random access. This classification comprises an iterator hierarchy:

- Forward iterators are also input and output iterators;

- Bidirectional iterators are also forward iterators, and therefore also input and output iterators;

- Random access iterators are also bidirectional iterators, and therefore also forward iterators and input and output iterators.

What this hierarchy essentially implies is that

- algorithms that require only input or output iterators can also be used with forward, bidirectional, or random access iterators;

- algorithms that require forward iterators can also be used with bidirectional or random access iterators;

- algorithms that require bidirectional iterators can also be used with random access iterators.

Iterator categories are thus used in the *specifications* of the containers and algorithms as follows:

- The description of container classes includes the category of the iterator types they provide;

- The description of generic algorithms includes the iterator categories with which they work.

Here are some examples:

1. `lists` provide bidirectional iterators, and the `find` algorithm just requires input iterators; hence `find` can be used with `lists`.

2. While `lists` provide bidirectional iterators, the `sort` algorithm requires random access iterators. Since bidirectional iterators are not required to have all the properties of random access iterators, `sort` *cannot* be used with lists. Code such as

```
list<int> list1;
... code to insert values in list1;
sort(list1.begin(), list1.end());
```

will not compile.

3. A `deque` does provide random access iterators, as required by `sort`. This means that `sort` will work with a `deque`; furthermore, the combination will be efficient.

4. `Set` iterators are bidirectional, and the `merge` algorithm requires input iterators or greater. Since bidirectional iterators are greater in the iterator hierarchy, we can immediately see that the `merge` algorithm can be applied to `sets`. The combination will be efficient and is allowed.

The iterator hierarchy highlights the fundamental idea behind the design of STL:

> *STL container and algorithm interfaces are designed to encourage combinations that are efficient and to discourage combinations that are inefficient.*

Iterator categories and efficiency issues are further discussed in Section 4.10 on page 63.

4.7 *Revisiting Input and Output: Stream Iterators*

We now take a slightly more detailed look at the input and output iterator categories. An important reason for including the input and output iterator categories in STL is to allow us to identify algorithms that can be used on iterators associated with I/O streams. Such iterators are provided by STL classes called `istream_iterator` (for input) and `ostream_iterator` (for output). Iterators constructed by `istream_iterator` are input iterators, but they are not output iterators. This means that `istream_iterator` objects can *read* data only in a single direction. Data cannot be *written* through an istream iterator object.

The type `istream_iterator<T>`[2] provides a constructor `istream_iterator(istream&)` that produces an input iterator for values of type `T` from a given input stream (such as the standard input stream `cin` in the next example).

The `istream_iterator<T>` class also provides a constructor `istream_iterator<T>()` that produces an input iterator that works as an *end marker* for istream iterators. This is simply a value to which istream iterators become equal when the istream they are scanning reports an end-of-stream condition.

An algorithm such as `merge` can be used with istream iterators because it needs to make only a single pass over the data and only read each data object, not assign to it. For example:

```
vector<int> vector1;
list<int> list1;
... code to insert values in vector1

merge(vector1.begin(), vector1.end(),
      istream_iterator<int>(cin),
      istream_iterator<int>(),
      back_inserter(list1));
```

This merges the integers in `vector1` with those on the standard input stream, `cin`, putting the result in `list1`. For storing into `list1` we use `back_inserter(list1)`, which is an example of an insert iterator. Insert iterators are output iterators and are described in Section 10.2.

The istream iterators in the preceding example could also be used for the first

---

2. This class has a default template parameter, `class Distance = ptrdiff_t`, which is a type that can store the distance between any two `istream_iterators` for the same stream. With STL versions for compilers that do not yet support default template parameters, you may be required to include the second parameter; e.g.,
   `istream_iterator<int, ptrdiff_t>(cin)`

pair of arguments to `merge`:

```
merge(istream_iterator<int>(cin), istream_iterator<int>(),
      vector1.begin(), vector1.end(), back_inserter(list1));
```

but we could not put an istream iterator in the *last* argument position, since `merge` needs to be able to assign new values through that iterator and it is not possible to do this through `istream_iterator` objects.

Iterators constructed by `ostream_iterator` are output iterators, but they are not input iterators. Again, an algorithm such as `merge` can be used with them. This time, though, the iterator must be used as the *result* parameter of `merge`:

```
vector<int> vector1;
list<int> lst;
... code to insert values in vector1 and list1

merge(vector1.begin(), vector1.end(),
      list1.begin(), list1.end(),
      ostream_iterator<int>(cout, " "));
```

The above example merges the integers in `vector1` with those in `list1` and places the result on the standard output stream, `cout`, inserting blanks between the values as they are output (that's what the second argument of the `ostream_iterator` constructor designates).

We cannot use an ostream iterator in any of the first four argument positions of `merge`, because `merge` needs to be able to read from objects obtained by dereferencing those iterators, and the `ostream_iterator` type does not provide such a capability.[3]

4.8 *Specification of Iterator Categories Required by STL Algorithms*

Let us take a closer look at how we determine, from the interface specifications of STL algorithms, which iterators can be used with an algorithm. The STL Generic Algorithm Reference Guide (Chapter 20) gives this interface for `merge`:

---

3. Another thing that would prevent us from using an `ostream_iterator` object in any of the first four argument positions of `merge` is the fact that the `ostream_iterator` type does not have a constructor like `istream_iterator()` that produces an end-marker (and even if it did, no equality-checking operator `==` or `!=` is defined on `ostream_iterator` objects).

```
template <class InputIterator1,
          class InputIterator2,
          class OutputIterator>
OutputIterator merge(InputIterator1 first1,
                     InputIterator1 last1,
                     InputIterator2 first2,
                     InputIterator2 last2,
                     OutputIterator result);
```

The conventions used in the STL Reference Guide are as follows:

- Template class parameter names that end in `Iterator`, or `Iterator`*n* for some integer *n*, signify that parameters of that type must be iterators; and

- The first part of the name is used to describe the category to which the iterator must belong.

So this interface description says that `merge` requires its first two parameters to be input iterators, of the same type; its third and fourth parameters also to be input iterators, of the same type (but a type possibly different from that of the first two parameters); and its last parameter to be an output iterator.

Just from reading this specification, without having to know exactly how `merge` is implemented, we can see that all the ways we've used it in previous examples are legal, including those using `istream_iterator` and `ostream_iterator` objects.

The `find` algorithm has this interface:

```
template <class InputIterator, class T>
InputIterator find(InputIterator first,
                   InputIterator last,
                   const T& value);
```

Thus, `find` requires its first two parameters to be input iterators, and it returns an input iterator. This means `find` works with virtually all iterators—input, forward, bidirectional, or random access. Only output iterators are excluded.

The specification of another algorithm, `search`, shows it to be a little more restrictive than `find`. The `search` algorithm looks for a subsequence within another sequence; it generalizes substring matching algorithms like `strstr`:

```
template<class ForwardIterator1, class ForwardIterator2>
ForwardIterator1 search(ForwardIterator1 first1,
                        ForwardIterator1 last1,
```

```
                        ForwardIterator2 first2,
                        ForwardIterator2 last2);
```

This says the arguments must be forward iterators, but why not input iterators? The reason is simply that the algorithm `search` uses is *multipass:* it saves iterators and uses them to rescan. So it would not work to try to use this algorithm with an `istream_iterator` or an `ostream_iterator`.

4.9 *Designing Generic Algorithms*

Once we understand how the interface specification for an algorithm tells us which iterators can be used, we don't really need to know the implementation of the algorithms. But let's reinforce our understanding of iterator categories by looking inside one algorithm and examining some of the design decisions that are dictated by the goal of making it as generic as possible, while still retaining its efficiency. Here again is the definition of the STL generic `find` algorithm:

```
template <class InputIterator, class T>
InputIterator find(InputIterator first,
                   InputIterator last,
                   const T& value) {
    while (first != last && *first != value)
         ++first;
    return first;
}
```

We see that such an implementation does indeed work with any input iterator, since

- it only applies `!=`, `*`, and `++` to its iterator parameters;

- it never tries to assign to objects it obtains using `*`; and

- it is a single-pass algorithm.

This `find` implementation makes the algorithm as generic as possible, but that's not true of other possible implementations. Suppose we make just one tiny change, using `<` instead of `!=` in the iterator comparison:

```
while (first < last && *first != value)
    ++first;
```

If we call this modified algorithm `find1`, we can see that many uses of `find1` would still work, such as with ordinary arrays, vectors, and deques. But if we try to use it with lists, as in

```
list<int> lst;
... code to insert values in lst

list<int>::iterator where = find1(lst.begin(),lst.end(),7);
```

it will fail because the implementation is trying to compute

```
lst.begin() < lst.end()
```

but no < operator is defined for `list` iterators (because such a < operator would be highly inefficient, as we will soon see). The failure shows up as a compile-time error.[4]

Put another way, since the presence of the operator < is guaranteed only by random access iterators, the interface to `find1` would have to be expressed as

```
template <class RandomAccessIterator, class T>
RandomAccessIterator find1(RandomAccessIterator first,
         RandomAccessIterator last, const T& value);
```

One of the key achievements in the design of STL is its demonstration that many algorithms like `find` can be coded with minimal requirements for access to data, thus making them generic. In all cases of implementations like that of `find1`, in which unnecessarily restrictive requirements are placed on their iterators, the implementations have been refined and reduced to ones like that of `find`—those that make the minimal possible assumptions and therefore are of the broadest possible utility.

4.10 *Why Some Algorithms Require More Powerful Iterators*

Some algorithms in the library require more of iterators than the minimal capabilities that input, output, or forward iterators provide. Such algorithms need the iterators supplied to them to be of the bidirectional or random access category; otherwise they simply won't compile. For example, `sort` has the following interface:

---

4. The compiler error message is something like "Could not find a match for `list<int>::iterator::operator<(list<int>::iterator)`."

```
template <class RandomAccessIterator>
void sort(RandomAccessIterator first,
          RandomAccessIterator last);
```

meaning that `sort` requires two iterators, both of the random access category. That's just what is supplied when we write

```
vector<int> vector1;
... code to insert values in vector1

sort(vector1.begin(), vector1.end());
```

As with the not-so-generic `find1` implementation, we now see why we run into problems when we try to apply `sort` to a `list`:

```
list<int> list1;
... code to insert values in list1

sort(list1.begin(), list1.end());  // incorrect
```

Since `list1.begin()` and `list1.end()` are only bidirectional iterators, they do not provide all of the operations that the implementation of `sort` tries to use, such as `+=`, so this code will not compile.

Why not extend `list` iterators, and those for the other container categories, to have operators `+=` and `<` and the other operations that random access iterators have? That would seem to simplify the task of writing generic algorithms, since we wouldn't have to worry so much about which operations we could apply to iterators. Again, the answer is *efficiency*. With `list`s, there's no way to do computations such as `lst.begin() + n` in constant time; we have only the obvious method of stepping through the list nodes one by one, taking time proportional to n (i.e., linear time) to do it. So even if we programmed that method and called it `+`, *we would not have achieved true random access*. Algorithms such as `sort` would then run much more slowly than other sorting algorithms that take special advantage of lists (such as the algorithm used by the `list` class `sort` member function).

4.11 *Choosing the Right Algorithm*

One final point about algorithm/container compatibility: although STL's iterator classification scheme encourages efficient combinations and discourages inefficient ones, it does not completely eliminate combinations that could be *inefficient in some cases*. That is, it may be *possible* to apply a generic algorithm to a container but it is not always wise to do so.

Perhaps the simplest example is once again the find algorithm, in combination with random access containers such as arrays, vectors or deques. As we've seen, find just steps through the objects in a sequence one by one, so it is a linear time algorithm (i.e., the time taken to find a value in a container of size N is proportional to N). If the objects in the sequence are not ordered in any particular way, this kind of search may be the best we can do. However, if we happen to have the objects in a random access container in sorted order, then another STL algorithm, binary_search, will do the job far more efficiently (in *logarithmic time,* that is, proportional to the logarithm of the size of the container).

A slightly more subtle case comes up when we consider the possibility of searching an associative container. Again, the generic find algorithm *could* be used, since associative containers provide a bidirectional iterator type. But STL associative containers are organized internally in such a way that they can be searched in logarithmic time. And they all provide a member function (it's also called find and takes one argument, the value for which to search) that does this efficient search. So for a large associative container, it would be very inefficient to use the generic find on the entire range of positions in the container:

```
set<int, less<int> > set1;
... code to insert some values in set1
set<int, less<int> >::iterator where;

where = find(set1.begin(), set1.end(), 7);
```

This works, but in linear time. It would be much better to write the following, since it runs in logarithmic time:

```
where = set1.find(7);
```

4.12 *Constant Versus Mutable Iterator Types*

There is an additional distinction that applies to forward, bidirectional, and random access iterators—they can be *mutable* or *constant* depending on whether the result of `operator*` is a reference or a reference to a constant.

All STL container types define not only the identifier `iterator` but also `const_iterator`. For example,

- `vector<T>::iterator` is a mutable random access iterator type, and

- `vector<T>::const_iterator` is the corresponding constant random access iterator type.

When the result of `operator*` on an iterator `i` is a reference, it is possible to do assignments `*i = ....` Such assignments, however, are impossible with a reference to a constant (i.e., such as in the case when the iterator is actually a constant iterator). The compiler will flag attempts to do such assignments as errors.

Other uses that might result in changing the object to which `*i` refers, such as passing `*i` to a function in place of a nonconstant reference parameter (i.e., `T&` but not `const T&`), are also disallowed.

In most cases we can use a container type's `iterator` type when declaring iterator variables:

```
vector<int> vector1;
... code to insert values in vector1

vector<int>::iterator i = vector1.begin(); // OK
```

This is correct because the `begin` member function returns an `iterator` when applied to a mutable container (i.e., a container that is not declared constant). Actually, it would also work to write

```
vector<int>::const_iterator i = vector1.begin(); // OK
```

since a conversion from `iterator` to `const_iterator` is provided.

But if we have a constant container, we have to use constant iterators with it:

```
// initialize vector2 with 100 zeros:
const vector<int> vector2(100, 0);

vector<int>::iterator i = vector2.begin(); // incorrect
```

Instead, the declaration should be

```
vector<int>::const_iterator i = vector2.begin();
```

In this case, using `iterator` is incorrect because the `begin` member function returns a `const_iterator` when applied to a container declared `const`. No conversion from `const_iterator` to `iterator` is provided, so the attempt to initialize i with the `const_iterator` returned by `begin` results in a compilation error message.

We won't often directly declare a container constant, since we usually want to insert elements into or erase elements from the container after it's created. But any time we pass a container to a function through a constant reference parameter, it is as though the container were declared constant:

```
template <class T>
void print(const vector<T>& v)
{
    for (vector<T>::const_iterator i = v.begin();
         i != v.end(); ++i)
       cout << *i << endl;
}
```

Attempting to use `vector<T>::iterator` in the above example would produce a compile-time error message, as would any attempt to use the container's `insert` or `erase` member functions.

If we have a function with an iterator parameter, the parameter should be declared `const_iterator` if possible:

```
void foo(list<T>::const_iterator i,
         deque<T>& d, deque<T>::iterator j)
{
    if (*i > *j++)
       *j = *i++;
    d.insert(j, *i);
}
```

Here we use * only to read the value to which i refers, not to assign through it, so declaring i to be a `const_iterator` is okay. It could also be declared `iterator`, but then for the corresponding actual parameter we would only be able to use `iterator` values. On the other hand, j must be declared `iterator`, since we assign through it and use it as a parameter to `insert` (either one alone would require an `iterator`).

Note that both i and j are subjected to incrementing with ++ in this example. The "const" in `const_iterator` doesn't mean that the iterator itself can't be changed; it only inhibits changing the value to which the iterator refers.

4.13 Iterator Categories Provided by STL Containers

Table 4-1 shows the category of each iterator type that the different containers in STL provide. Note that for `sets` and `multisets`, both the `iterator` and `const_iterator` types are constant bidirectional types—in fact, they are the same type. The reason for this is as follows: for sets and multisets, the only allowed method of changing a stored key is to first delete it (using the `erase` member function) and then insert a different key (with the `insert` member function). If the set and multiset iterators were not constant iterators, then it would be possible to modify the keys without going through the `erase` and `insert` member functions. The following example illustrates this point:

```
#include <set.h>

set<int, less<int> > s;
s.insert(3);
s.insert(5);
s.insert(7);

set<int, less<int> >::iterator i = s.begin();
*i = 4;  // incorrect
```

This will not compile since `i` is a constant iterator and elements cannot be modified through constant iterators. Instead, we must write

```
s.erase(i);
s.insert(4);
```

A similar restriction applies with maps and multimaps. A `map<Key, T, less<Key>` > object stores values of type `pair<const Key, T>`. The key part of such a pair cannot be directly modified but it is possible to modify the value of type `T`. The following example illustrates this:

```
#include <map.h>

typedef multimap<int, double, less<int> > multimap_1;
multimap_1 m;
m.insert(pair<const int, double>(3, 4.1));
multimap_1::iterator i = m.begin();
*i = pair<const int, double>(3, 5.1);  // incorrect
```

This is an incorrect method of modifying values in maps and multimaps, and it will not compile. A correct method is to erase the value to which i points, then insert the new pair:

```
m.erase(i);
m.insert(pair<const int, double>(3, 5.1));
```

It would also be correct to write

```
(*i).second = 5.1;
```

since the values associated with keys in a map or multimap can be modified using nonconstant iterators. This latter method is preferred, since it is more efficient than using erase and insert. It would not be permitted, though, if we had declared i as a multimap_1::const_iterator, since constant iterators do not allow modification of the values to which they refer.

TABLE 4-1. Category of Each Iterator Type the STL Containers Provide

Container	Iterator	Iterator category
T a[n]	T*	mutable random access
T a[n]	const T*	constant random access
vector<T>	vector<T>::iterator	mutable random access
vector<T>	vector<T>::const_iterator	constant random access
deque<T>	deque<T>::iterator	mutable random access
deque<T>	deque<T>::const_iterator	constant random access
list<T>	list<T>::iterator	mutable bidirectional
list<T>	list<T>::const_iterator	constant bidirectional
set<T>	set<T>::iterator	constant bidirectional
set<T>	set<T>::const_iterator	constant bidirectional
multiset<T>	multiset<T>::iterator	constant bidirectional
multiset<T>	multiset<T>::const_iterator	constant bidirectional
map<Key,T>	map<Key,T>::iterator	mutable bidirectional
map<Key,T>	map<Key,T>::const_iterator	constant bidirectional
multimap<Key,T>	multimap<Key,T>::iterator	mutable bidirectional
multimap<Key,T>	multimap<Key,T>::const_iterator	constant bidirectional

CHAPTER 5

Generic Algorithms

STL provides a rich set of algorithms that operate on data structures defined within the STL framework. As we saw in Section 2.2, STL algorithms are *generic*: each algorithm can operate not just on a single data structure but on a variety of data structures.

STL generic algorithms fall into four broad categories, based loosely on their semantics. *Nonmutating sequence algorithms* operate on containers without, in general, modifying the contents of the container, while *mutating sequence algorithms* typically modify the containers on which they operate. The *sorting-related algorithms* include sorting and merging algorithms, binary searching algorithms, and set operations on sorted sequences. Finally, there is a small collection of *generalized numeric algorithms*. We will consider each of these in turn.

The previous chapter explained how iterators are used to allow different classes of algorithms to work with a variety of data structures. In this chapter we explore the various categories of algorithms and explain their usage through examples. For further details on each algorithm, the reader is referred to the generic algorithm reference guide in Chapter 20.

5.1 Basic Algorithm Organization in STL

Before taking a detailed look at the four main categories of STL algorithms, we give a brief overview of the different variations that a particular algorithm may have. The different variations include in-place and copying versions, and versions that take predicate parameters.

5.1.1 In-Place and Copying Versions

For certain STL algorithms, both *in-place* and *copying* versions are provided. An in-place version of the algorithm places its result into the same container on which it operates.

Example 5-1 Using an in-place generic `sort` algorithm.

```
#include <algo.h>
#include <assert.h>
```

```
int main() {
  int a[1000];
  for (int i = 0; i < 1000; i++)
    a[i] = 1000 - i - 1;

  sort(&a[0], &a[1000]);

  for (i = 0; i < 1000; i++)
    assert(a[i] == i);
}
```

This program sorts the array a and puts the sorted sequence back into a. That is, the array is replaced with a sorted version of itself, since the generic sort algorithm is an in-place algorithm.

A copying version of an algorithm copies its result to a different container or to a nonoverlapping portion of the same container on which it operates. For example, in the following program, reverse_copy leaves the array a unchanged and puts a reversed copy of it into the array b.

Example 5-2 Using reverse_copy, **a copying version of the generic reverse algorithm.**

```
#include <algo.h>
#include <assert.h>

int main() {
  int a[1000], b[1000];
  for (int i = 0; i < 1000; i++)
    a[i] = i;

  reverse_copy(&a[0], &a[1000], &b[0]);

  for (i = 0; i < 1000; i++)
    assert(a[i] == i && b[i] == 1000 - i - 1);
}
```

In STL, the decision whether to include a copying version of an algorithm is based on complexity considerations. For example, sort_copy is *not* provided, since the cost of sorting is much greater than the cost of copying, and users might as well do copy followed by sort. On the other hand, replace_copy is provided, since the cost of copying is greater than the cost of replacing a value in a container.

Whenever a copying version is provided for *algorithm* in STL, it is called *algorithm*_copy. For example, the copying version of replace is called replace_copy.

5.1.2 Algorithms with Function Parameters

Many of STL's generic algorithms have a version that accepts a function as a parameter. In most cases these functions are *predicates* (a predicate is a function that returns a `bool` value). For example, all of the sorting-related algorithms accept a binary predicate parameter and use it to compare two values x and y to determine whether x is less than y in some ordering. By supplying different functions for this parameter, we can produce different orders in the resulting sequence.[1]

One convenient way to obtain a function to pass to a generic algorithm is to use one of STL's function object types, as discussed briefly in Section 2.4 and in more detail in Chapter 8. Function objects are a form of function representation that makes function passing especially efficient because it can be done at compile time. In the following example, a function object `greater<int>()`, constructed with the default constructor of the template class `greater`, is used as a binary predicate and passed to the generic `sort` algorithm to sort an array into descending order. This function object class is defined in the STL header `function.h`. The array is initialized using the STL generic `random_shuffle` algorithm[2] to rearrange array elements into a random permutation of the original order.

Example 5-3 Using the generic `sort` algorithm with a binary predicate.

```
#include <algo.h>
#include <function.h>
#include <assert.h>

int main() {
  int a[1000];
  for (int i = 0; i < 1000; i++)
    a[i] = i;
  random_shuffle(&a[0], &a[1000]);

  // Sort into ascending order:
  sort(&a[0], &a[1000]);

  for (i = 0; i < 1000; i++)
    assert(a[i] == i);

  random_shuffle(&a[0], &a[1000]);
```

---

1. Functions used for comparison in sorting-related algorithms must obey certain laws, as will be discussed in Section 5.4.

2. Use of this algorithm, from header `algo.h`, may require compilation and linking of another file, as will be discussed in Section 5.3.5.

```
// Sort into descending order:
sort(&a[0], &a[1000], greater<int>());

for (i = 0; i < 1000; i++)
    assert(a[i] == 1000 - i - 1);
}
```

The version of `sort` with two iterator parameters makes comparisons of values in the sequence using the < operator defined on the value type. The version with two iterator parameters and a binary predicate parameter makes comparisons with the binary predicate. The same name, `sort`, is used for both since the two versions are distinguishable by the difference in their parameter lists. In a few cases, though, there would be an ambiguity that could not be resolved, and different names must be used. For example, the predicate version of `find` is called `find_if` so that there is no ambiguity between the two interfaces:

```
template <class InputIterator, class T>
find(InputIterator first, InputIterator last,
     const T& value);

template <class InputIterator, class Predicate>
find_if(InputIterator first, InputIterator last,
        Predicate pred);
```

In the example programs in this chapter, we give examples of either the predicate or the nonpredicate versions of an algorithm, or in a few cases both. A predicate version whose name ends with `_if` is discussed in the subsection labeled with the base name; for example, `find_if` is discussed in Section 5.2.1, called "Find."

5.2 *Nonmutating Sequence Algorithms*

Nonmutating sequence algorithms are those that do not directly modify the containers on which they operate. They include algorithms to search for elements in sequences, to check for equality, and to count sequence elements.

The nonmutating sequence algorithms are `find`, `adjacent_find`, `count`, `for_each`, `mismatch`, `equal`, and `search`. We examine each of these in this section.

5.2.1 Find

In Section 2.2 we saw several examples of the generic `find` algorithm. Its predicate version, `find_if`, searches a sequence for the first occurrence of an element for which the given predicate is true.

Example 5-4 Illustrating the generic `find_if` algorithm.

```
#include <algo.h>
#include <vector.h>
#include <assert.h>

// Define a unary predicate object type:
class GreaterThan50 {
 public:
   bool operator()(int x) const { return x > 50; }
};

int main()
{
  // Create a vector with values 0, 1, 4, 9, 16, ..., 144:
  vector<int> vector1;
  for (int i = 0; i < 13; ++i)
    vector1.push_back(i * i);

  vector<int>::iterator where;
  where = find_if(vector1.begin(), vector1.end(),
                  GreaterThan50());

  assert(*where == 64);
}
```

In this program we define a unary predicate object type, `GreaterThan50`, and pass an object constructed with its default constructor to `find_if`. (Instead of defining `GreaterThan50` as a new class, we could have assembled an equivalent function object type using STL function objects and function adaptors, as discussed in Chapter 8.)

The time complexity of the `find` and `find_if` algorithms is linear.

5.2.2 Adjacent_find

The `adjacent_find` algorithm searches a sequence for adjacent pairs of equal elements. When it finds two adjacent equal elements, it returns an iterator pointing to the first of the pair.

75

Example 5-5 Illustrating the generic `adjacent_find` **algorithm.**

```
#include <algo.h>
#include <bstring.h>
#include <deque.h>
#include <function.h>
#include <assert.h>

int main()
{
   deque<string> player(5, string());
   deque<string>::iterator diter;

   // Initialize the deque:
   player[0] = "Pele";
   player[1] = "Platini";
   player[2] = "Maradona";
   player[3] = "Maradona";
   player[4] = "Rossi";

   // Find the first pair of equal consecutive names:
   diter = adjacent_find(player.begin(), player.end());

   assert(*diter == "Maradona" && *(diter+1) == "Maradona");

   // Find the first name that is lexicographically
   // greater than the following name:
   diter = adjacent_find(player.begin(), player.end(),
         greater<string>());

   assert(*diter == "Platini" && *(diter+1) == "Maradona");
}
```

This program first uses the nonpredicate version of `adjacent_find`, which uses `string::operator==` for the comparisons and thus finds the first pair of equal elements. It then conducts another search using the predicate version of `adjacent_find` and the binary predicate `greater<string>()` to do the comparisons. It thus finds the first pair of consecutive strings in the deque such that the first string is lexicographically greater than the second.

The time complexity of the `adjacent_find` algorithm is linear.

5.2.3 Count

`Count` is a nonmutating sequence algorithm that searches a sequence and counts the number of elements equal to a specified value.

Example 5-6   Demonstrating the generic count algorithm.

```
#include <function.h>
#include <algo.h>
#include <assert.h>

int main()
{
  int a[] = {0, 0, 0, 1, 1, 1, 2, 2, 2};
  int final_count = 0;

  // Count the number of values in the array a
  // that are equal to 1:
  count(&a[0], &a[9], 1, final_count);

  assert(final_count == 3);

  // Determine the number of array elements that are not
  // equal to 1:
  final_count = 0;
  count_if(&a[0], &a[9], bind2nd(not_equal_to<int>(), 1),
           final_count);

  assert(final_count == 6);
  // There are 6 elements not equal to 1.
}
```

The first call to count determines the number of elements in the array a that are equal to 1. Note that count *increases its last argument* by the number it computes, rather than returning it as a function value. Although it would be more natural to return the number as a function value, that would require deducing its type from that of the iterator arguments, which is impossible with built-in iterator types like int*.

The second call is to count_if, the unary predicate version of the algorithm, to determine the number of elements in the array that are not equal to 1. The unary predicate is constructed by passing the binary predicate not_equal_to<int> to the *function adaptor* bind2nd, along with the argument 1, as follows:

```
bind2nd(not_equal_to<int>(), 1)
```

Both not_equal_to and bind2nd are defined in the header file function.h.

Note that by simply changing the arguments to the predicate, we can easily accomplish a completely different task. For example, to find the number of elements in the array greater than 5, we use the predicate

```
bind2nd(greater<int>(), 5)
```

The time complexity of the `count` and `count_if` algorithms is linear.

5.2.4 For_each

The generic `for_each` algorithm applies a function `f` to each element of a sequence.

Example 5-7 Illustrating the generic `for_each` algorithm.
```
#include <algo.h>
#include <bstring.h>
#include <list.h>
#include <iostream.h>

void print_list(string s)
{
  cout << s << endl;
}

int main()
{
  list<string> dlist;
  dlist.insert(dlist.end(), "Clark");
  dlist.insert(dlist.end(), "Rindt");
  dlist.insert(dlist.end(), "Senna");

  // Print out each list element.
  for_each(dlist.begin(), dlist.end(), print_list);
}
```

Output from Example 5-7:
```
    Clark
    Rindt
    Senna
```

In this example we use the `for_each` algorithm to print all elements of a list. The function `print_list` is applied to the result of dereferencing each iterator in the range [`dlist.begin()`, `dlist.end()`).[3] The result of the function applied by `for_each` on the container elements is ignored.

---

3. The iterator range concept and notation were introduced on page 49.

The time complexity of the `for_each` algorithm is linear.

5.2.5   Mismatch and equal

The `mismatch` and `equal` algorithms are used to compare two ranges. Each accepts three iterator parameters: `first1`, `last1`, and `first2`. The `equal` algorithm returns true if the elements at corresponding positions `first1 +` i and `first2 +` i are equal for all positions `first1 +` i in the range [`first1`, `last1`), and false otherwise. The `mismatch` algorithm returns a `pair` of iterators, `first1 +` i and `first2 +` i, which are the first corresponding positions where unequal elements occur. If there are no unequal elements in corresponding positions, `last1` and `first2 +` (`last1` – `first1`) are returned. Thus

```
equal(first1, last1, first2)
```

is equivalent to

```
mismatch(first1, last1, first2).first == last1
```

Example 5-8   Illustrating the generic `equal` and `mismatch` algorithms.

```
#include <algo.h>
#include <bstring.h>
#include <list.h>
#include <deque.h>
#include <assert.h>

int main()
{
   list<string> driver_list;
   vector<string> vec;
   deque<string> deq;

   driver_list.insert(driver_list.end(), "Clark");
   driver_list.insert(driver_list.end(), "Rindt");
   driver_list.insert(driver_list.end(), "Senna");

   vec.insert(vec.end(), "Clark");
   vec.insert(vec.end(), "Rindt");
   vec.insert(vec.end(), "Senna");
   vec.insert(vec.end(), "Berger");

   deq.insert(deq.end(), "Clark");
   deq.insert(deq.end(), "Berger");
```

```
// Show that driver_list and the first 3 elements of
// vec are equal in all corresponding positions:
assert(equal(driver_list.begin(), driver_list.end(),
             vec.begin()));

// Show that deq and the first 2 elements of driver_list
// are not equal in all corresponding positions:
assert(!equal(deq.begin(), deq.end(),
              driver_list.begin()));

// Find the corresponding positions in deq and driver_list
// at which unequal elements first occur:
pair<deque<string>::iterator, list<string>::iterator>
   pair1 = mismatch(deq.begin(), deq.end(),
                    driver_list.begin());

if (pair1.first != deq.end())
   cout << "First disagreement in deq and driver_list:\n  "
        << *(pair1.first) << " and " << *(pair1.second)
        << endl;
}
```

Output from Example 5-8:
```
First disagreement in deq and driver_list:
  Berger and Rindt
```

In this example, although the list `driver_list` is not equal to the entire vector `vec`, the first assertion shows that `equal` determines that `driver_list` does agree with the initial three-element range in `vec`. In the second assertion, `equal` returns false since `deq` and `driver_list` disagree in their second positions. Calling `equal` does not yield any information about where the disagreement occurs, but the final part of the program shows how `mismatch` can be called, and its return value used, to display the elements that disagree.

Note that neither of these algorithms can serve as a complete check for the equality of two containers, since there is no check for the containers having the same size. To check if two containers `c1` and `c2` have equal contents, we can write

```
c1.size() == c2.size() &&
   equal(c1.begin, c1.end(), c2.begin())
```

This works even if `c1` and `c2` are of different types, but if they are of the same type, we only have to write

```
c1 == c2
```

since, as we'll see in Section 6.1.6, the == operator is defined on containers of the same type by exactly the preceding expression using size and equal.

One other point should be noted about the size of the ranges given to equal or mismatch. The number of dereferenceable positions reachable from first2 should be at least the size of [first1, last1), or else there should be a disagreement between some reachable, dereferenceable position and the corresponding position in [first1, last1). If neither of these conditions holds, the result of equal or mismatch is undefined. For example, it would be incorrect to write the first call to equal in Example 5-8 as

```
equal(vec.begin(), vec.end(), driver_list.begin())
```

since the end of driver_list would be reached without finding a disagreement.

Both algorithms have predicate versions, in which the meaning of equality can be replaced by a binary predicate given as the fourth argument.

The time complexity of both equal and mismatch is linear.

5.2.6 Search

Given two ranges, the generic search algorithm finds the first position in the first range in which the second range occurs as a subsequence. It generalizes string matching functions like the C library function strstr. Its interface is

```
template <class ForwardIterator1, class ForwardIterator2>
  ForwardIterator1
      search(ForwardIterator1 first1, ForwardIterator1 last1,
             ForwardIterator2 first2, ForwardIterator2 last2);
```

where the two sequences are determined by the ranges [first1, last1) and [first2, last2). If the second range does occur as a subsequence of the first, the beginning position in [first1, last1) of the first occurrence is returned; otherwise, last1 is returned.

Example 5-9 Illustrating the generic search algorithm.
```
#include <algo.h>
#include <vector.h>
#include <deque.h>
#include <assert.h>

int main()
{
  vector<int> vec(20);
```

```
    deque<int> deq(5);
    // Initialize vector with 0, 1, ..., 19:
    for (int i = 0; i < 20; ++i)
      vec[i] = i;

    // Initialize deque deq with 5, 6, 7, 8, 9:
    for (i = 0; i < 5; ++i)
      deq[i] = i + 5;

    // Search for first occurrence of the deque contents
    // as a subsequence of the vector contents:
    vector<int>::iterator viter =
      search(vec.begin(), vec.end(), deq.begin(), deq.end());

    for (i = 0; i < 5; ++i)
      assert(*(viter + i) == i + 5);
}
```

The call to the `search` algorithm looks for the first position in the vector where the deque elements (5, 6, 7, 8, 9) are contained as a range. It returns an iterator object of type `vector<int>::iterator`, pointing to the element 5 within the vector.

The algorithm also has a predicate version, taking a binary predicate as a fifth argument and using it as the meaning of equality.

The time complexity of the `search` algorithm is only required to be quadratic, and that's the case with the HP reference implementation of STL. This implementation does not use the famous Knuth-Morris-Pratt (KMP) algorithm, because although the KMP algorithm guarantees linear time, it tends to be slower in most practical cases than the naive algorithm with worst-case quadratic behavior. The worst case is extremely unlikely.

5.3 Mutating Sequence Algorithms

Mutating sequence algorithms are those that modify the contents of the containers on which they operate. They include algorithms to copy, replace, transform, remove, and rotate elements in data structures, and several other algorithms as well.

5.3.1 Copy and copy_backward

The generic `copy` and `copy_backward` algorithms are used to copy elements from one range to another. The call

```
copy(first1, last1, first2)
```

copies [first1, last1) to [first2, last2), where last2 == first2 + (last1 - first1), and returns last2. The algorithm proceeds forward, copying source elements in the order first1, first1 + 1, . . . , last1 - 1, with the consequence that the destination range can overlap with the source range provided it doesn't contain first2. Thus, for example, copy can be used to shift a range one position to the left but not to the right. The opposite is true of copy_backward:

```
copy_backward(first1, last1, last2)
```

copies [first1, last1) to [first2, last2), where first2 == last2 - (last1 - first1), and returns first2. It proceeds backward, copying source elements in the order last1 - 1, last1 - 2, . . . , first1. The copying thus works properly as long as the source range doesn't contain last2.

For example, to shift a range left by one position, use

```
copy(first1, last1, first1 - 1)
```

which copies first1 to first1 - 1, first1 + 1 to first1, . . . , last1 - 1 to last1 - 2, and returns last1 - 1. To shift a range right by one position, use

```
copy_backward(first1, last1, last1 + 1)
```

which copies last1 - 1 to last1, last1 - 2 to last1 - 1, . . . , first1 to first1 + 1, and returns first1 + 1.

Example 5-10   Illustrating the generic copy **and** copy_backward **algorithms.**

```
#include <vector.h>
#include <algo.h>
#include <iostream.h>
#include <bstring.h>
#include <assert.h>
int main()
{
  vector<char> vector1 =
    string("abcdefghihklmnopqrstuvwxyz");

  vector<char> vector2(vector1.size());

  // Copy vector1 to vector2:
  copy(vector1.begin(), vector1.end(),
      vector2.begin());
```

```
    assert(vector1 == vector2);

    // Shift the contents of vector1 left by 4 positions:
    copy(vector1.begin() + 4, vector1.end(),
        vector1.begin());

    assert(string(vector1) ==
           string("efghihklmnopqrstuvwxyzwxyz"));

    // Shift it right by 2 positions:
    copy_backward(vector1.begin(), vector1.end() - 2,
                  vector1.end());

    assert(string(vector1) ==
           string("efefghihklmnopqrstuvwxyzwx"));
}
```

In this program the initialization in the declaration of vector1 takes advantage of a type conversion provided by the string class, from string to vector<char>. The first example of copy copies from vector1 to vector2.

The second example illustrates copying to an overlapping range, shifting the contents of vector1 to the left by 4 positions. The assertion that follows this copy call uses another type conversion provided by the string class, from vector<char> to string. Note that, after the shift, the first four characters, abcd, have been lost, and the last four characters, wxyz, are repeated at the end.

The example of copy_backward is a shift by 2 positions to the right; this shift could not be done with copy. In this case, the first 2 characters, ef, of the previous string are now repeated at the beginning, and the last two, yz, are lost.

The copy and copy_backward algorithms have linear time bounds.

5.3.2 Fill

The fill and fill_n algorithms put copies of a given value in all positions of a range. The call

```
fill(first, last, value)
```

puts last - first copies of value in [first, last). The call

```
fill_n(first, n, value)
```

puts n copies of value in [first, first + n).

Example 5-11 Illustrating the generic `fill` **and** `fill_n` **algorithms.**

```
#include <algo.h>
#include <vector.h>
#include <bstring.h>
#include <assert.h>

int main()
{
  vector<char> vector1 = string("Hello there");

  // Fill first 5 positions of vector1 with X's:
  fill(vector1.begin(), vector1.begin() + 5, 'X');

  assert(string(vector1) == string("XXXXX there"));

  // Fill 3 more positions with Y's.
  fill_n(vector1.begin() + 5, 3, 'Y');

  assert(string(vector1) == string("XXXXXYYYere"));
}
```

The time complexity of the `fill` and `fill_n` algorithms is linear.

5.3.3 Generate

The `generate` algorithm fills a range `[first, last)` with the values returned by `last - first` successive calls to a function `gen`. It is assumed that `gen` takes no arguments.

Example 5-12 Illustrating the generic `generate` **algorithm.**

```
#include <algo.h>
#include <vector.h>
#include <assert.h>

class calc_square {
  int i;
 public:
  calc_square(): i(0) {}
  int operator()() { ++i; return i * i; }
};

int main()
{
  vector<int> vector1(10);
```

```
    // Fill vector1 with 1, 4, 9, 16, ..., 100
    generate(vector1.begin(), vector1.end(), calc_square());

    for (int j = 0; j < 10; ++j)
      assert(vector1[j] == (j+1)*(j+1));
}
```

The call to `generate` fills the vector `vector1` with the values returned by 10 successive calls of the function object `calc_square()`. Note that each of these calls is

```
    calc_square()()
```

since the function called is the one defined as `operator()` in class `calc_square`. Though the call is the same each time, it returns a different value because the data member `i` is incremented during each call. Function objects used with `generate` are typically defined to change some data member on which the return value depends, so that successive calls produce different values.

The time complexity of the `generate` algorithm is linear.

5.3.4 Partition

Given a range [`first, last`) and a unary predicate `pred`, the generic partition algorithm rearranges the elements in the range such that all elements that satisfy `pred` are placed before all elements that do not satisfy it. There is a version of the algorithm called `stable_partition`, which guarantees that within each group the relative positions of the elements are preserved. Each function returns an iterator marking the end of the first group and the beginning of the second.

Example 5-13 Illustrating the generic `partition` and `stable_partition` algorithms.

```
#include <algo.h>
#include <vector.h>
#include <bstring.h>
#include <iostream.h>

bool above40(int n) { return (n > 40); }

int main()
{
  const int N = 7;
  int array0[N] = {50, 30, 10, 70, 60, 40, 20};
  int array1[N];
```

```
copy(&array0[0], &array0[N], &array1[0]);
ostream_iterator<int> out(cout, " ");

cout << "Original sequence:                  ";
copy(&array1[0], &array1[N], out), cout << endl;

// Partition array1, putting numbers greater than 40
// first, followed by those less than or equal to 40:
int* split = partition(&array1[0], &array1[N], above40);

cout << "Result of (unstable) partitioning: ";
copy(&array1[0], split, out), cout << "| ";
copy(split, &array1[N], out), cout << endl;

// Restore array1 to array0 contents:
copy(&array0[0], &array0[N], &array1[0]);

// Again partition array1, putting numbers greater than 40
// first, followed by those less than or equal to 40,
// preserving relative order in each group:
split = stable_partition(&array1[0], &array1[N], above40);

cout << "Result of stable partitioning:      ";
copy(&array1[0], split, out), cout << "| ";
copy(split, &array1[N], out), cout << endl;
}
```

Output from Example 5-13:
```
Original sequence:                  50 30 10 70 60 40 20
Result of (unstable) partitioning: 50 60 70 | 10 30 40 20
Result of stable partitioning:     50 70 60 | 30 10 40 20
```

In this program the call to partition rearranges the values in array1 into two groups: first, those that are greater than 40, and second, those that are 40 or less. The partition algorithm makes no guarantee about the relative order in each group, and indeed we see that in the result 70 and 60 are permuted.[4] With stable_partition, on the other hand, the elements in each group appear in the result in the same order as they did in the original sequence.

In compiling this program with the HP reference implementation of STL, we had to compile and link the file tembuf.cpp, which is part of the HP STL distri-

---

4. The exact order produced by partition might vary with different STL implementations.

bution. This file declares an array, `__stl_temp_buffer`, which is used by the `stable_partition` algorithm. The declaration is in a separate file so that this buffer can be shared when several separately compiled files are linked to produce a single executable file. Other STL implementations might handle this compilation issue differently.

The time complexity is linear for both `partition` and `stable_partition`.

5.3.5 Random Shuffle

The generic `random_shuffle` algorithm randomly shuffles the elements in a range [`first`, `last`), using a pseudo-random number generating function. The permutations produced by `random_shuffle` are approximately uniformly distributed; that is, the probability of each of the $N!$ permutations of a range of size N is approximately $1/N!$.

Example 5-14 Illustrating the generic `random_shuffle` **algorithm.**

```
#include <algo.h>
#include <vector.h>
#include <function.h>
#include <iostream.h>

int main() {
  const int N = 20;
  vector<int> vector1(N);
  for (int i = 0; i < N; ++i)
    vector1[i] = i;

  for (int j = 0; j < 3; ++j) {
    // Randomly shuffle the integers in vector1:
    random_shuffle(vector1.begin(), vector1.end());

    // Output the contents of vector1:
    copy(vector1.begin(), vector1.end(),
        ostream_iterator<int>(cout, " "));
    cout << endl;
  }
}
```

Output from Example 5-14:
```
6 11 9 2 18 12 17 7 0 15 4 8 10 5 1 19 13 3 14 16
14 19 18 12 0 2 3 5 4 13 15 8 17 11 1 16 9 6 10 7
15 10 5 14 6 11 17 9 13 8 16 4 1 19 7 12 2 18 3 0
```

The order in the output will, of course, vary depending on the details of the particular pseudo-random number generator used. The random_shuffle algorithm in the HP reference implementation of STL uses a generator defined in the file random.cpp, which is part of the HP STL distribution. In compiling Example 5-14 with the HP implementation, we had to compile and link random.cpp; other STL implementations may handle this compilation issue differently.

There is also a random_shuffle version that takes a function object argument, so that one can supply a different generator. The function passed to random_shuffle should return a double value in the range [0, 1), chosen randomly with approximately uniform distribution.

The time complexity of random_shuffle is linear.

5.3.6   Remove

The generic remove algorithm removes those elements from a range that are equal to a particular value. It is a stable algorithm—it preserves the relative order of the elements that are not removed from the sequence.

Example 5-15   Illustrating the generic remove algorithm.

```
#include <algo.h>
#include <vector.h>
#include <assert.h>
int main()
{
  const int N = 11;
  int array1[N] = {1, 2, 0, 3, 4, 0, 5, 6, 7, 0, 8};
  vector<int> vector1;
  for (int i = 0; i < N; ++i)
    vector1.push_back(array1[i]);

  // Remove the zeros from vector1:
  vector<int>::iterator new_end;
  new_end = remove(vector1.begin(), vector1.end(), 0);

  // The size of vector1 remains the same:
  assert(vector1.size() == N);

  // The nonzero elements are left in
  // [vector1.begin(), new_end).  Erase the rest:
  vector1.erase(new_end, vector1.end());

  // Show that 3 elements were removed and the
  // nonzero elements remain, in their original order:
  assert(vector1.size() == N - 3);
```

```
    for (i = 0; i < vector1.size(); ++i)
      assert(vector1[i] == i+1);
}
```

It is important to note that `remove` does not alter the size of the container on which it operates. Thus, in the example above, `vector1` still has N elements after the `remove` call, which has merely copied the elements not equal to the given value into a smaller range and returned the end of the smaller range. Using this new end marker and the `erase` member function of the `vector` class, the program then erases the elements from that point to the end of the vector.

There are also copying and predicate versions of `remove`. The time complexity is linear for all versions of the algorithm.

5.3.7 Replace

The generic `replace` algorithm replaces elements in a range that are equal to a particular value with another value.

Example 5-16 Illustrating the generic `replace` algorithm.

```
#include <algo.h>
#include <vector.h>
#include <assert.h>
#include <bstring.h>

int main()
{
  vector<char> vecChar = string("FERRARI");

  // Replace all occurrences of R by S:
  replace(vecChar.begin(), vecChar.end(), 'R', 'S');

  assert(string(vecChar) == string("FESSASI"));
}
```

In this example, all occurrences of R are replaced with S. All other characters in the sequence remain the same.

There are copying and predicate versions of `replace`. The time complexity is linear for all versions.

5.3.8 Reverse

The generic `reverse` algorithm reverses the order of elements in a range. The iterators specifying the range must be bidirectional. See the examples in Section 1.6. The time complexity for the `reverse` algorithm is linear.

5.3.9 Rotate

The generic `rotate` algorithm rotates a range. The call

```
rotate(first, middle, last)
```

rotates the elements in the range [`first`, `last`) left by `middle` - `first` positions. After the call the elements originally in [`middle`, `last`) appear in [`first`, `first` + k), where k = `last` - `middle`, and the elements originally in [`first`, `middle`) appear in [`first` + k, `last`). The arguments to `rotate` must be bidirectional iterators.

Example 5-17 Illustrating the generic `rotate` algorithm.

```
#include <algo.h>
#include <vector.h>
#include <assert.h>
#include <bstring.h>

int main()
{
   vector<char> vecChar = string("Software Engineering ");

   // Rotate the vector so that "Engineering " comes first:
   rotate(vecChar.begin(), vecChar.begin() + 9,
          vecChar.end());

   assert(string(vecChar) ==
          string("Engineering Software "));
}
```

The time complexity for the `rotate` algorithm is linear.

5.3.10 Swap

The generic `swap` algorithm exchanges two values.

Example 5-18 Illustrating the generic `swap` algorithm.

```
#include <algo.h>
#include <assert.h>

int main()
{
   int high = 250, low = 0;

   swap(high, low);
```

```
    assert(high == 0 && low == 250);
}
```

The `swap` algorithm has constant time complexity.

5.3.11   Swap Ranges

The generic `swap_ranges` algorithm exchanges two ranges of values, which can be in different containers. The call

```
swap_ranges(first1, last1, first2)
```

exchanges the contents of `[first1, last1)` with that of `[first2, first2 + N)`, where N = `last1 - first1`. It is assumed that these ranges do not overlap.

Example 5-19   Illustrating the generic `swap_ranges` **algorithm.**

```
#include <algo.h>
#include <vector.h>
#include <assert.h>

int main()
{
  vector<char> vector1, vector2;

  char elem1[5] = {'H', 'E', 'L', 'L', 'O'};
  char elem2[5] = {'T', 'H', 'E', 'R', 'E'};

  // Initialize vectors:
  for (int i = 0; i < 5; i++) {
    vector1.push_back(elem1[i]);
    vector2.push_back(elem2[i]);
  }

  // Save vector1 and vector2 contents, for checking:
  vector<char> temp1 = vector1, temp2 = vector2;

  // Swap the contents of vector1 and vector2:
  swap_ranges(vector1.begin(), vector1.end(),
              vector2.begin());

  assert(vector1 == temp2 && vector2 == temp1);
}
```

The time complexity is linear for the swap_ranges algorithm.

5.3.12   Transform

The generic transform algorithm applies a function to each element in a range and stores the values it returns in another range. One version of the algorithm applies a unary function to each element of a range, while another version applies a binary function to corresponding pairs of elements from two ranges. The binary function version of transform is illustrated below.

Example 5-20   Illustrating the generic transform algorithm.

```
#include <algo.h>
#include <iostream.h>

int sum(int val1, int val2) { return val2 + val1; }

int main()
{
   int array1[5] = {0, 1, 2, 3, 4};
   int array2[5] = {6, 7, 8, 9, 10};
   ostream_iterator<int> out(cout, " ");

   // Put sums of corresponding array1 and array2 elements
   // into output stream
   transform(&array1[0], &array1[5], &array2[0], out, sum);

   cout << endl;
}
```

Output from Example 5-20:

```
6 8 10 12 14
```

In this program we use transform to produce the sums of corresponding pairs of elements from array1 and array2. The resulting sequence of values is placed on the standard output stream using an ostream iterator.

The time complexity for the transform algorithm is linear.

5.3.13   Unique

The generic unique algorithm eliminates all consecutive duplicate elements from an input sequence. An element is considered to be a consecutive duplicate if it is equal to the element to its immediate left in the sequence, so all but the first element of a group of consecutive elements is removed. As with the remove algorithm (see Section 5.3.6 on page 89), unique does not change the size of the container on which it operates; it merely copies the elements that are not consecutive duplicates into a smaller range and returns the end of the smaller range.

Example 5-21   Illustrating the generic unique algorithm.

```
#include <algo.h>
#include <vector.h>
#include <assert.h>
#include <iostream.h>

int main()
{
  const int N = 11;
  int array1[N] = {1, 2, 0, 3, 3, 0, 7, 7, 7, 0, 8};
  vector<int> vector1;
  for (int i = 0; i < N; ++i)
    vector1.push_back(array1[i]);

  // Eliminate consecutive duplicates from vector1:
  vector<int>::iterator new_end;
  new_end = unique(vector1.begin(), vector1.end());

  // The size of vector1 remains the same;
  assert(vector1.size() == N);

  // The nonconsecutive duplicate elements are left in
  // [vector1.begin(), new_end).  Erase the rest:
  vector1.erase(new_end, vector1.end());

  // Put the resulting vector1 contents on the
  // standard output stream:
  copy(vector1.begin(), vector1.end(),
       ostream_iterator<int>(cout, " "));
  cout << endl;
}
```

Output from Example 5-21:

```
1 2 0 3 0 7 0 8
```

Note that in the output none of the occurrences of 0 has been eliminated, because they are not consecutive duplicates. If you want to eliminate all duplicates, and you do not need to preserve the order of the nonduplicates, first sort the range so that all duplicates occur in consecutive positions, and then apply unique.

The time complexity is linear for all versions of unique.

5.4   *Sorting-Related Algorithms*

STL includes several algorithms that are in some way related to sorting. There are algorithms for sorting and merging sequences and for searching and performing set-like operations on sorted sequences. In this section we take a look at all of these algorithms. Before doing that, we need to understand some of the means by which the generality of these algorithms is achieved.

Comparison relations. An essential ingredient for these algorithms is comparison of sequence elements. Each algorithm has a version that uses the < operator, and another version takes a comparison object as one of its parameters. In this section, whenever we talk about requirements on comparison objects, the same requirements are placed on the < operator.

A comparison object should be a binary predicate object, and the binary relation it defines must obey some fundamental laws, in order to obtain well-defined results from the sorting-related algorithms.

Let's first consider a set of requirements that is a bit stronger than actually needed. Let R be a binary relation on a set S; then we say that R is a *strict total ordering* on S if R obeys the following two laws:

1. (Transitivity) For every x, y, z in S, if $x \, R \, y$ and $y \, R \, z$, then $x \, R \, z$.

2. (Trichotomy) For every x and y in S, exactly one of the following is true: $x \, R \, y$, $y \, R \, x$, or $x = y$.

Comparison relations that are strict total orderings may be used with the STL sorting-related algorithms. For example, the requirements are satisfied by the comparison relations defined by the C++ built-in < or > operators on built-in numeric types.[5] When defining a comparison object, it's usually not difficult to obtain a strict total ordering if we merely define it in terms of some previously defined operator whose relation obeys these laws. STL provides two function object types less and greater (in header function.h), with template type parameter T, that use the < or > operator for T, respectively. So, for example,

---

5. Note that the trichotomy law is *not* satisfied by the built-in <= or >= operators, since these operators satisfy the reflexive law, $x \, R \, x$. The word "strict" in "strict total ordering" refers to the fact that the definition requires R to be irreflexive, that is, such that $x \, R \, x$ is false for all x. Irreflexivity follows from trichotomy. The term "total ordering" (not modified by "strict") usually refers to a reflexive relation that is also transitive and *antisymmetric*, which means "if $x \, R \, y$ and $y \, R \, x$, then $x = y$." If R is an irreflexive relation and R' is defined as $x \, R' \, y$ if and only if $x \, R \, y$ or $x = y$" then it can be shown that R' is a total ordering if and only if R is a strict total ordering.

```
sort(vector1.begin(), vector1.end(), less<int>());
```

sorts the `vector<int> vector1`, and so does

```
sort(vector1.begin(), vector1.end(), greater<int>());
```

As we'll see ahead, with `less<int>()`, the result is put into ascending order, and with `greater<int>()` it is put into descending order. As another example, the C++ standard `string` class defines `operator<` on strings as alphabetical ordering, which is a total ordering on strings;

```
sort(vector2.begin(), vector2.end(), less<string>());
```

sorts the `vector<string> vector2` into ascending order (normal alphabetical order); and

```
sort(vector2.begin(), vector2.end(), greater<string>());
```

sorts it into descending order (reverse alphabetical order).

A strict total ordering completely defines the order in which elements can appear in a sequence (hence the name, "total"), but sometimes we may not care about the order of some elements. For example, if we have

```
struct Person {
  string last_name;
  string first_name;
};
```

we might only need to sort according to last names, not caring about the order in which two people with the same last name but different first names appear. This can be done by defining

```
class LastNameLess {
 public:
  bool operator()(const Person& p, const Person& q) const
  {
    return p.last_name < q.last_name;
  }
};
```

and sorting, say, a `deque<Person> deque1` with

```
sort(deque1.begin(), deque1.end(), LastNameLess());
```

The fact that this works does not follow from the previous discussion, since the relation R defined by `LastNameLess()` is *not* a strict total ordering. It fails to impose any order on some pairs of persons (those with the same last name). That is, for some distinct persons p and q, both $p\ R\ q$ and $q\ R\ p$ are false. Effectively, it is treating such persons as equivalent, though they are not identical. The need for this kind of sorting operation is common enough that the STL sorting-related algorithms have all been designed to work with a relation weaker than a strict total ordering.

The actual requirements are for what is called a "strict weak ordering," where "weak" refers to the fact that the requirements are not strong enough to determine the order of all elements. Any two elements whose relative order is not determined are considered equivalent: given R, let E be the relation defined by

$$x\ E\ y \text{ if and only if both } x\ R\ y \text{ and } y\ R\ x \text{ are false;} \qquad (*)$$

then we say R is a *strict weak ordering* if it is asymmetric and transitive and E is an equivalence relation. It can be shown that these properties imply that R induces a strict total ordering on the equivalence classes defined by E. See also the discussion in Section 20.23.

Given a comparison object defining a strict weak ordering R, the STL sorting algorithms sort a sequence into an order determined by the induced strict total ordering. If E is ordinary equality (identity), then R itself is a strict total ordering. But if E makes some distinct elements equivalent, then the ordering of these elements in the result is not determined.

Again note that the strict weak ordering requirements cannot be satisfied by a reflexive R (since it follows from (*) that if $x\ R\ x$ is true then $x\ E\ x$ is false, contradicting the requirement that E be an equivalence relation). Thus it is still the case that comparison objects to be used with the sorting-related algorithms *cannot* be defined in terms of operators like the built-in `<=` or `>=` operators, since these are reflexive relations. In fact, if you attempt to do so, say with

```
sort(first, last, less_equal<int>());   // incorrect
```

the computation *may even fail to terminate.*

Another important point is that the sorting-related algorithms make no use of operator `==`. In *describing* the results these algorithms produce, we nonetheless often talk about "equivalence" between elements, but what we mean is *independent of the meaning of the* `==` *operator.* Instead, we mean the equivalence relation E defined by (*).

An example is the way we describe the "stability" property of a sorting algorithm. Usually, a sorting algorithm is said to be *stable* if it preserves the relative order of equal elements. We extend this definition to mean preserving the order of elements that are equivalent according to E as defined by (*) above.

Nondecreasing (ascending) order versus nonincreasing (descending) order. The STL sorting and merging algorithms put their results into *nondecreasing order* according to the given comparison relation R. This means that for every iterator i referring to a sequence element x and every nonnegative integer n such that i + n refers to a sequence element y, $y R x$ is false.

Suppose that we need the opposite order—*nonincreasing order*—according to R. For this we need R's *converse relation*. In general, if R is a binary relation on S, its converse is the relation C on S defined by "$x C y$ if and only if $y R x$." Thus the converse relation of the < operator for built-in types is the same relation as that computed by the > operator. For a user-defined type, if < is defined, then an STL template function definition (in header `function.h`) ensures that > is defined as the converse relation of <:

```
template <class T>
inline bool operator>(const T& x, const T& y) {
    return y < x;
}
```

(There are similar definitions of <= and >= in terms of <, so that one only needs to define <. As already noted, these relations cannot be used with the STL sorting-related algorithms, but they may be useful for other purposes.)

The STL predicate object `greater<T>()` encapsulates the > operator for type T in a function object that can be passed to a sorting algorithm. Thus, for example, we can sort a range [`first`, `last`) of integers into nonincreasing order with

```
sort(first, last, greater<int>());
```

Suppose that instead of < we are using a comparison object `comp` as the less-than relation on some user-defined type U. That is, assume we have defined

```
class comp {
 public:
  bool operator()(const U& x, const U& y) const
  { // ...
  }
};
```

Then we can code its converse relation explicitly, by defining

```
class comp_reverse {
 public:
  bool operator()(const U& x, const U& y) const
  {
```

```
        return comp(y, x);
    }
};
```

and we can sort into nonincreasing order with

```
    sort(first, last, comp_reverse());
```

We sometimes use the term *ascending* as a synonym for nondecreasing, and *descending* for nonincreasing.

5.4.1   Sort, stable_sort, and partial_sort

The generic sorting algorithms sort a random access sequence. There are three varieties: `sort`, based on quicksort; `stable_sort`, which uses an adaptive merge sort algorithm; and `partial_sort`, based on the principle of the heapsort algorithm but more efficient if only a fraction of the sorted sequence is needed. All of these are illustrated in Example 5-22 ahead.

The various sorting algorithms differ in their computing times and stability. The `sort` function uses an underlying quicksort algorithm, which sorts a sequence of length N using $O(N \log N)$ comparisons on the average. While this sorting algorithm is fast on the average, one cannot completely rely on it for fast performance, since there are a few input sequences that cause it to blow up to quadratic time.[6] For *guaranteed* $O(N \log N)$ behavior, one can use *heapsort*, either by doing `make_heap` followed by `sort_heap`, as shown in Section 5.4.6, or by using a special case of `partial_sort`, as described below. For most sequences, heapsort takes about twice as long as quicksort, but it never blows up to quadratic time.

Another generic sorting algorithm STL provides is `stable_sort`, which runs in $O(N(\log N)^2)$ time. This algorithm is based on the principle of merge sorting, but it adds another significant technique, *adaptation to memory constraints*: it attempts to allocate and use extra memory in order to improve its running time. If memory for at least $N/2$ elements is available, then the time is $O(N \log N)$. In some cases, `stable_sort` can be faster even than `sort`. As its name suggests, it also has the advantage of being *stable*; that is, the relative position of equivalent elements is maintained. This property is often important when the elements have several fields on which they are being sorted, for example, a last name field and a city field. If sorted by city first, and then by last name with a stable algorithm, each set of records with the same last name will still be in order according to the city fields. Neither quicksort nor heapsort has this stability property.

---

6. A median-of-three algorithm is used for choosing pivots, so the computing time is still $O(N \log N)$ for already-sorted sequences, which can cause simpler versions of quicksort to take quadratic time.

Sometimes we only need partial sorting; for example, we might want to know only the top 100 scores among 20,000 test grades. Calling the `partial_sort` algorithm as

```
partial_sort(first, middle, last)
```

puts into [`first, middle`) the k = `middle - first` smallest elements of the entire range [`first, last`), but without actually sorting the entire range. The elements in [`middle, last`) are left in an undetermined order. Thus if the test scores are in `vector<float>` scores,

```
partial_sort(scores.begin(), scores.begin() + 100,
             scores.end(), greater<float>())
```

puts the 100 largest scores into descending order in the range [`scores.begin(), scores.begin() + 100`).

The computing time for partial_sort is $O(N \log k)$, where N = `last - first` and k = `middle - first`.

It follows from the above specification that

```
partial_sort(first, last, last)
```

sorts the entire range [`first, last`). This special case is the normal heapsort algorithm, with $O(N \log N)$ computing time.

The following program illustrates all three of these algorithms, applying them to a vector of integers and using a comparison object `comp_last()`, which compares two integers based on the size of their last base-10 digits. Thus, for example, `comp_last()(13, 6)` is true since 3 < 6, but both `comp_last()(13, 3)` and `comp_last()(3, 13)` are false, so 3 and 13 are considered equivalent. Using sort, 3 and 13 may not be left in the same relative order in which they occurred in the sequence before sorting (in fact, we see from the output in this case that they are not), but `stable_sort` leaves these and other groups of equivalent elements in their original relative order.

Example 5-22   Illustrating the generic sort, stable_sort, **and** partial_sort **algorithms.**

```
#include <vector.h>
#include <algo.h>
#include <iostream.h>

class comp_last {
 public:
   bool operator()(int x, int y)
     // Compare x and y based on their last base-10 digits:
```

```cpp
    {
      return x % 10 < y % 10;
    }
};

int main()
{
  const int N = 20;

  vector<int> vector0;
  for (int i = 0; i != N; ++i)
   vector0.push_back(i);

  vector<int> vector1 = vector0;

  ostream_iterator<int> out(cout, " ");

  cout << "Before sorting:\n";
  copy(vector1.begin(), vector1.end(), out);
  cout << endl;

  sort(vector1.begin(), vector1.end(), comp_last());

  cout << "After sorting by last digits with sort:\n";
  copy(vector1.begin(), vector1.end(), out);
  cout << endl << endl;

  vector1 = vector0;
  cout << "Before sorting:\n";
  copy(vector1.begin(), vector1.end(), out);
  cout << endl;

  stable_sort(vector1.begin(), vector1.end(), comp_last());

  cout << "After sorting by last digits with stable_sort:\n";
  copy(vector1.begin(), vector1.end(), out);
  cout << endl << endl;

  vector1 = vector0;
  reverse(vector1.begin(), vector1.end());
  cout << "Before sorting:\n";
  copy(vector1.begin(), vector1.end(), out);
  cout << endl << endl;
```

```
partial_sort(vector1.begin(), vector1.begin() + 5,
            vector1.end(), comp_last());

cout << "After sorting with partial_sort to get\n"
     << "5 values with smallest last digits:\n";
copy(vector1.begin(), vector1.end(), out);
cout << endl << endl;
}
```

Output from Example 5-22:
```
Before sorting:
0 1 2 3 4 5 6 7 8 9 10 11 12 13 14 15 16 17 18 19

After sorting by last digits with sort:
10 0 11 1 12 2 13 3 4 14 5 15 6 16 7 17 8 18 9 19

Before sorting:
0 1 2 3 4 5 6 7 8 9 10 11 12 13 14 15 16 17 18 19

After sorting by last digits with stable_sort:
0 10 1 11 2 12 3 13 4 14 5 15 6 16 7 17 8 18 9 19

Before sorting:
19 18 17 16 15 14 13 12 11 10 9 8 7 6 5 4 3 2 1 0

After sorting with partial_sort to get
5 values with smallest last digits:
10 0 11 1 12 19 18 17 16 15 9 8 7 6 5 4 14 13 3 2
```

5.4.2   Nth_element

The generic `nth_element` algorithm places an element of a sequence in the location where it would be if the sequence were sorted. The algorithm also partitions the sequence in such a way that all elements to the left of the *n*th element are less than or equal to those to its right.

Example 5-23   Illustrating the generic `nth_element` algorithm.
```
#include <vector.h>
#include <algo.h>
#include <assert.h>

int main()
```

```
{
  vector<int> v(7);

  v[0] = 25; v[1] = 7; v[2] = 9;
  v[3] = 2; v[4] = 0; v[5] = 5; v[6] = 21;

  const int N = 4;

  // Use nth_element to place the Nth smallest
  // element in v in the Nth position, v.begin() + N:

  nth_element(v.begin(), v.begin() + N, v.end());

  // Check that the element at v.begin() + N, v[N], is
  // greater than or equal to each of the preceding elements:
  for (int i = 0; i != N; ++i)
    assert(v[N] >= v[i]);

  // Check that the element at v.begin() + N, v[N], is
  // less than or equal to each of the following elements:
  for (i = N + 1; i != 7; ++i)
    assert(v[N] <= v[i]);
}
```

In this example, the call to nth_element places in position v.begin() + N the element that would appear there if the vector were completely sorted. This element, v[N], is the Nth smallest element if elements are counted starting with 0, or the (N + 1)st smallest if they are counted starting with 1. That the element in v[N] is the Nth smallest element is verified by the assertions, which also show that the elements have been partitioned so that v[0],...,v[N] are all less than or equal to v[N + 1],...,v[6].

The average computing time for nth_element is linear.

5.4.3   Binary_search, lower_bound, upper_bound, and equal_range

The generic binary search algorithms use a traditional binary search to find an element in a sorted sequence. Given a sorted range [first, last), the generic binary_search algorithm returns true if it finds the input value in the container, false otherwise. The lower_bound and upper_bound algorithms return an iterator i referring to the *first* or *last* position, respectively, into which the value may be inserted while still maintaining the sorted ordering. The equal_range algorithm returns the pair of iterators that would be computed by lower_bound and upper_bound.

For random access containers, the binary_search function makes at most log N + 2 comparisons; lower_bound and upper_bound make at most log N + 1 comparisons, and equal_range makes at most 2 log N + 1 comparisons.

Note that random access containers can also be searched with the generic find algorithm, described in Section 2.2. The find algorithm takes linear time to determine whether an element is present in a sequence, regardless of whether the sequence is sorted. The advantage of using find over the binary search algorithms is that find can be used on nonsorted sequences. Also, since find operates on input iterators, it can be used to search for elements in data structures such as input streams, singly and doubly linked lists, and so forth, on which the binary search algorithms cannot operate in logarithmic time.

It must be noted that although the binary search algorithms are efficient (i.e., they perform in logarithmic time) only for sorted random access sequences, the algorithms are written to work for nonrandom access containers such as lists as well. For all nonrandom access data structures, the time the binary search algorithms take is linear, but the number of comparisons is only logarithmic. In cases in which comparisons are expensive, it could be better, by some constant factor, to use one of the binary search algorithms rather than find.

All of the binary search algorithms are illustrated in the following example.

Example 5-24 Illustrating the generic binary search algorithms.

```
#include <algo.h>
#include <vector.h>
#include <assert.h>

int main()
{
  vector<int> v(5);
  bool found;

  // Initialize:
  for(int i = 0; i < 5; i++) v[i] = i;

  // Search for each of the integers 0, 1, 2, 3, 4:
  for (i = 0; i < 5; i++) {
    found = binary_search(v.begin(), v.end(), i);
    assert(found == true);
  }

  // Try searching for a value that's not present:
  found = binary_search (v.begin(), v.end(), 9);
  assert(found == false);

  v[1] = 7; v[2] = 7; v[3] = 7; v[4] = 8;
```

```
  // Vector v now contains:  0 7 7 7 8

  typedef vector<int>::iterator iter;
  iter viter;

  // Apply upper_bound, lower_bound and equal_range on v:

  viter = lower_bound(v.begin(), v.end(), 7);
  assert(viter == v.begin() + 1 && *viter == 7);

  viter = upper_bound(v.begin(), v.end(), 7);
  assert(viter == v.end() - 1 && *viter == 8);

  pair<iter, iter> pIter =
      equal_range(v.begin(), v.end(), 7);

  assert(pIter.first == v.begin() + 1);
  assert(pIter.second == v.end() - 1);
}
```

5.4.4 Merge

The generic `merge` algorithm merges two sorted ranges and places the result in a range that does not overlap either of the two input ranges. The `inplace_merge` algorithm merges two sorted consecutive ranges and replaces both ranges with the resulting merged sequence.

The time complexity of the `merge` algorithm is linear. For `inplace_merge` the time complexity depends on the amount of additional memory available. If no additional memory is available, the algorithm can take $O(N \log N)$ time; otherwise, it takes linear time.

Example 5-25 Illustrating the generic `merge` algorithms.

```
#include <vector.h>
#include <algo.h>
#include <assert.h>

int main()
{
  // Initialize vector of integers:
  vector<int> vecInt1(5);
  vector<int> vecInt2(5);
  vector<int> vecInt3(10);

  for (int i = 0; i < 5; i++)
```

```
        vecInt1[i] = 2 * i;

    for (i = 0; i < 5; i++)
        vecInt2[i] = 1 + 2 * i;

    // Merge contents of vecInt1 and vecInt2,
    // putting result in vecInt3:
    merge(vecInt1.begin(), vecInt1.end(),
          vecInt2.begin(), vecInt2.end(),
          vecInt3.begin());

    for (i = 0; i < 10; i++)
        assert(vecInt3[i] == i);

    for (i = 0; i < 5; i++)
        vecInt3[i] = vecInt1[i];
    for (i = 0; i < 5; i++)
        vecInt3[i + 5] = vecInt2[i];

    // Merge the two sorted halves of vecInt3
    // in place to obtain a sorted vecInt3:
    inplace_merge(vecInt3.begin(), vecInt3.begin() + 5,
                  vecInt3.end());

    for (i = 0; i < 10; i++)
        assert(vecInt3[i] == i);
}
```

5.4.5 Set Operations on Sorted Structures

STL provides five algorithms that perform set-like operations on sorted sequences: `includes`, `set_union`, `set_intersection`, `set_difference`, and `set_symmetric_difference`.

The `includes` algorithm checks whether one sequence is contained in another and returns a boolean value accordingly. Given two ranges, `[first1, last1)` and `[first2, last2)`, representing sets, the `set_union` algorithm generates the union of the two sets into the range `[result, last)` and returns `last`, the past-the-end location of the resulting sequence.

The `set_difference` function creates a set of elements that are in the first range but not in the second; `set_intersection` creates a set from elements that are common to both input sequences; and `set_symmetric_difference` creates a set of elements that are in one but not in both of the input sequences. Like `set_union`, all of these functions place the resulting sequence into the range [result, last) and return last, the past-the-end location of the resulting sequence.

For all of the set operations, the time complexity is linear. Each algorithm performs at most 2(*N1* + *N2*) – 1 comparisons, where *N1* = last1 - first1 and *N2* = last2 - first2.

Example 5-26   Illustrating the generic set operations.

```
#include <vector.h>
#include <algo.h>
#include <assert.h>

int main()
{
  bool result;

  // Initialize a vectors of characters:
  vector<char> vecChar1(5);
  vector<char> vecChar2(5);
  char elem1[5] = { 'a', 'b', 'c', 'd', 'e' };
  char elem2[5] = { 'a', 'e', 'i', 'o', 'u' };

  for(int i = 0; i < 5; i++) vecChar1[i] = elem1[i];
  for(i = 0; i < 5; i++) vecChar2[i] = elem2[i];

  // Illustrate includes:
  result = includes(vecChar1.begin(), vecChar1.end(),
        vecChar2.begin(), vecChar2.end());
  assert(result == false);

  // Illustrate set_union():
  vector<char> setUnion(8);
  set_union(vecChar1.begin(), vecChar1.end(),
        vecChar2.begin(), vecChar2.end(),
        setUnion.begin());

  assert(setUnion[0] == 'a');
  assert(setUnion[1] == 'b');
  assert(setUnion[2] == 'c');
  assert(setUnion[3] == 'd');
  assert(setUnion[4] == 'e');
  assert(setUnion[5] == 'i');
  assert(setUnion[6] == 'o');
  assert(setUnion[7] == 'u');
```

```
// Illustrate set_intersection:
vector<char> setIntersection(2);
set_intersection(vecChar1.begin(), vecChar1.end(),
     vecChar2.begin(), vecChar2.end(),
     setIntersection.begin());

assert(setIntersection[0] == 'a');
assert(setIntersection[1] == 'e');

// Illustrate set_symmetric_difference:
vector<char> setDiff(6);

set_symmetric_difference(vecChar1.begin(),
     vecChar1.end(),
     vecChar2.begin(), vecChar2.end(),
     setDiff.begin());

assert(setDiff[0] == 'b');
assert(setDiff[1] == 'c');
assert(setDiff[2] == 'd');
assert(setDiff[3] == 'i');
assert(setDiff[4] == 'o');
assert(setDiff[5] == 'u');
}
```

5.4.6 Heap Operations

A *heap* represents a particular organization of a random access data structure. Given a range [first, last), we say that the range represents a heap if two key properties are satisfied:

- the value pointed to by first is the largest value in the range;

- the value pointed to by first may be removed by a pop operation, or a new element added by a push operation, in logarithmic time. Both the pop and push operations return valid heaps.

STL provides four algorithms to create and manipulate heaps: make_heap, pop_heap, push_heap, and sort_heap.

The push_heap algorithm assumes [first, last - 1) contains a valid heap and rearranges [first, last) into a heap (thus pushing the value at last - 1 into the heap). pop_heap assumes [first, last) is a valid heap, swaps the value at first with the value at last - 1, and transforms the range [first, last - 1) into a heap. The time complexity for push_heap and pop_heap is $O(\log N)$.

make_heap constructs a heap in the range [first, last) using elements in [first, last), and sort_heap sorts the elements that are stored in the heap. The time complexity for make_heap is linear, requiring at most 3N comparisons, while the sort_heap algorithm requires $O(N \log N)$ time with a maximum of $N \log N$ comparisons. All of these algorithms are illustrated in the next example.

Example 5-27   Illustrating the generic heap operations.

```
#include <vector.h>
#include <algo.h>
#include <assert.h>

int main()
{
  // Initialize a vector of integers:
  vector<int> vecInt(5);
  for (int i = 0; i < 5; i++)
    vecInt[i] = i;

  random_shuffle(vecInt.begin(), vecInt.end());

  // Sort the vector using push_heap and pop_heap:
  for (i = 2; i < 5; i++)
    push_heap(vecInt.begin(), vecInt.begin() + i);

  for (i = 5; i >= 2; i--)
    pop_heap(vecInt.begin(), vecInt.begin() + i);

  // Verify that the array is sorted:
  for (i = 0; i < 5; i++)
    assert(vecInt[i] == i);

  // Shuffle the elements again:
  random_shuffle(vecInt.begin(), vecInt.end());

  // Sort the vector using make_heap and sort_heap:
  make_heap(vecInt.begin(), vecInt.end());
  sort_heap(vecInt.begin(), vecInt.end());

  // Verify that the array is sorted:
  for (i = 0; i < 5; i++) assert(vecInt[i] == i);
}
```

Sorting with push_heap and pop_heap is done as follows. The element v[0] is assumed to be a valid heap; push_heap is then called three times to arrange the vector elements into a heap. Once the heap has been thus created, pop_heap is called four times. On each call, `pop_heap` takes the first heap element (which is known to be the largest element in the sequence) and places it at the end of the sequence. After all calls to `pop_heap` are complete, the sequence is thus sorted.

5.4.7 Minimum and Maximum

The generic `min` and `max` algorithms are passed two elements and they return the one that is smaller or larger, respectively. The `min_element` and `max_element` algorithms return an iterator pointing to a minimum or maximum, respectively, of the elements in an input sequence, as illustrated in the following example.

Example 5-28   Illustrating the generic `min_element` **and** `max_element` **algorithms.**

```
#include <vector.h>
#include <algo.h>
#include <assert.h>

int main()
{
  // Initialize a vector of integers:
  vector<int> vecInt(5);
  for(int i = 0; i < 5; i++)
    vecInt[i] = i;
  random_shuffle(vecInt.begin(), vecInt.end());

  // Find the max_element in the container:
  vector<int>::iterator vecIter;

  vecIter = max_element(vecInt.begin(), vecInt.end());
  assert(*vecIter == 4);

  // Find the min_element in the container:
  vecIter = min_element(vecInt.begin(), vecInt.end());
  assert(*vecIter == 0);
}
```

5.4.8 Lexicographical Comparison

The generic `lexicographical_compare` algorithm compares two input sequences as follows. Corresponding pairs of elements, e1 and e2 (from sequences 1 and 2), are compared. If e1 < e2, then the algorithm returns true immediately; if e2 < e1, the algorithm returns false immediately. Otherwise, comparison proceeds to the next pair of elements. If the first sequence is exhausted but the second is not, then the algorithm returns true; otherwise it returns false. The < operator must be defined on the sequence elements as a strict weak ordering (or one can pass to `lexicographical_compare` a comparison object that defines a strict weak ordering). If < or the comparison object defines a strict total ordering, the ordering determined by `lexicographical_compare` is also a strict total ordering; otherwise, it is a strict weak ordering.

Example 5-29   Illustrating the generic `lexicographical_compare` algorithm.

```
#include <vector.h>
#include <algo.h>
#include <assert.h>

int main()
{
  bool result;

  // Initialize vectors of characters:
  vector<char> vecChar1(5);
  char elem1[5] = {'h', 'e', 'l', 'i', 'o'};
  for(int i = 0; i<5; i++)
    vecChar1[i] = elem1[i];

  vector<char> vecChar2(5);
  char elem2[5] = {'h', 'e', 'l', 'l', 'o'};

  for(i = 0; i<5; i++)
    vecChar2[i] = elem2[i];

  // Show that vecChar1 is lexicographically less than
  // vecChar2:
  result = lexicographical_compare(vecChar1.begin(),
      vecChar1.end(), vecChar2.begin(), vecChar2.end());

  assert(result == true);
}
```

5.4.9   Permutation Generators

STL provides two permutation generation algorithms: `next_permutation` changes a sequence into the next permutation in lexicographical order, while `prev_permutation` changes into the previous permutation in lexicographical order. The input sequence must support bidirectional iterators. Because of their definition in terms of lexicographical ordering, < must be defined on the sequence elements as a strict weak ordering (alternatively, one can pass to these algorithms a comparison object that defines a strict weak ordering). The algorithms are illustrated in the example below.

Example 5-30   Illustrating the generic permutation algorithms.
```
#include <vector.h>
#include <algo.h>
#include <assert.h>

int main()
{
    // Initialize a vector of integers:
    vector<int> vecInt(3);
    for(int i = 0; i < 3; i++) vecInt[i] = i;

    // In lexicographical order the permutations of 0 1 2 are
    // 0 1 2, 0 2 1, 1 0 2, 1 2 0, 2 0 1, 2 1 0.
    // Show that from 0 1 2 next_permutation produces 0 2 1:
    next_permutation(vecInt.begin(), vecInt.end());
    assert(vecInt[0] == 0);
    assert(vecInt[1] == 2);
    assert(vecInt[2] == 1);

    // Show that from 0 2 1 prev_permutation() produces 0 1 2:
    prev_permutation(vecInt.begin(), vecInt.end());
    assert(vecInt[0] == 0);
    assert(vecInt[1] == 1);
    assert(vecInt[2] == 2);
}
```

5.5 *Generalized Numeric Algorithms*

STL provides four generalized numeric algorithms: `accumulate`, `partial_sum`, `adjacent_difference`, and `inner_product`. In the following sections, we take a look at examples of each of these algorithms.

5.5.1 Accumulate

The generic `accumulate` function adds the values in a given range.

Example 5-31   Illustrating the generic `accumulate` algorithm.
```
#include <algo.h>
#include <function.h>
```

```
#include <assert.h>

int main()
{
  int result;
  int x[20];

  for (int i = 0; i < 20; i++)
    x[i] = i;

  // Show that 5 + 0 + 1 + 2 + ... + 19 == 195:
  result = accumulate(&x[0], &x[20], 5);
  assert(result == 195);

  // Show that 10 * 1 * 2 * 3 * 4 == 240:
  result = accumulate(&x[1], &x[5], 10, times<int>());
  assert(result == 240);
}
```

In the second call of `accumulate` we use multiplication in place of addition, and we accumulate the values in `x[1]` through `x[4]`. Other examples of `accumulate` are given in Examples 2-9 through 2-12.

5.5.2 Partial_sum

Given a sequence $x_0, x_1, ..., x_{n-1}$, the generic `partial_sum` algorithm computes the sequence of sums $x_0, x_0 + x_1, x_0 + x_1 + x_2, ..., x_0 + x_1 + ... + x_{n-1}$. The algorithm can store these partial sums either in place of the original sequence or in another range.

Example 5-32 Illustrating the generic `partial_sum` algorithm.

```
#include <algo.h>
#include <iostream.h>

int main()
{
  const int N = 20;
  int x1[N], x2[N];
  for (int i = 0; i != N; ++i)
    x1[i] = i;

  // Compute the partial sums of 0, 1, 2, 3, ..., N - 1,
  // putting the result in x2:
```

```
    partial_sum(&x1[0], &x1[N], &x2[0]);

    for (i = 0; i != N; ++i)
      cout << x2[i] << " ";
    cout << endl;
}
```

Output from Example 5-32:
0 1 3 6 10 15 21 28 36 45 55 66 78 91 105 120 136 153 171 190

5.5.3 Adjacent_difference

The generic `adjacent_difference` algorithm calculates the difference between adjacent pairs of values in a sequence, and places the result into the same or another sequence.

Example 5-33 Illustrating the generic `adjacent_difference` **algorithm.**
```
#include <algo.h>
#include <assert.h>

int main()
{
  const int N = 20;
  int x1[N], x2[N];
  for (int i = 0; i != N; ++i)
    x1[i] = i;

  // Compute the partial sums of 0, 1, 2, 3, ..., N - 1,
  // putting the result in x2:
  partial_sum(&x1[0], &x1[N], &x2[0]);

  // Compute the adjacent differences of elements in x2,
  // placing the result back in x2:
  adjacent_difference(&x2[0], &x2[N], &x2[0]);

  // The result is the original 0, 1, 2, 3, ..., N - 1:
  for (i = 0; i != N; i++)
      assert(x2[i] == i);
}
```

The program first calls `partial_sum` on a sequence 0, 1, . . . , N – 1. When `adjacent_difference` is applied to the resulting sequence of partial sums (see the output of Example 5-32), the original sequence is reproduced.

5.5.4 Inner_product

The generic `inner_product` algorithm computes the inner product of two input sequences. The following program first computes the inner product of 1, 2, 3, 4, 5, and 2, 3, 4, 5, 6 using its normal definition in terms of + and *, obtaining

$$1 * 2 + 2 * 3 + 3 * 4 + 4 * 5 + 5 * 6 == 70.$$

The algorithm uses the two operators involved in this calculation, + and *, by default, but other operators can be used instead by passing function objects to `inner_product`. The program illustrates this fact in a second call of `inner_product` that reverses the roles of + and * to compute

$$(1 + 2)* (2 + 3) * (3 + 4) * (4 + 5) * (5 + 6) == 10395.$$

Example 5-34 Illustrating the generic `inner_product` **algorithm.**

```
#include <algo.h>
#include <iostream.h>
#include <function.h>

int main()
{
  const int N = 5;
  int x1[N], x2[N];
  for (int i = 0; i != N; ++i) {
    x1[i] = i + 1;
    x2[i] = i + 2;
  }

  // Compute inner product of 1, 2, ..., N and 2, 3, ..., N+1
  int result = inner_product(&x1[0], &x1[N], &x2[0], 0);

  cout << "Inner product as normally defined: "
       << result << endl;

  // Again compute "inner product," with roles of + and *
  // reversed:
  result = inner_product(&x1[0], &x1[N], &x2[0], 1,
    times<int>(), plus<int>());

  cout << "Inner product with roles of + and * reversed: "
       << result << endl;
}
```

Output from Example 5-34:

```
Inner product as normally defined: 70
Inner product with roles of + and * reversed: 10395
```

The fourth argument to `inner_product` is the value for initializing the sum of products. Normally this initial value should be the identity element for the first of the two operators involved. Thus we use 0 for this initial value when we compute the sum of products, but we use 1 when we compute the product of sums.

CHAPTER 6 *Sequence Containers*

In this chapter and the next we take a comprehensive tour of STL containers, describing and illustrating most of their features. More importantly, we consider criteria for choosing one kind of container in preference to others.

All of STL's container classes are examples of one of the most important concepts in software, *data abstraction* or *abstract data types*. An abstract data type provides a set of objects and a set of operations on those objects, both of which have a publicly defined abstract meaning that is separated from the way the objects are represented and the operations are implemented. By keeping their representation and implementation private (a goal supported by the C++ class feature), abstract data types prevent programmers from writing code that depends on particular internal details, which in turn means greater flexibility in modifying and maintaining the software over its lifetime.

Many software libraries embody the data abstraction concept, but the design of STL's container classes takes an important further step by employing an even higher-level concept, that of a *family of abstractions* that share a core of specifications. STL provides two families of abstractions, *sequence containers* and *sorted associative containers*. The sequence containers are `vector`, `deque`, and `list`, and the sorted associative containers are `set`, `multiset`, `map`, and `multimap`. In terms of functions provided, different members of a family may differ "at the margins"; for example, deques and lists provide a function called `push_front`, but vectors do not. But with the sequence abstraction family, the fundamental differences are in terms of performance, which is what dictates decisions to include or omit certain operations—the reason `push_front` is not included in vector is that it would have to take linear time, whereas in deques and lists it can be implemented as a constant time operation.

None of the three members of the sequence abstraction family dominates the others in terms of performance of *all* operations (if one did, there would be little reason to provide all three). When we learn about the differences between vectors, deques, and lists, one of our most important goals should be to understand when one is likely to be superior to the others. That is, when programming some application that involves building and using sequences, we need to think about what mix of operations needs to be done on the sequences and choose the sequence representation accordingly. Of course, in our initial thinking about a problem, we may only have a vague idea of the operation mix, and we may want to start programming experimentally before we know the answer. One of the advantages of the STL library is that it not only provides different representations of sequences but it also provides them with almost the same interfaces—the family of abstractions idea. This allows switching between different representations to experiment with which one gives the best overall performance, with only a few changes in the program. Where there *are* differences between two interfaces, it's because they're designed that way purposely to make you think about which is the best representation to use.

The `set`, `multiset`, `map`, and `multimap` members of the sorted associative abstraction family have some real differences in the meanings of their operations, rather than differing mainly in terms of performance the way the sequence abstractions do. Between `set` and `multiset`, the main difference is in the meaning of `insert`. Insertion into a set has no effect if the value being inserted is already present, but with a multiset duplicates are stored. The same distinction exists between `map` and `multimap`, and these two containers share a substantial difference from `set` and `multiset` in that they associate values of another type with keys; with `set` and `multiset` just the keys themselves are stored. The performance requirements on all of these sorted associative containers are essentially the same, requiring logarithmic time bounds on insertion, deletion, and search operations.[1]

STL also provides several containers that are more restrictive in the access they provide—stacks, queues, and priority queues. However, these are provided by means of container adaptors and will be described in Chapter 9.

In describing the sequence containers, we will describe vectors in fullest detail and then discuss deques and lists mainly in terms of how they differ from vectors. More self-contained descriptions of all container classes can be found in the Container Reference Guide in Chapter 19.

6.1 Vectors

Vectors are sequence containers that provide fast random access to sequences of varying length in addition to fast insertions and deletions at the end. They are the sequence container of choice when the fastest possible random access is needed, and few if any insertions or deletions are required at any point other than the end. If insertions and deletions must also be done at the beginning of a sequence, they

---

1. The sorted associative containers described here are those that have been accepted as part of the ANSI/ISO C++ (Draft) Standard Library. Another closely related abstraction family is *hashed associative containers,* which trade some of the functionality of sorted associative containers for improvements in performance. The requirements for these containers permit hash table representations that have *constant average time* performance for storage and retrieval operations. Specifications and reference implementations for hashed associative containers are available from the Web sites and FTP sites described in Appendix B .

will take linear time when using a vector. If many such operations are required, a better choice is a deque, which provides constant time insertions and deletions at both ends, together with random access. (The trade-off is that the constant bound for accessing elements is somewhat larger with a deque than with a vector.) Finally, if insertions and deletions must be done at interior positions, it may be better to use a list than a vector or deque. (With lists one gives up random access, but many kinds of computations can get by with stepping through a container sequentially, which lists support well.)

6.1.1   Types

The template parameters of each of the sequences classes are given by

```
template <class T, class Allocator = allocator>
```

The first parameter is the type of data to be stored, and the second is the type of storage allocator to be used, which defaults to a standard allocator.[2]

Each STL container class defines and makes public several types:

- `value_type`, which is the type of elements the container stores;

- `reference`, which is the type of locations of elements of the container (usually `T&` but more generally it is determined by the allocator type);

- `iterator`, which is an iterator type referring to values of type `reference`; for vectors this type is of the random access category;

- `difference_type`, which is a signed integral type that can represent the difference between two iterators;

- `size_type`, which is an unsigned integral type that can represent any non-negative value of difference type;

- `reverse_iterator`, which is an iterator type referring to values of type `reference` and which defines incrementing and decrementing opposite to their normal `iterator` definitions; for vectors this type is of the random access category.

The reference and iterator types also have corresponding constant reference and constant iterator types, `const_reference` and `const_iterator`. Finally, there is also a constant reverse iterator type, `const_reverse_iterator`.

With vectors the iterator types are all random access types, the most powerful

---

2. See the caveat in Section 1.3.4 on page 11 regarding lack of current compiler support for default template parameters.

category. This means that *all* STL generic algorithms can be used with vectors. Consequently, the only operations that the vector class needs to define as member functions are those for constructing vectors, inserting and deleting vector elements, and accessing basic information such as the iterators marking the vector's beginning and end.

6.1.2   Constructing Sequences

Vectors have several kinds of constructors. The default constructor, as used in expressions like `vector<T>()` or in declarations like

```
vector<T> vector1;
```

produces a sequence that is initially empty. An expression `vector<T>(n, value)` or a declaration

```
vector<T> vector1(n, value);
```

produces a sequence initialized with N = n copies of `value`, which must be of type `T` or convertible to type `T`. The second parameter of this constructor is actually a default parameter, with `T()` as the default; that is, `vector<T>(n)` or

```
vector<T> vector1(n);
```

produces a sequence initialized with N = n copies of the result of calling the default constructor of type `T`.[3]

Constructing an empty sequence with the default constructor takes constant time, and constructing a sequence with N elements takes time proportional to N.

There are two other ways of constructing vectors, but before looking at them, let's see some simple examples of the three ways considered so far. The following program illustrates the first two ways; it also makes use of both a member function `size`, which returns the number of elements in a vector, and the ability to use array-like notation for accessing the *i*th element of a vector.

Example 6-1   Demonstrating the simplest STL vector constructors.
```
#include <iostream.h>
#include <vector.h>
```

---

3. According to the ANSI/ISO (Draft) C++ Standard, this works even if `T` is a built-in type such as `int`, since `int()` and other such expressions are required to be defined (as 0 converted to type `T`, by default initialization). Beware, though, because existing compilers might not yet meet this requirement. If `T` is defined by a class, that class must have a default constructor.

```
#include <assert.h>

int main()
{
  cout << "Demonstrating simplest vector constructors"
       << endl;
  vector<char> vector1, vector2(3, 'x');
  assert(vector1.size() == 0);
  assert(vector2.size() == 3);
  assert(vector2[0] == 'x' && vector2[1] == 'x' &&
         vector2[2] == 'x');
  assert(vector2 == vector<char>(3, 'x') &&
         vector2 != vector<char>(4, 'x'));
}
```

Here's an example of constructing a vector of elements of a user-defined type, including a case of defaulting the initial value by passing only one argument to the constructor.

Example 6-2   Demonstrating STL vector constructors with a user-defined type.

```
#include <iostream.h>
#include <vector.h>
#include <assert.h>

class U {
public:
  unsigned long id;
  U() : id(0) { }
  U(unsigned long x) : id(x) { }
};

bool operator==(const U& x, const U& y)
{
  return x.id == y.id;
}

int main()
{
  cout << "Demonstrating STL vector constructors with "
       << "a user-defined type." << endl;
  vector<U> vector1, vector2(3);
  assert(vector1.size() == 0);
  assert(vector2.size() == 3);
  assert(vector2[0] == U() && vector2[1] == U() &&
```

```
            vector2[2] == U());
     assert(vector2 == vector<U>(3, U()));
}
```

In this example, for the user-defined type we use a type U with almost minimal properties (as discussed in Section 1.6.3 on page 20); we'll also use this type in several subsequent examples. We define the == operator on U for use in the assertions about vector2[i].

When creating N copies of the initial value, the vector constructor calls the copy constructor of the element type. To demonstrate that this is the case, let's define the copy constructor for type U to keep track of which "generation" a copy is (an originally constructed value is generation 0, a copy of it is generation 1, a copy of a copy of it is generation 2, etc.). We also keep track of the total number of times U's copy constructor has been called, in a static variable.

Example 6-3 Demonstrating STL vector constructors with a user-defined type and showing copying explicitly.

```
#include <iostream.h>
#include <vector.h>
#include <assert.h>

class U {
public:
  unsigned long id;
  unsigned long generation;
  static unsigned long total_copies;
  U() : id(0), generation(0) { }
  U(unsigned long n) : id(n), generation(0) { }
  U(const U& z) : id(z.id), generation(z.generation + 1) {
    ++total_copies;
  }
};

bool operator==(const U& x, const U& y)
{
  return x.id == y.id;
}

unsigned long U::total_copies = 0;

int main()
{
  cout << "Demonstrating STL vector constructors with "
```

```
           << "a user-defined type and showing copying "
           << "explicitly." << endl;
      vector<U> vector1, vector2(3);

      assert(vector1.size() == 0);
      assert(vector2.size() == 3);

      assert(vector2[0] == U() && vector2[1] == U() &&
             vector2[2] == U());

      for (int i = 0; i != 3; ++i)
        cout << "vector2[" << i << "].generation: "
             << vector2[i].generation << endl;
      cout << "Total copies: " << U::total_copies << endl;
    }
```

Output from Example 6-3:
```
Demonstrating STL vector constructors with a user-defined
type and showing copying explicitly.
vector2[0].generation: 1
vector2[1].generation: 1
vector2[2].generation: 1
Total Copies: 3
```

This program's output shows that each U value stored in the vector is a generation 1 copy, and U's copy constructor was called once for each of the 3 values stored.

Of course, the vector class itself provides a copy constructor for copying another vector. The following program shows uses of the copy constructor along with uses of another constructor for copying any range of values from another vector.

Example 6-4   Demonstrating STL vector copying constructors.
```
#include <iostream.h>
#include <vector.h>
#include <assert.h>

int main()
{
  cout << "Demonstrating STL vector copying constructors"
       << endl;
  char* name = "George Foreman";
  vector<char> George(name, name + 6);

  vector<char> anotherGeorge(George.begin(), George.end());
  assert(anotherGeorge == George);
```

```
vector<char> son1(George); // Uses copy constructor
assert(son1 == anotherGeorge);

vector<char> son2 = George; // Also uses copy constructor
assert(son2 == anotherGeorge);
}
```

The constructor for copying a range of values via iterators is more general than this example illustrates; it can be used with iterators for other containers to copy, for example, a range of values from a list or from a deque.

```
list<char> list1;
... code to insert characters in list1;
vector<char> vector1(list1.begin(), list1.end());
```

However, this capability requires a feature only recently added to the ANSI/ISO (Draft) C++ Standard, namely *template member functions*. The constructor member that would permit the code above is specified in the standard with the following interface:

```
template <class InputIterator>
vector(InputIterator first, InputIterator last);
```

At the time of this writing, most compilers do not support this template member function feature, and consequently versions of STL for those compilers may only provide a more limited facility, for copying a range from an array:

```
vector(const T* first, const T* last);
```

or for copying a range from another vector:

```
vector(const_iterator first, const_iterator last);
```

where const_iterator is the vector<T>::const_iterator type defined in class vector. Actually, these two interfaces will be equivalent and only one will be present if const T* and vector<T>::const_iterator are the same type, as is the case in most implementations of vector.

If the template copying constructor is not available, the preceding code for copying from a list would have to be written with a for loop:

```
list<char> list1;
... code to insert characters in list1;
vector<char> vector1;
```

```
vector<char>::iterator i;
for (i = list1.begin(); i != list1.end(); ++i)
  vector1.push_back(*i);
```

or, more succinctly, with the aid of the generic copy algorithm and an insert iterator:

```
list<char> list1;
... code to insert characters in list1;
vector<char> vector1;
copy(list1.begin(), list1.end(), back_inserter(vector1));
```

6.1.3 Insertion

The most useful vector member function for inserting elements is push_back, which inserts a single element at the end of the sequence. We've already seen this function used just above and several times in earlier sections. The following program contains yet another use, along with one of a more general insert member function.

Example 6-5 Demonstrating STL vector push_back **and** insert **functions.**

```
#include <iostream.h>
#include <vector.h>
#include <algo.h>
#include <assert.h>

vector<char> vec(char* s)
  // Return vector<char> containing the characters of s
  // (not including the terminating null).
{
  vector<char> x;
  while (*s != '\0')
    x.push_back(*s++);
  return x;
}

int main()
{
  cout << "Demonstrating vector push_back function" << endl;

  vector<char> vector1 = vec("Bjarne Stroustrup"), vector2;
  vector<char>::iterator i;
```

```
for (i = vector1.begin(); i != vector1.end(); ++i)
    vector2.push_back(*i);
assert(vector1 == vector2);

vector1 = vec("Bjarne Stroustrup");
vector2 = vec("");

cout << "Demonstrating vector insertion at beginning"
     << endl;

for (i = vector1.begin(); i != vector1.end(); ++i)
    vector2.insert(vector2.begin(), *i);
assert(vector2 == vec("purtsuortS enrajB"));

// Show that vector2 is the reverse of vector1, by using
// STL generic reverse function to reverse vector1.
reverse(vector1.begin(), vector1.end());
assert(vector2 == vector1);
}
```

In the `vec` function, as we've seen before, we use `push_back` to build a vector by inserting characters from a string one by one at its end. We then use `push_back` in the same way in the first part of the main program. The second part reinitializes and takes characters from the same string and inserts them one by one at the beginning of `vector2`, which makes `vector2` hold the reverse of the original string. We can see that from the assertion

```
assert(vector2 == vec("purtsuortS enrajB"));
```

but we also show it in another way by using the STL generic `reverse` function to reverse the original string and then asserting equality between the result and `vector2`.

Inserting elements into a vector at positions other than the end is okay in a small example like this, but it should be avoided when working with large vectors since it requires linear time (because every element at or past the insertion point has to be moved over to make room for the new element). If your application requires such insertions, a deque or a list probably should be used instead.

By the way, `vector1.push_back(x)` is functionally equivalent to `vector1.insert(vector1.end(), x)`; the performance might be slightly different, but both take constant time (amortized).

Vectors also provide `insert` member functions for inserting n = N copies of an element or a range of elements from another sequence:

```
vector1.insert(position, n, x);
```

This is functionally equivalent to a loop:

```
for (int k = 0; k < n; ++k)
  vector1.insert(position, x);
```

but is much faster if `position` is not at the end. (If there are M elements at or past `position`, then in the loop version each of the N insert calls causes these M elements to be moved, requiring a total of NM moves. The insert member function with parameter N is only allowed to take $O(N + M)$ time, but it can achieve this by moving the M elements only once, making space for the N new elements, for a total of $N + M$ element moves. If, say, $M = N = 1,000$, there are only 2,000 moves rather than 1 million.)

There is also a vector member function for inserting a range of elements from another sequence: if `first` and `last` are iterators of some type `iterator_type` and they define a range, then

```
vector1.insert(position, first, last)
```

is functionally equivalent to

```
for (iterator_type i = first; i != last; ++i)
  vector1.insert(position, *i);
```

but is much faster if `position` is not at the end—provided `iterator_type` is of the forward, bidirectional, or random access category. With iterators of these categories, it is possible to compute the distance from `first` to `last` and reserve that much space for the new elements, but otherwise the insertions have to be done one by one, as in the loop.

This last member function is actually a template member function:

```
template <class InputIterator>
void insert(iterator position, InputIterator first,
            InputIterator last);
```

As we noted for the similar case of the templated vector constructor, most current compilers do not yet support templated member functions. STL versions for such compilers should include the following member instead:

```
void insert(iterator position, const T* first,
            const T* last)
```

This permits inserting a range of elements from an array (or another vector in the common case that const T* and vector<T>::const_iterator are the same type). For inserting a range from some other kind of sequence, if the templated version is not available, the insertions could be done with a loop or using copy and inserter, an insert iterator:

```
copy(first, last, inserter(vector1, position));
```

Note, however, that either the loop or the copy takes O(nm) time to insert n elements at a position m elements from the end. There are faster ways of doing it, but once again, if many such insertions appear to be necessary in some application, a deque or a list should probably be used instead of a vector.

Using insert can cause reallocation; i.e., the vector elements may be stored in a different area after the insert. The reason is that the elements are stored in a block of contiguous storage. If there is no room left in the current block for the new element, then a larger block is requested from the storage allocator, all of the old elements and the new element are copied to the new block, and the old block is deallocated. The new block size is twice the old size,[4] which means that for a vector holding N elements, reallocation will not be required again until N more elements are inserted. Thus, although reallocation can make the insertions that cause it expensive, they are infrequent enough that the amortized cost of insertion is constant (see also the discussion in Section 1.4.2 on page 14).

You can exercise some control over when reallocation occurs by using the capacity and reserve member functions. The capacity member function returns the size of the currently allocated block (the number of elements it can hold). The call

```
    vector1.reserve(n);
```

ensures that vector1.capacity() after the call is at least N = n; it causes reallocation if (and only if) the current capacity is less than N. In any case, it does not change the current size of the vector (i.e., the number of elements actually stored).

If you know in advance that you are about to insert N elements (with push_back or one of the forms of insert), you can speed up your program by doing the reserve call beforehand, rather than letting repeated reallocations occur. It is guaranteed that no reallocations take place during the insertions that happen after reserve until the time when the vector's size reaches N.

---

4. However, if the vector is empty, then a block of some implementation-defined size is allocated. The factor 2 is used in the Hewlett-Packard reference implementation, but any constant factor greater than 1 would yield amortized constant time for insertion.

Example 6-6 Demonstrating STL vector capacity **and** reserve **functions.**

```cpp
#include <vector.h>
#include <algo.h>
#include <assert.h>

class U {
 public:
  unsigned long id;
  U() : id(0) { }
  U(unsigned long x) : id(x) { }
};

int main()
{
  cout << "Demonstrating STL vector capacity and reserve "
          "functions." << endl;

  const int N = 10000; // size of vectors

  vector<U> vector1, vector2;

  cout << "Doing " << N << " insertions in vector1,\n"
       << "with no advance reservation.\n";
  for (int k = 0; k != N; ++k) {
    vector<U>::size_type cap = vector1.capacity();
    vector1.push_back(U(k));
    if (vector1.capacity() != cap)
      cout << "k: " << k << ", new capacity: "
           << vector1.capacity() << endl;
  }

  vector2.reserve(N);
  cout << "\nNow doing the same thing with vector2,\n"
       << "after starting with reserve(" << N << ").\n";
  for (k = 0; k != N; ++k) {
    vector<U>::size_type cap = vector2.capacity();
    vector2.push_back(U(k));
    if (vector2.capacity() != cap)
      cout << "k: " << k << ", new capacity: "
           << vector2.capacity() << endl;
  }
}
```

Output from Example 6-6:

```
Demonstrating STL vector capacity and reserve functions.
Doing 10000 insertions in vector1,
with no advance reservation.
k:  0, new capacity: 1024
k: 1024, new capacity: 2048
k: 2048, new capacity: 4096
k: 4096, new capacity: 8192
k: 8192, new capacity: 16384

Now doing the same thing with vector2,
after starting with reserve(10000).
```

In the loop inserting into `vector1`, the points at which reallocations occur might differ with different implementations of STL. There is no output from the loop inserting into `vector2`, since calling `reserve` prevents reallocations from occurring.

Besides efficiency, there is another reason you may want to use `reserve`. *Reallocation invalidates all iterators and references to positions in the vector*, since the elements may be moved to a different storage area. If no reallocation occurs, though, it is guaranteed that insertions at the end of a vector do not invalidate any iterators or references, and those in the middle invalidate just those iterators and references to or after the insertion point. If there is some section of your program in which you need to maintain several iterators to different parts of a vector while doing insertions, you should use `reserve` with a sufficiently large size in order to avoid reallocations while that section is executing.

6.1.4 Erasure (Deletion)

Just as `push_back` is the most useful vector insertion member function, the most useful member function for erasure is `pop_back`, which removes one element from the end of a sequence, in constant time. These two functions together, along with another member function, `back`, allow a vector to be used as a stack; i.e., data can be stored and retrieved in a last-in, first-out order. (A true stack data abstraction is much more restricted than a vector, as access is limited to the last element. STL provides the more restricted notion via a container adapter, as described in Chapter 9.)

Example 6-7 Demonstrating STL vector `back` **and** `pop_back` **operations.**

```cpp
#include <iostream.h>
#include <vector.h>
#include <assert.h>

vector<char> vec(char* s)
```

```
      // Return vector<char> containing the characters of s
      // (not including the terminating null).
   {
     vector<char> x;
     while (*s != '\0')
       x.push_back(*s++);
     return x;
   }

   int main()
   {
     cout << "Demonstrating STL vector back "
          << "and pop_back operations." << endl;
     vector<char> vector1 = vec("abcdefghij");

     cout << "Popping characters off the back produces: ";

     while (vector1.size() > 0) {
       cout << vector1.back();
       vector1.pop_back();
     }
     cout << endl;
   }
```

Output from Example 6-7:
```
Demonstrating STL vector back and pop_back operations.
Popping characters off the back produces: jihgfedcba
```

This program repeatedly retrieves the last element, prints it, and erases it, until the vector becomes empty.

As with insertion, vectors do provide a more general ability to erase an element at any position. For example, we could replace the while loop in the previous program by one that retrieves, prints, and erases the first element rather than the last:

```
   while (vector1.size() > 0) {
     cout << vector1.front();
     vector1.erase(vector1.begin());
   }
```

Note that to erase the first element we use erase, as there is no pop_front member function corresponding to pop_back for vectors. The reason pop_front isn't provided for vectors (this function *is* provided for deques and lists) is to discourage using a vector in this way, since erasure at the beginning of a vector is inefficient. With a deque or a list, erasure at the beginning takes only constant time, but with a vector it can only be accomplished by moving all of the elements that are past the erasure point over by one to fill the gap, and that takes linear time. That means, for example, that the above loop would take quadratic time.

Nevertheless, the general erasure capability is provided for vectors, for situations in which a vector is overall a better choice than a deque or a list but an occasional erasure is needed at positions other than the end. The following program shows various uses of the vector `erase` member function, including one in which the version

```
void erase(iterator first, iterator last)
```

is used. This erases all elements from the range of positions [`first`, `last`) (the element at `last`, if any, is not erased).

Example 6-8 Demonstrating the STL vector `erase` function.
```
#include <iostream.h>
#include <vector.h>
#include <algo.h>
#include <assert.h>

vector<char> vec(char* s)
  // Return vector<char> containing the characters of s
  // (not including the terminating null).
{
  vector<char> x;
  while (*s != '\0')
    x.push_back(*s++);
  return x;
}

int main()
{
  cout << "Demonstrating STL vector erase function." << endl;

  vector<char> vector1 = vec("remembering");
  vector<char>::iterator j;

  j = find(vector1.begin(), vector1.end(), 'm');

  // j now points to the first 'm'
  assert(*j == 'm' && *(j+1) == 'e');
```

```
            vector1.erase(j--);
            assert(vector1 == vec("reembering"));

            // j now points to the first 'e'
            assert(*j == 'e' && *(j+1) == 'e');

            vector1.erase(j--);
            assert(vector1 == vec("rembering"));
            assert(*j == 'r');

            // Erase first 3 characters:
            vector1.erase(j, j + 3);
            assert(vector1 == vec("bering"));

            vector1.erase(vector1.begin() + 1);
            assert(vector1 == vec("bring"));
        }
```

There is one rather subtle point illustrated in this program about the interaction between erase and iterators. The erase function *invalidates all iterators to all positions past the point of erasure*, but it leaves valid those referring to preceding positions or to the erased position. That's why the line

```
            vector1.erase(j--);
```

works correctly, but the similar code

```
            vector1.erase(j++);
```

wouldn't work, because j would be invalid after the erasure.

All STL containers have insert and erase member functions, but the way they interact with iterators varies considerably. We will revisit this issue when we consider other containers in later sections.

The erase member for erasing a range (which is used in the next-to-last step of the preceding program) is more efficient than erasing elements one by one. The time it takes is $O(p)$, where p is the number of elements past the erased elements, whereas the time for erasing them one by one would be $O(ep)$, where e is the number of erased elements.

6.1.5 Accessors

Container accessors are member functions that return information about a container, without changing it. We've already seen most of the vector accessors in earlier discussions and examples. Here is the complete list:

- `iterator begin()`, which returns an iterator referring to the beginning of the vector;

- `iterator end()`, which returns an iterator referring to the end of the vector;

- `iterator rbegin()`, which returns a reverse iterator referring to the beginning of the vector for reverse order traversal;

- `iterator rend()`, which returns a reverse iterator referring to the end of the vector for reverse order traversal;

- `size_type size() const`, which returns the number of elements in the vector;

- `size_type max_size() const`, which returns the maximum number of elements that could be stored in the vector;

- `size_type capacity() const`, which returns the number of elements that can be stored in the vector without reallocation;

- `bool empty() const`, which returns true if the vector contains no elements, false otherwise;

- `reference front()`, which returns a reference to the element at the beginning of the vector;

- `reference back()`, which returns a reference to the element at the end of the vector;

- `reference operator[](size_type n)`, which returns a reference to the element n elements from the beginning of the vector;

- `reference at(size_type n)`, which returns a reference to the element n elements from the beginning of the vector, if n is in range; otherwise, an exception is raised.

Those member functions in this list that return iterators also have versions that return constant iterators when applied to constant vectors, and similarly for reverse iterator and reference-returning member functions:

- `const_iterator begin() const`, which returns a constant iterator referring to the beginning of a constant vector;

- `const_iterator end() const`, which returns a constant iterator referring to the end of a constant vector;

- `const_iterator rbegin() const`, which returns a constant reverse iterator referring to the beginning of a constant vector for reverse order traversal;

- `const_iterator rend() const`, which returns a constant reverse iterator referring to the end of a constant vector for reverse order traversal;

- `const_reference front() const`, which returns a constant reference to the element at the beginning of a constant vector;

- `const_reference operator[](size_type n) const`, which returns a constant reference to the element n elements from the beginning of a constant vector;

- `const_reference at(size_type n) const`, which returns a reference to the element n elements from the beginning of the vector, if n is in range; otherwise, an exception is raised.

All of these accessors take constant time.

6.1.6   Equality and Less-Than Relations

We've already seen numerous examples of vector equality in assertions in our example programs. STL employs a general definition of container equality, one that allows equality comparison between *any* two containers of the same type (not just vectors):

- the sequences they contain must be of the same size, and

- elements in corresponding positions must be equal, as determined by the `==` operator of the element type.

In fact, the official definition of container equality is expressed in terms of the `size` member function and the generic `equal` algorithm: for any two containers a and b of the same type, a `==` b is defined by:

```
a.size() == b.size() && equal(a.begin(), a.end(), b.begin())
```

The number of `==` operations applied to pairs of elements is at most `a.size()`.
   Similarly, a general definition of `<` is used: for any two containers a and b of the same type, if T is the type of elements they contain and there is a `<` on T that defines a strict weak ordering relation (see Section 5.4), then a `<` b is defined by

```
lexicographical_compare(a.begin(), a.end(),
                        b.begin(), b.end())
```

This uses the generic `lexicographical_compare` function on the sequences in a and b. The number of < operations applied to pairs of elements is at most $2 \min(a.size(), b.size())$.

Both the equality and less-than definitions apply not only to sequence containers but also to associative containers, since associative containers include a notion of containing a sequence.

Other ordering relations (>, <=, >=) are defined in terms of <, so the definition above suffices to determine them all.

6.1.7 Assignment

The assignment operator = is defined for all STL containers. Immediately after an assignment x = y, it is always the case that x == y. The computing time is $O(\max(x.size(), y.size()))$.

For sequence containers there is also an `assign` template member function for assigning from an iterator range:

```
template <class InputIterator>
assign(InputIterator first, InputIterator last);
```

It is functionally equivalent to

```
erase(begin(), end());
insert(begin(), first, last);
```

Finally, there is a `swap` member function such that x.swap(y) exchanges the values of x and y. It is functionally equivalent to swap(x, y) but operates in constant time.

6.2 *Deques*

Deques have few differences from vectors in terms of functionality. The main difference is in performance: insertion and erasure at the beginning of a deque are much faster than with a vector, taking only constant time rather than linear time, while other operations are the same as, or are slower by a constant factor than, the corresponding vector operations. Like vectors, deques provide random access iterators, and thus all STL generic algorithms can be applied to them. They are therefore the sequence abstraction of choice when enough insertions and deletions are required at both ends of sequences to offset a small slowdown in other operations, in comparison with vectors. Although deques also support insertions and deletions in the middle, these operations take linear time. If many such operations will be required, the list abstraction may be a better choice.

The deque class interface is so similar to the vector class interface that many programs that use vectors could be converted to use deques instead with only a few syntactic changes, mainly in declarations and other uses of constructors. Certainly, all of the example programs demonstrating vectors in the preceding section fit this description. Here is one example: we edit the program in Example 6-5 on page 125 and simply replace all occurrences of "vector" with "deque." The result will compile and execute properly; no other changes are necessary. In the following version we have made two other changes: we replaced all occurrences of "vec" with "deq," and we changed the section

```
cout << "Demonstrating deque insertion at beginning"
      << endl;
for (i = deque1.begin(); i != deque1.end(); ++i)
  deque2.insert(deque2.begin(), *i);
```

to use the `push_front` member function that deque provides but vector does not:

```
cout << "Demonstrating deque push_front function" << endl;
for (i = deque1.begin(); i != deque1.end(); ++i)
  deque2.push_front(*i);
```

Here is the result:

Example 6-9   Demonstrating STL deque `push_back` **and** `push_front` **functions.**

```
#include <iostream.h>
#include <deque.h>
#include <algo.h>
#include <assert.h>

deque<char> deq(char* s)
  // Return deque<char> containing the characters of s
  // (not including the terminating null).
{
  deque<char> x;
  while (*s != '\0')
    x.push_back(*s++);
  return x;
}

int main()
{
  deque<char> deque1 = deq("Bjarne Stroustrup"), deque2;
  deque<char>::iterator i;
```

```
    cout << "Demonstrating deque push_back function" << endl;
    for (i = deque1.begin(); i != deque1.end(); ++i)
      deque2.push_back(*i);

    assert(deque1 == deque2);

    deque1 = deq("Bjarne Stroustrup");
    deque2 = deq("");

    cout << "Demonstrating deque push_front function" << endl;
    for (i = deque1.begin(); i != deque1.end(); ++i)
      deque2.push_front(*i);

    assert(deque2 == deq("purtsuortS enrajB"));

    // Show that deque2 is the reverse of deque1, by using
    // STL generic reverse function to reverse deque1
    reverse(deque1.begin(), deque1.end());

    assert(deque2 == deque1);
}
```

Note that the generic `reverse` algorithm works with deque iterators just as it does with vector iterators.

The only essential change required to convert programs using vectors into programs using deques, other than using "deque" instead of "vector" in declarations and constructors, would be to remove any uses of the vector `capacity` and `reserve` member functions. The deque class does not provide these members, as they are not needed for improving performance in the way they are for vectors. We must be careful here, though, to examine the way `reserve` was being used. If the only purpose was to improve performance by avoiding repeated reallocations, it will not affect the correctness of the original uses of vectors or the corresponding uses of deques to just drop the `reserve` statements. On the other hand, if the purpose was to avoid reallocations in order to preserve the validity of iterators, then a careful examination of the ways in which iterators are used is necessary, since deque insertions and erasures are not guaranteed to preserve the validity of iterators in the (limited) way that vector insertions and erasures are. This point is discussed in more detail in the sections on insertion (Section 6.2.3 on page 139) and erasure (Section 6.2.4 on page 140).

An implementation approach that meets all of the deque requirements is to use a two-level storage structure consisting of blocks of fixed size and a directory containing the block addresses.[5] The directory block is initialized so that its active entries occupy the middle and expand toward the directory boundaries. When inserting at the beginning of the deque, if there is no room in the first block, a new block is allocated and a pointer to it added to the directory in the position before the current first directory entry. Inserting at the end is handled symmetrically. It is only when a directory boundary is hit that reallocation must occur, and then only the directory block is reallocated, not the data-containing blocks. Reallocation is thus infrequent and inexpensive, in comparison with vector reallocation. Nevertheless, when it does occur, it can invalidate all iterators and references into the deque,[6] so we must be careful not to write code that depends on iterators or references remaining valid while insertions are occurring.

6.2.1   Types

The deque class has the same template parameters, T and Allocator, as the vector class, and it provides definitions of the same types: value_type, iterator, reference, size_type, difference_type, const_iterator, const_reference, and const_reverse_iterator. These types have the same abstract meaning as in the vector class, although the implementation can be quite different. Like vector iterators, deque iterators are of the random access category.

6.2.2   Constructors

The deque class provides exactly the same variety of constructors as the vector class. As with vectors, the constructor that initializes a deque using a range is a template member function, and versions of STL developed for compilers that do not yet support this feature may only have a more limited version of this constructor. See Section 19.4.5 on page 280 for details.

6.2.3   Insertion

There is also the same variety of insert member functions as with vectors, and it adds a push_front function for inserting at the beginning of a deque, as shown in Example 6-9 on page 137. As we already noted, however, there is no reserve member function. The differences from vectors are in performance and in instances when iterators and references may be invalidated by insertions.

Inserting at either the beginning or the end of a deque is a constant time operation. Inserting in the interior of a deque takes time proportional to the distance from the insertion point to the closest end. Thus, for example,

---

5. This is the approach used in the Hewlett-Packard reference implementation.

6. In the HP implementation no references are invalidated when reallocation occurs, but they would be if deques were implemented as a single block of memory, with the data in the middle and able to grow in either direction.

```
deque1.insert(deque1.begin() + 5, x)
```

would be a constant time operation, whereas the corresponding operation on a vector would take linear time.

As with vectors, insertion may cause reallocation of the storage associated with a deque. See the discussion (on page 138) of the implications for validity of iterators. Insertions in the interior invalidate all iterators and references, regardless of whether reallocation occurs. This is different from the situation with vectors, where insertions that don't cause reallocation leave iterators and references before the insertion point valid.

6.2.4   Erasure (Deletion)

Again, there is the same variety of `erase` member functions as with vectors, plus there is a `pop_front` function for erasing from the beginning of a deque. The same remarks about insertion performance and effect on validity of iterators and references apply to erasures also.

6.2.5   Accessors

The deque class provides all the same container accessors as the vector class—except `capacity`—namely `begin`, `end`, `rbegin`, `rend`, `size`, `max_size`, `empty`, `operator[]`, `at`, `front`, and `back`. As with vectors, these are all constant time operations. The `capacity` member is omitted because it is not needed.

6.2.6   Equality and Less-Than Relations

The definitions of equality and ordering relations given in Section 6.1.6 on page 135 are for all STL containers and thus apply to deques.

6.2.7   Assignment

The definitions of =, `assign`, and `swap` member functions given in Section 6.1.7 on page 136 are for all STL sequence containers and thus apply to deques.

6.3   Lists

We've seen that the vector and deque sequence abstractions are almost identical in terms of functionality; their only essential difference is in performance of insertions at the beginning of a sequence. The `list` sequence abstraction, by contrast, does have some real differences from vectors or deques in terms of member functions provided. The reason is that lists give up random access iterators in order to allow constant time insertions and deletions; without random access, some key generic algorithms, such as those for sorting, cannot be used. Hence, these operations are provided instead as member functions of the list class.

Also provided as member functions are some operations such as reversing a sequence, which *can* be done using the generic `reverse` algorithm and the bidirectional iterators that the list class does provide, but which can be done somewhat more efficiently with special algorithms that take advantage of the linked structures used to represent lists.

Insertion and deletion member functions are provided with essentially the same interface as in vectors and deques, but with major differences in performance. Insertions and deletions at *any* position in a list are constant time operations, not just at one or both ends. The linked representation of lists also permits some additional operations called *splicing*, for transferring elements from one sequence to another in constant time, and these are also provided as member functions.

Another major difference from vectors and deques is that list insertions never invalidate any iterators, and deletions invalidate only those referring to the element deleted.

Lists are certainly the sequence abstraction of choice when many insertions and/or deletions are required in interior positions and there is little need to jump around randomly from one position to another. Such linked structures have also been frequently used in favor of arrays simply for their ability to grow dynamically, but vectors and deques also have this property and probably should be used instead if that is the sole reason for using linked structures.

Let's begin our tour of the list class by taking the same example program we considered when discussing the differences between vectors and deques (Example 6-5 on page 125 and Example 6-9 on page 137).

Example 6-10 Demonstrating STL list `push_back` and `push_front` functions.

```
#include <iostream.h>
#include <list.h>
#include <algo.h>
#include <assert.h>

list<char> lst(char* s)
  // Return list<char> containing the characters of s
  // (not including the terminating null).
{
  list<char> x;
  while (*s != '\0')
    x.push_back(*s++);
  return x;
}
```

```
int main()
{
  list<char> list1 = lst("Bjarne Stroustrup"), list2;
  list<char>::iterator i;

  cout << "Demonstrating list push_back function" << endl;
  for (i = list1.begin(); i != list1.end(); ++i)
    list2.push_back(*i);

  assert(list1 == list2);

  list1 = lst("Bjarne Stroustrup");
  list2 = lst("");

  cout << "Demonstrating list push_front function" << endl;
  for (i = list1.begin(); i != list1.end(); ++i)
    list2.push_front(*i);

  assert(list2 == lst("purtsuortS enrajB"));

  // Show that list2 is the reverse of list1, by using
  // STL generic reverse function to reverse list1
  reverse(list1.begin(), list1.end());

  assert(list2 == list1);
}
```

This program was obtained from the deque version simply by substituting "list" everywhere for "deque" and "lst" for "deq." Note that the generic reverse algorithm is still applicable, since the bidirectional iterators it requires are exactly what lists supply. It does the sequence reversal by moving sequence elements from one position to another with assignments, but it may be better for some kinds of data to accomplish the reversal by relinking the list structure instead. When the data are characters, as they are here, the assignments are inexpensive, but relinking would be more efficient for large data elements. The relinking algorithm is provided as a list member function, and the generic reverse algorithm call could be replaced by

```
  // Show that list2 is the reverse of list1, by using
  // the list reverse member function to reverse list1
  list1.reverse();
```

In other cases, such changes from using generic algorithms to list member functions may be required rather than optional. We'll see examples as we go through the member functions provided.

6.3.1 Types

The list class has the same template parameters, T and Allocator, as the vector and deque classes and provides definitions of the same types: value_type, iterator, reference, size_type, difference_type, reverse_iterator, const_iterator, const_reference, and const_reverse_iterator. The list iterator types are of the bidirectional category rather than random access, which means that some generic algorithms, such as those for sorting, cannot be applied to lists.

6.3.2 Constructors

The list class provides exactly the same variety of constructors as the vector and deque classes. As with vectors and lists, the constructor that initializes a list using a range is a template member function, and versions of STL developed for compilers that do not yet support this feature may only have a more limited version of this constructor. See Section 19.5.5 on page 286 for details.

6.3.3 Insertion

The insert member functions the list class provides have the same functionality as those the vector and deque provide, but they always take only constant time per element inserted. There is also a significant difference in their abstract meaning: they never invalidate any iterators or references. There is no reserve member function, as it is unnecessary with lists. The splice member functions (Section 6.3.5 on page 145) also perform insertion-like operations.

6.3.4 Erasure (Deletion)

The list class provides the same erase member functions as the vector and deque classes. With lists they always take only constant time per element erased, and the only iterators and references invalidated are those to the erased elements.

   Here is an example similar to one we considered for vectors (Example 6-8 on page 132):

Example 6-11 Demonstrating STL list erase function.
```
#include <iostream.h>
#include <list.h>
#include <algo.h>
#include <assert.h>
list<char> lst(char* s)
    // Return list<char> containing the characters of s
```

```
                 // (not including the terminating null).
{
    list<char> x;
    while (*s != '\0')
        x.push_back(*s++);
    return x;
}

int main()
{
    cout << "Demonstrating STL list erase function." << endl;
    list<char> list1 = lst("remembering");
    list<char>::iterator j;

    j = find(list1.begin(), list1.end(), 'i');

    list1.erase(j++);
    assert(list1 == lst("rememberng"));

    // j now points to the 'n'.
    list1.erase(j++);
    assert(list1 == lst("rememberg"));

    // j now points to the 'g'.
    list1.erase(j++);
    assert(list1 == lst("remember"));
    list1.erase(list1.begin());
    assert(list1 == lst("emember"));

    list1.erase(list1.begin());
    assert(list1 == lst("member"));
}
```

In the calls

```
    list1.erase(j++);
```

we are doing something that neither vectors nor deques support, because they would invalidate iterators to the position after the one erased. With lists the iterator returned by j++, which is the iterator j held before it was incremented, is invalidated but the incremented value is not, and we can continue computing with it in subsequent statements (in the vector version we used j-- and carried out a somewhat different computation). Note that the following code

```
list1.erase(j); j++;
```

which might seem equivalent, is incorrect because the `erase` call invalidates `j` before we have a chance to increment it.

The `splice` member functions described next also perform erasure-like operations.

6.3.5 Splicing

One of the big performance advantages of linked structures over storing data in contiguous positions is that sequences can be rearranged by relinking, which takes only constant time regardless of the number of elements involved. The list class provides for this kind of rearrangement with its `splice` member functions. There are three versions (examples of all three are given ahead):

- `list1.splice(i1, list2)`, where `i1` is a valid iterator for `list1`, inserts the contents of `list2` before `i1` and leaves `list2` empty. `list1` and `list2` must not be the same list.

- `list1.splice(i1, list2, i2)`, where `i1` is a valid iterator for `list1` and `i2` is a valid dereferenceable iterator for `list2`, removes the element to which `i2` refers and inserts it before `i1` in `list1`. `list1` and `list2` may be the same list.

- `list1.splice(i1, list2, i2, j2)`, where `i1` is a valid iterator for `list1` and `[i2, j2)` is a valid range in `list2`, removes the elements of the range and inserts them before `i1` in `list1`. `list1` and `list2` may be the same list.

The first two variants always take constant time. The third does if `list1` and `list2` are the same list; otherwise it takes linear time.

Example 6-12 Demonstrating STL list `splice` functions.

```
#include <iostream.h>
#include <list.h>
#include <algo.h>
#include <assert.h>

list<char> lst(char* s)
   // Return list<char> containing the characters of s
   // (not including the terminating null).
{
   list<char> x;
   while (*s != '\0')
```

```
       x.push_back(*s++);
   return x;
}

int main()
{
   cout << "Demonstrating STL splice functions." << endl;
   list<char> list1, list2, list3;
   list<char>::iterator i, j, k;

   // Example of splice(iterator, list<char>&)
   list1 = lst("There is something about science.");
   list2 = lst("fascinating ");
   i = find(list1.begin(), list1.end(), 'a');
   list1.splice(i, list2);
   assert(list1 ==
       lst("There is something fascinating about science."));
   assert(list2 == lst(""));

   // Example of splice(iterator, list<char>&, iterator)
   list1 =
       lst("One gets such wholesale return of conjecture");
   list2 =
       lst("out of ssuch a trifling investment of fact.");
   list3 = lst(" of");
   i = search(list1.begin(), list1.end(), list3.begin(),
            list3.end());
   // i points to the blank before "of";
   j = find(list2.begin(), list2.end(), 's');
   list1.splice(i, list2, j);
   assert(list1 ==
       lst("One gets such wholesale returns of conjecture"));
   assert(list2 ==
       lst("out of such a trifling investment of fact."));

   // Example of splice(iterator, list<char>&, iterator,
   //                   iterator)
   list1 = lst("Mark Twain");
   list2 = lst(" --- ");
   j = find(list2.begin(), list2.end(), ' ');
   k = find(++j, list2.end(), ' ');   // Find second blank.
   list1.splice(list1.begin(), list2, j, k);// Move the ---.
   assert(list1 == lst("---Mark Twain"));
```

```
      assert(list2 == lst("  "));
}
```

6.3.6 Sorting-Related Member Functions

As we've already noted, the generic `sort` algorithm requires random access itera-tors and thus cannot be used with lists, which only supply bidirectional iterators. Instead, to sort a list one can use its `sort` member function. The following example shows a simple use of `sort` along with another member function, `unique`, which removes consecutive duplicate elements.

Example 6-13 Demonstrating STL list `sort` and `unique` functions.

```
#include <iostream.h>
#include <list.h>
#include <algo.h>
#include <assert.h>

list<char> lst(char* s)
  // Return list<char> containing the characters of s
  // (not including the terminating null).
{
  list<char> x;
  while (*s != '\0')
    x.push_back(*s++);
  return x;
}

int main()
{
    cout << "Demonstrating STL list sort and unique "
         << "functions." << endl;
    list<char> list1 = lst("Stroustrup");

    list1.sort();
    assert(list1 == lst("Soprrsttuu"));

    list1.unique();
    assert(list1 == lst("Soprstu"));
}
```

The `sort` member function has another version for sorting with a given compari-son function:

```
template <class Compare>
  void sort(Compare comp);
```

147

STL versions for compilers that don't yet support template member functions have to omit this template member. That's true also with `unique`, which has a version with a template parameter in order to allow the comparison between consecutive elements to be done with a given binary predicate:

```
template <class Compare>
  void unique(BinaryPredicate comp);
```

Another sorting-related operation that is supplied as a list member function is `merge`, which merges the current list with another list, where both lists are assumed to be sorted. Again, it has a template version:

```
merge(const list<T>& otherList);
template <class Compare>
  void merge(const list<T>& otherList, Compare comp);
```

As in the case of `reverse`, the generic `merge` algorithm can be used with lists (as it only requires input iterators), but the merge operation is also supplied as a member function in order to provide an algorithm based on relinking rather than moving elements by assignment.

6.3.7 Removal

One other operation supplied as a member function, for the same reason as `reverse` and `merge`, is `remove`, which erases all elements in the list equal to some given value or for which some given predicate holds:

```
void remove(const T& value);
template <class Predicate>
  void remove_if(Predicate pred);
```

6.3.8 Accessors

The list class provides all the same container accessors as the vector class—except `capacity`, `operator[]`, and `at`—namely `begin`, `end`, `rbegin`, `rend`, `size`, `max_size`, `empty`, `front`, and `back`. As with vectors, these are all constant time operations. The `capacity` member is omitted because it is not needed, and `at` and `operator[]` are omitted because they would have to take linear time.

6.3.9 Equality and Less-Than Relations

The definitions of equality and ordering relations given in Section 6.1.6 on page 135 are for all STL containers and thus apply to lists.

6.3.10   Assignment

The definitions of =, `assign`, and `swap` member functions given in Section 6.1.7 on page 136 are for all STL sequence containers and thus apply to lists.

CHAPTER 7

Sorted Associative Containers

We now come to *sorted associative containers*, which are a different family of abstractions from the sequence family we considered in Chapter 6. Whereas sequence containers store data items in a linear arrangement that preserves the relative positions into which the items are inserted, sorted associative containers dispense with this order and instead concentrate on being able to retrieve items as quickly as possible based on *keys* that are stored in the item (or in some cases *are* the items themselves).

One general approach to associative retrieval is to keep keys sorted according to some total order, such as numeric order if the items are numbers or lexicographical order if the keys are strings, and use a binary search algorithm. Another approach is hashing: divide the key space into some number of subsets, insert each key into its designated subset, and correspondingly confine each search to just one subset, with the association of a key to a subset being done by a "hash" function (so-called because it appears to be somewhat arbitrary or random in its assignments). The former approach—called *sorted* associative containers—can be implemented with balanced binary search trees, and the latter—called *hashed* associative containers—in any of a variety of hash table representations.

The main advantage of the hashed approach is constant average time for storage and retrieval, while that of the sorted approach is reliable performance (worst-case performance of hash table operations can be very bad—linear in the size, N, of the table—under some circumstances, but that of balanced binary trees is always $O(\log N)$).

Ideally, both sorted and hashed associative containers should be in the C++ Standard Library, but only the specification of sorted associative containers has been accepted (unofficial STL-based hash table specifications and implementations are available; see the footnote on page 118 and Appendix B).

The STL sorted associative container classes are `set`, `multiset`, `map` and `multimap`. With sets and multisets, the data items are just the keys themselves, and multisets allow duplicate keys while sets do not. With maps and multimaps, the data items are pairs of keys and data of some other type, and multimaps allow duplicate keys while maps do not. We consider sets and multisets together in Section 7.1, and then maps and multimaps together in Section 7.2.

Though their fundamental nature is different, sorted associative containers do share many features with sequence containers because they support traversal of the data items as a linear sequence using the same container accessors as are de-fined for sequence containers. Bidirectional iterators are provided, and traversals using them produce the items in sorted order. Indeed, in some cases sorting a se-quence of items may be accomplished more efficiently by inserting them in a mul-tiset and traversing the multiset than by using the generic sort algorithm or list sort member function (for example, if the data items are large structures).

7.1 Sets and Multisets

7.1.1 Types

The template parameters of both the `set` and the `multiset` classes are given by

```
template <class Key, class Compare = less<Key>,
          class Allocator = allocator>
```

The first parameter is the type of keys to be stored, the second is the type of com-parison function to be used in determining order, and the third is the type of stor-age allocator to be used.[1]

Both classes provide definitions of the same types as the sequence containers: `value_type` (which is defined as type `Key`), `iterator`, `reference`, `size_type`, `difference_type`, `const_iterator`, `const_reference`, and `const_reverse_iterator`, plus

- `key_type`, which is defined as type `Key`,

- `key_compare`, which is defined as type `Compare`,

- `value_compare`, which is also defined as type `Compare`.

These classes define both `key_compare` and `value_compare` for compatibility with `map` and `multimap`, where they are distinct types.

The comparison function must define an ordering relation on keys, which is used to determine their order in the linear traversals the container's iterator types support. The requirements on this relation are the same as we've already discussed for relations used with STL's sorting-related algorithms (in Section 5.4 on page 95). The ordering relation is also used to determine when two keys are considered equivalent. That is, two keys k1 and k2 are considered equivalent if

```
key_compare(k1, k2) == false && key_compare(k2, k1) == false
```

---

1. See the caveat in Section 1.3.4 on page 11 regarding lack of current compiler support for default template parameters.

In most simple cases, this definition of equivalence will coincide with that of the `==` operator. For example, if the keys are any built-in numeric type and `key_compare(k1, k2) == (k1 < k2)`, the definition of key equivalence amounts to

```
!(k1 < k2) && !(k2 < k1)
```

which is the same relation as that computed by `k1 == k2`. Certainly, though, it's possible for the two definitions to disagree. As a trivial example, suppose the keys are `vector<int>` containers and we define `key_compare` to compare just their first elements. Then any two vectors that have the same first element will be considered equal by `key_compare` but not by the `==` operator for vectors if they disagree in any other position.

It's important to keep this (potential) distinction in mind because, as we'll see, the notion of key equivalence comes into play in a variety of ways with all of the sorted associative containers. These ways include determining whether to insert an element based on whether its key duplicates (is equivalent to) one already present or the results of searching a multiset for all keys equivalent to a given key. In every case, when we talk about key equivalence, we mean the definition given here, not `==`.

The set and multiset iterator types are of the bidirectional category rather than random access, which means that some generic algorithms, such as those for sorting, cannot be applied to sets or multisets. But there's no need to apply a sorting algorithm anyway, since these containers maintain sorted order at all times.

7.1.2 Constructors

The set constructors are

```
set(const Compare& comp = Compare());

template <class InputIterator>
  set(InputIterator first, InputIterator last,
      const Compare& comp = Compare());

set(const set<Key, Compare, Allocator>& otherSet);
```

The first of these produces an empty set, the second a set with copies of elements from the range `[first, last)` (with duplicates eliminated), and the third (the copy constructor) a set with the same elements as `otherSet`. The first and second constructors take an optional argument of type `Compare`, which defaults to `Compare()`. The multiset constructors have the same form and meaning, except that they retain duplicate elements.

STL versions for compilers that do not support default template arguments may substitute a more limited constructor for initializing from a range, typically one for initializing from values in an array:

```
set(const Key* first, const Key* last,
    const Compare& comp = Compare());
```

7.1.3   Insertion

The simplest `insert` member function for `set` and `multiset` takes a single argument of type `value_type`, which is type `Key`, and inserts a copy of the argument.

Example 7-1   Demonstrating `set` construction and insertion.

```
#include <list.h>
#include <set.h>
#include <assert.h>

list<char> lst(char* s)
  // Return list containing the characters of s
  // (not including the terminating null).
{
  list<char> x;
  while (*s != '\0')
    x.push_back(*s++);
  return x;
}

int main()
{
  cout << "Demonstrating set construction and insertion."
       << endl;
  list<char> list1 = lst("There is no distinctly native "
                         "American criminal class");

  // Put the characters in list1 into set1:
  set<char, less<char> > set1;
  list<char>::iterator i;
  for (i = list1.begin(); i != list1.end(); ++i)
    set1.insert(*i);

  // Put the characters in set1 into list2:
  list<char> list2;
  set<char, less<char> >::iterator k;
```

```
    for (k = set1.begin(); k != set1.end(); ++k)
        list2.push_back(*k);

    assert(list2 == lst(" ATacdehilmnorstvy"));
}
```

In this program we write[2]

```
    set<char, less<char> >
```

where we apparently could have written just

```
    set<char>
```

since the second template parameter of `set` defaults to `less<char>`. But with STL versions for compilers that do not support default template arguments, the `set` class is typically defined as having both `Key` and `Compare` as explicit parameters, so the second parameter must be explicitly instantiated. (As with the sequence containers, the `Allocator` parameter is typically omitted from the class declaration, and substitution of different allocators is handled using preprocessor macros instead.)

After inserting the characters in `list1` into `set1`, we examine the contents of this set by copying its contents back into `list2` using a loop variable of the iterator type `set<char, less<char> >::iterator` and the `begin` and `end` member functions, which are provided for associative containers just as they are for sequence containers. The assertion shows that the sequence of characters in `list2`, and thus also in `set1`, is in sorted order, and there are no duplicates.

Here is a program that does the same thing using a multiset instead of a set.

Example 7-2 Demonstrating `multiset` **construction and insertion.**
```
#include <list.h>
#include <multiset.h>
#include <assert.h>

list<char> lst(char* s)
    // Return list containing the characters of s
    // (not including the terminating null).
{
    list<char> x;
    while (*s != '\0')
```

---

2. Note that the extra space before the closing > is necessary since >> would be parsed as a single token by most compilers, resulting in an error message.

155

```
        x.push_back(*s++);
    return x;
}

int main()
{
    cout << "Demonstrating multiset construction "
        << "and insertion." << endl;
    list<char> list1 = lst("There is no distinctly native "
                            "American criminal class");

    // Put the characters in list1 into multiset1:
    multiset<char, less<char> > multiset1;
    list<char>::iterator i;
    for (i = list1.begin(); i != list1.end(); ++i)
      multiset1.insert(*i);

    // Put the characters in multiset1 into list2:
    list<char> list2;
    multiset<char, less<char> >::iterator k;
    for (k = multiset1.begin(); k != multiset1.end(); ++k)
      list2.push_back(*k);

    assert(list2 == lst("        ATaaaaccccdeeeehiiiiiiiilll"
                        "mmnnnnnorrrssssstttvy"));
}
```

In this case, the assertion shows that duplicates are retained.

The `insert` member function used in these examples has different return types in the `set` and `multiset` classes. In class `set`, its interface is

```
pair<iterator, bool> insert(const value_type& x);
```

while in class `multiset` it is

```
iterator insert(const value_type& x);
```

In the `set` version, the iterator returned refers to the position of `x` in the set, whether or not it was already there, and the `bool` value is `true` if the element was inserted, `false` if it was already there. In the `multiset` version, the element is always inserted, and so the `bool` value is unnecessary.

The time required by `insert` is $O(\log N)$, where N is the number of elements stored in the set or multiset.

The `insert` member above differs from any of the sequence `insert` members in that no iterator must be passed to it to tell where the newly inserted element goes. Instead, the new element's position is whatever the comparison function requires to maintain sorted order. There is, however, another set and multiset `insert` member that does take an iterator argument, giving it the same interface as in the sequence containers.

```
iterator insert(iterator position, const value_type& x);
```

This function still puts x in the position required to maintain sorted order, treating `position` only as a "hint" as to where to begin searching. It takes only amortized constant time, rather than $O(\log N)$ time, if x is inserted, or is already present, at `position`. A simple case in which this performance property is useful is copying some already sorted container into a set or multiset, for example, with

```
vector<int>::iterator i;
for (i = vector1.begin(); i != vector1.end(); ++i)
  set1.insert(set1.end(), *i);
```

This code works whether or not `vector1` is in sorted order, taking $O(N \log N)$ time (where N is `vector1.size()`) if it is not sorted, but only $O(N)$ time if it is.

Since the `inserter` iterator adaptor is expressed in terms of the `insert` function, the preceding code above could also be written as

```
copy(vector1.begin(), vector1.end(),
     inserter(set1, set1.end()));
```

More generally, the "hint" version of set and multiset `insert` is useful in conjunction with the generic algorithms for set operations on sorted structures (`set_union`, `set_intersection`, `set_difference`, and `set_symmetric_-difference`). For example,

```
set_union(set1.begin(), set1.end(),
          set2.begin(), set2.end(),
          inserter(set3, set3.end()));
```

puts the union of `set1` and `set2` into `set3` in time $O(N1 + N2)$, where $N1$ and $N2$ are the sizes of `set1` and `set2`.

There is one other `insert` member function for sets and multisets, for inserting elements from a range:

```
template <class InputIterator>
  void insert(InputIterator first, InputIterator last);
```

It takes time $O(M \log (N + M))$, where M is the size of the range and N is the size of the set or multiset.

7.1.4 Erasure (Deletion)

Elements can be erased from a set or multiset either by key or by position: to erase all elements with key k from a set or multiset set1, use

```
set1.erase(k);
```

If set1 is a set, there can be at most one element with key k; if there is none, this function call does nothing. If i is a valid dereferenceable iterator for set1, use

```
set1.erase(i);
```

to erase the element to which i refers. In case set1 is a multiset and there are other copies of *i in set1, only the copy to which i refers is erased. To illustrate this in the following program, we define a new version of the 1st function we've been using to make lists from character strings. The new version is a template function that makes a list of characters from any STL container holding characters.[3] This example also uses one of the multiset accessor member functions, find, for finding an element by key.

Example 7-3 Demonstrating multiset erase functions.

```
#include <list.h>
#include <multiset.h>
#include <assert.h>

list<char> 1st(char* s)
  // Return list containing the characters of s
  // (not including the terminating null).
{
  list<char> x;
  while (*s != '\0')
    x.push_back(*s++);
  return x;
}
```

---

3. Note that the Container parameter of this function is a const reference parameter. When parameters are potentially large containers, it is crucial in terms of efficiency to make them constant reference parameters rather than value parameters. Passing by value (e.g., list<char> 1st(Container m)) means that the argument will be copied, taking time and space proportional to the size of the container.

```
template <class Container>
list<char> lst1(const Container& m)
  // Return list containing the characters in m.
{
  list<char> x;
  copy(m.begin(), m.end(), back_inserter(x));
  return x;
}

int main()
{
  cout << "Demonstrating multiset erase functions" << endl;
  list<char> list1 = lst("There is no distinctly native "
                         "American criminal class");

  // Put the characters in list1 into multiset1:
  multiset<char, less<char> > multiset1;
  copy(list1.begin(), list1.end(),
       inserter(multiset1, multiset1.end()));

  assert(lst1(multiset1) ==
         lst("       ATaaaaccccdeeeehiiiiiiilll"
             "mmnnnnnorrrssssstttvy"));

  multiset1.erase('a');
  assert(lst1(multiset1) ==
         lst("       ATccccdeeeehiiiiiiilll"
             "mmnnnnnorrrsssssttttvy"));

  multiset<char, less<char> >::iterator i =
    multiset1.find('e');

  multiset1.erase(i);
  assert(lst1(multiset1) ==
         lst("       ATccccdeeehiiiiiiilll"
             "mmnnnnnorrrsssssttttvy"));
}
```

The first `erase` call passes a key a, and all elements in `multiset1` with that key are erased. The second `erase` call passes an iterator i returned by the `find` call, referring to the element containing one of the e's, causing just that element to be erased. By the way, we could have written the `find` call and `erase` call together in one line:

```
multiset1.erase(multiset1.find('e'));
```

This would avoid having to declare an iterator variable.

The `set` and `multiset` classes provide one other `erase` member function, for erasing all elements in a range. For example, we might add the following lines to the end of the above program:

```
i = multiset1.find('T');
multiset<char, less<char> >::iterator j =
  multiset1.find('v');

multiset1.erase(i, j);
assert(lst(multiset1) == lst("        Avy"));
```

All of the `erase` member functions take $O(\log N + E)$ time, where N is the size of the set or multiset and E is the number of elements erased.

7.1.5 Accessors

Sets and multisets have most of the accessors that are common to the sequence containers, for accessing information about the elements as a linear, sorted sequence: `begin`, `end`, `rbegin`, `rend`, `empty`, `size`, and `max_size`. As usual, the iterator-returning accessors also have a version that returns a constant iterator when applied to a constant set or multiset. But these containers also have several member functions for accessing information by key: `find`, `lower_bound`, `upper_bound`, `equal_range`, and `count`.

We've already seen examples of `find` in Section 7.1.4. It's important to understand the differences between this member function and the generic `find` algorithm. As we already pointed out in Section 4.11 on page 65, the major difference is in efficiency: the set or multiset `find` member function takes only $O(\log N)$ time, where N is the size of the container, while the generic `find` algorithm takes $O(N)$ time. The `find` member is more efficient because it can take advantage of the keys' sorted order to do a binary search (implemented in terms of a binary search tree), while the generic `find` does a linear search.

Another difference between the `find` member and the generic `find`, in the case of multisets, is in the element to which the returned iterator refers. The generic `find` returns the position of the first member with the given key, but it is unspecified which position the `find` member returns, among those containing the given key. If it is important to get the first position, that is what the lower_bound member returns, and upper_bound returns the end of the range of positions containing the given key.

Example 7-4   Demonstrating multiset search member functions.

```
#include <list.h>
#include <multiset.h>
#include <assert.h>

list<char> lst(char* s)
  // Return list containing the characters of s
  // (not including the terminating null).
{
  list<char> x;
  while (*s != '\0')
    x.push_back(*s++);
  return x;
}

template <class Container>
list<char> lst(const Container& m)
  // Return list containing the characters in m
{
  list<char> x;
  copy(m.begin(), m.end(), back_inserter(x));
  return x;
}

int main()
{
  cout << "Demonstrating multiset search member functions."
       << endl;
  list<char> list1 = lst("There is no distinctly native "
                         "American criminal class"),
             list2 = lst("except Congress. - Mark Twain");

  // Put the characters in list1 into multiset1:
  multiset<char, less<char> > multiset1;
  copy(list1.begin(), list1.end(),
       inserter(multiset1, multiset1.end()));

  assert(lst(multiset1) ==
         lst("       ATaaaaccccdeeeehiiiiiiiilll"
             "mmnnnnnorrrsssssttttvy"));
```

```
      multiset<char, less<char> >::iterator i =
        multiset1.lower_bound('c');
      multiset<char, less<char> >::iterator j =
        multiset1.upper_bound('r');

      multiset1.erase(i, j);

      assert(lst(multiset1) == lst("          ATaaaassssttvy"));

      list<char> found, not_found;
      list<char>::iterator k;
      for (k = list2.begin(); k != list2.end(); ++k)
        if (multiset1.find(*k) != multiset1.end())
          found.push_back(*k);
        else
          not_found.push_back(*k);

    assert(found == lst("t ss  a Ta"));
    assert(not_found == lst("excepCongre.-Mrkwin"));
  }
```

We can think of `lower_bound` as returning the first position where the key could be inserted while still maintaining sorted order, and of `upper_bound` as returning the last such position. These statements are true regardless of whether the key is already present. (This is the same meaning that the generic `lower_bound` and `upper_bound` algorithms have on sorted sequences.)

The last part of the previous program searches `multiset1` for each of the characters in `list2` and puts those it finds in `found` and the others in `not_found`. The final assertions show that `find` returns the end position if the key is not present in the program.

If we need the results of `lower_bound` and `upper_bound` for the same key, we can get them both in one call with `equal_range`, which returns a pair of iterators. This latter function gets its name from the fact that the iterators it returns determine the range of elements equivalent to the given key. This range is empty (the iterators are equal) if there are no such elements in the container.

Finally, `count` returns the distance from the `lower_bound` position to the `upper_bound` position, which is the number of elements equivalent to the given key. For examples of both `equal_range` and `count`, we could add the following to the end of the previous program:

```
    assert(lst(multiset1) == lst("          ATaaaassssttttvy"));
```

```
i = multiset1.lower_bound('s');
j = multiset1.upper_bound('s');

pair<multiset<char, less<char> >::iterator,
     multiset<char, less<char> >::iterator>
  p = multiset1.equal_range('s');

assert(p.first == i && p.second == j);

assert(multiset1.count('s') == 4);

multiset1.erase(p.first, p.second);

assert(multiset1.count('s') == 0);

assert(lst(multiset1) == lst("       ATaaaatttvy"));
```

Each of these search functions (except `count`) has a version that returns a constant iterator when applied to a constant container (or, in the case of `equal_range`, a pair of constant iterators). Note that although we've illustrated them only for multisets, each is defined for sets as well. On sets, `count` always returns either 0 or 1.

With all of these search functions, one should keep in mind that their meaning depends on the meaning of equivalence as defined in terms of the `key_compare` function, not as defined by the `==` operator.

All of the search member functions take $O(\log N)$ time, where N is the size of the set or multiset, except `count`, which takes $O(\log N + E)$ time, where E is the number of elements with the given key.

7.1.6   Equality and Less-than Relations

Let's recall the definition of container equality that's used with all STL containers (from Section 6.1.6 on page 135):

- The sequences they contain must be of the same length; and

- Elements in corresponding positions must be equal, as determined by the `==` operator of the element type.

When applied to STL set and multiset containers, with their property of maintaining their elements in sorted order, this definition amounts to just what we expect from the names "set" and "multiset," based on their usage in mathematics. That is, two sets are equal if they contain the same elements—order is ignored. Two multisets are equal if they contain the same number of occurrences of each element, again regardless of order. Taken together with the STL generic algorithms for set operations on sorted structures (`set_union`, `set_intersection`, `set_difference`, and `set_symmetric_difference`), these properties enable all of the most basic and useful computations with sets and multisets.

Actually, though, things are not quite that simple, because the notion of "sameness" involved here is the key equivalence relation, as determined by the `key_compare` function: two keys `k1` and `k2` are considered equivalent if

```
key_compare(k1, k2) == false && key_compare(k2, k1) == false
```

As noted in Section 7.1.1 on page 152, this is not always identical to the relation computed by the `==` operator on the elements. If the two relations don't agree, we may get some unexpected results from set and multiset equality.

A similar situation exists with `operator<` on sets and multisets, since the general definition of this operator on all containers uses the generic `lexicographical_compare` algorithm, which uses the `<` operator of the element type. If `key_compare` does not compare keys the same way the element type `<` operator does, comparisons of sets and multisets might not give the results you expect.

7.1.7 Assignment

As already noted in Section 6.1.7 on page 136, `operator=` is defined for all STL containers, such that `x = y` makes it true that `x == y`. There is no `assign` member function for sorted associative containers, but there is a `swap` member function such that `x.swap(y)` exchanges the values of `x` and `y`. These are linear time operations.

7.2 *Maps and Multimaps*

Map containers can be viewed as arrays that are indexed by keys of some arbitrary type `Key` rather than by integers 0, 1, 2, ... They are sorted associative containers that provide for fast retrieval of information of some type `T` based on keys of a separate type `Key`, with the keys being stored uniquely. Multimaps do the same but allow duplicate keys. Their relationship to maps is the same as that of multisets to sets.

Maps and multimaps can be understood as sets and multisets in which there is additional information of type `T` along with each key. This additional data does not affect the way the containers are searched or traversed and only comes into play in a few additional operations that are provided specifically for storing or retrieving it. Our discussion in this section will be based on this insight and will therefore be brief.

Alternatively, we could have started with a full treatment of maps/multimaps and then said that sets/ multisets could be understood simply as maps and multimaps in which the associated data was not used. This might have been a more natural order of presentation, since maps/multimaps have a wider range of applications than sets/multisets, but we choose to discuss sets/multisets first because they are a little simpler and are easier to illustrate in small example programs. We present only a few examples of maps and multimaps in this chapter, but you'll find them used in a more significant way in Chapters 14 and 15.

Turning around the analogy with which we began, arrays (and vectors and deques) provide a map-like capability in which the keys are integers in some range $0, 1, 2, \dots, n - 1$, for some nonnegative integer n. While they handle such associations very efficiently, they are severely limited compared to the map container, first by allowing only integers as keys, and second by requiring storage proportional to n even if only a small percentage of the integers in the range $0, 1, 2, \dots,$ $n - 1$ have useful data associated with them. Maps and multimaps break away from both of these restrictions, allowing keys of almost any type and using storage only in proportion to the number of keys actually stored.

Even with integer keys, the "sparse representation" that maps and multimaps permit can enable huge savings in storage and computing time, as we'll show in a simple case in Section 7.2.3, with an example of computing the inner product of two sparse vectors (where by "vector" we mean an n-tuple of numbers; it will be represented as a `map`, not a `vector`). We'll come to examples of maps and multimaps with noninteger keys in Chapters 15 and 16.

7.2.1 Types

The template parameters of both the `map` and the `multimap` classes are given by

```
template <class Key, class T, class Compare = less<Key>,
          class Allocator = allocator>
```

The first parameter is the type of keys to be stored, the second is the type of objects to be associated with the keys, the third is the comparison function to be used in determining order, and the fourth is the storage allocator to be used. These are the same parameters as for sets and multisets except for the addition of `T`.

Both classes provide definitions of the same types as the sequence containers: `value_type` (which is defined as type `pair<const Key, T>`), `iterator`, `reference`, `size_type`, `difference_type`, `const_iterator`, `const_reference`, and `const_reverse_iterator`, plus

- `key_type`, which is defined as type `Key`,

- `key_compare`, which is defined as type `Compare`, and

- value_compare, which is the function type defined to compare two value_type objects based just on their keys:

```
class value_compare
  : public binary_function<value_type, value_type, bool> {
 protected:
  Compare comp;
  value_compare(Compare c) : comp(c) { }
 public:
  bool operator()(const value_type& x,
                  const value_type& y) const {
    return comp(x.first, y.first);
  }
};
```

As with sets and multisets, the map and multimap iterator types are of the bidirectional category rather than the random access category.

7.2.2   Constructors

The map and multimap constructors have the same form as those for sets and multisets and have the same distinction in their meanings, that constructing a map from a range eliminates copies with duplicate keys, but a multimap retains them. Time bounds are the same as for sets and multisets.

7.2.3   Insertion

Insertion into maps and multimaps can be accomplished with insert member functions, which have the same interfaces as for sets and multisets. Note, however, that here value_type is not just Key but pair<const Key, T>; that is, the single value_type argument passed to insert contains both a Key and a T value. We are allowed to change already-inserted pairs (by assignment; see below), but only in their T members; the const in front of Key prevents changing a key. This restriction is crucial to the integrity of the internal map representation (a binary search tree with ordering based on key_compare).

Another way to insert into a map (but not a multimap) is with operator[]:

```
map1[k] = t;
```

If there is no pair already in map1 with key k, then the pair (k, t) is inserted. If there is already a pair (k, t0) for some t0, then t0 is replaced by t. One other way to accomplish this replacement (departing for the moment from the subject of insertion) is

```
(*i).second = t;
```

where i is a map<Key, T>::iterator such that (*i).first == k. (But we could not write (*i).first = k1, since (*i).first is a constant member of value_type.)

Returning to operator[], there is one perhaps surprising behavior of this operator: it can cause an insertion into a map even when it just appears in an expression, and not only when it appears on the left-hand side of an assignment. That is, an occurrence of

```
map1[k]
```

in any expression returns the T value associated with key k if there is one—but if there isn't, *it inserts a pair* (k, T()) *and returns* T(). See also the footnote on page 120 regarding the meaning of T() when T is a built-in type like int.

Let's look at some examples of insertion using operator[]. In the process we will note similarities and differences between the map container and the array, vector, and deque containers. Consider the problem of computing the *inner product* of two vectors of real numbers. Here we are using the word "vector" in one of its traditional senses, meaning tuples of real numbers, not STL vectors. In the following we use the word "tuple" for this meaning to avoid confusion. If $x = (x_0, x_1, ..., x_{n-1})$ and $y = (y_0, y_1, ..., y_{n-1})$, then the inner product of x and y is defined as

$$x \bullet y = \sum_{i=0}^{n-1} x_i \cdot y_i$$

If x and y are stored in arrays, vectors, or deques, this is of course easily computed with

```
for (sum = 0, int i = 0; i < n; ++i)
    sum += x[i] * y[i];
```

There's also an STL generic inner_product algorithm that could be used (see Section 5.5.4 on page 115). But suppose we want to deal with sparse tuples, that is, those in which most elements are 0. For example, suppose n is 1 million but there are only a few thousand nonzero elements in either x or y. Neither the above for loop nor the STL generic inner_product algorithm takes advantage of sparseness; both would blindly compute each of the million products and sum them.

By storing x and y in maps rather than vectors, and storing only the nonzero elements, first we can cut the storage requirements dramatically. Second, we can make the same kind of reduction in the time for computing the inner product, by traversing the nonzero elements in one of the tuples.

Before looking at the version with maps, let's do it with vectors:

Example 7-5 Computing an inner product of tuples represented as vectors.

```
#include <vector.h>
#include <iostream.h>

int main()
{
  cout << "Computing an inner product of tuples "
       << "represented as vectors." << endl;

  const long N = 600000; // Length of tuples x and y
  const long S = 10; // Sparseness factor

  cout << "\nInitializing..." << flush;
  vector<double> x(N, 0.0), y(N, 0.0);

  for (long k = 0; 3 * k * S < N; ++k)
    x[3 * k * S] = 1.0;
  for (k = 0; 5 * k * S < N; ++k)
    y[5 * k * S] = 1.0;

  cout << "\n\nComputing inner product by brute force: "
       << flush;
  double sum;
  for (sum = 0.0, k = 0; k < N; ++k)
    sum += x[k] * y[k];

  cout << sum << endl;
}
```

Output from Example 7-5:
```
Computing an inner product of tuples represented as vectors.
Initializing...
Computing inner product by brute force: 4000
```

In this program we use the vector constructor that takes two arguments to initialize x and y to have N elements, all equal to 0.0. This is essential since the vector operator[] does not grow the vector if the index is larger than the current size.

Maps do not require this initialization since there is no bound on the size of indices (keys) other than that imposed by the key type itself. We can simply start off with x and y as empty maps:

```
map<long, double, less<long> > x, y;
```

The inner-product calculation can now be written as

```
map<long, double, less<long> >::iterator ix, iy;

for (sum = 0.0, ix = x.begin(); ix != x.end(); ++ix) {
   long k = (*ix).first;
   if (y.find(k) != y.end())
      sum += x[k] * y[k];
}
```

where we use the map find member function, which has the same meaning as with sets and multisets: it searches for a given key and returns an iterator referring to the entry with that key if it finds one or to the end position if it doesn't find the given key.

The computation of y[k] involves essentially the same search, but we can avoid repeating it by saving the iterator returned by y.find(k) and dereferencing it to help get the value of y[k]. We can likewise avoid the search implicit in x[k] by dereferencing ix.

Example 7-6   Computing an inner product of tuples represented as maps.

```
#include <map.h>
#include <iostream.h>

int main()
{
   cout << "Computing an inner product of tuples "
        << "represented as maps." << endl;

   const long N = 600000; // Length of tuples x and y
   const long S = 10; // Sparseness factor

   cout << "\nInitializing..." << flush;
   map<long, double, less<long> > x, y;
   for (long k = 0; 3 * k * S < N; ++k)
      x[3 * k * S] = 1.0;
   for (k = 0; 5 * k * S < N; ++k)
      y[5 * k * S] = 1.0;
```

```
cout << "\n\nComputing inner product taking advantage "
     << "of sparseness: " << flush;

double sum;
map<long, double, less<long> >::iterator ix, iy;
for (sum = 0.0, ix = x.begin(); ix != x.end(); ++ix) {
  long i = (*ix).first;
  iy = y.find(i);
  if (iy != y.end())
    sum += (*ix).second * (*iy).second;
}
cout << sum << endl;
}
```

Output from Example 7-6:
Computing an inner product of tuples represented as maps.
Initializing...
Computing inner product taking advantage of sparseness: 4000

7.2.4 Erasure (Deletion)

As with sets/multisets, elements can be erased from a map or multimap either by key or by position. The type T data plays no role in erasure operations, and they behave exactly as they do for sets and multisets and have the same computing time bound ($O(\log N + E)$ time, where N is the size of the map or multimap and E is the number of elements erased).

7.2.5 Accessors

Again, the story here is very similar to sets/multisets. Maps/multimaps have the same accessors as sets/multisets for accessing information about the elements as a linear, sorted sequence: begin, end, rbegin, rend, empty, size, and max_size. They also have the same member functions for accessing information by key: find, lower_bound, upper_bound, and equal_range, and count. Maps have the new accessor operator[]. This accessor does not apply to multimaps since there may be more than one element associated with a particular key value. The time bounds for all search operations, including operator[], are all $O(\log N)$, where N is the size of the map or multimap. The single exception is count, which takes $O(\log N + E)$ time, where E is the number of elements with the given key.

7.2.6   Equality and Less-Than Relations

Basically, equality and less-than relations on maps/multimaps have all the same properties as sets/multisets do. The only distinction is that the presence of the extra type `T` information means that the key equivalence will agree less often with the meaning of `value_type::operator==`, since the latter will (usually) take the `T` member into account, while `key_compare` cannot. A similar remark applies to the distinction between `key_compare` and `value_type::operator<`.

7.2.7   Assignment

Again, `operator=` and `swap` are defined as they are for all other STL containers; see Section 6.1.7 on page 136.

CHAPTER 8

Function Objects

We now come to the fourth major kind of components STL provides, function objects. A *function object* encapsulates a function in an object for use by other components. In C++ programming, we define a function object to be an object of any class (or struct) that *overloads the function call operator*, `operator()`.

Most STL generic algorithms (and some container classes) accept a function object as a parameter, in order to make it possible to vary their computations in other ways besides those controlled by iterators.

8.1 *Example: Function Objects That Do Comparisons*

For example, the `sort` algorithm can be called with a third parameter, `comp`, a function object that tells `sort` how to compare two objects.

```
// Sort based on < as the comparison operation:
sort(first, last);

// Sort based on comp as the comparison operation:
sort(first, last, comp);
```

When given `comp`, `sort` uses it whenever it compares two values of the type `T` of the data being sorted. Without the `comp` argument, `sort` uses whatever function is associated with the operator < for type `T`.

Since < is already defined for built-in numeric types and it's possible to define the < operator for user-defined types, the two-argument version of `sort` is adequate in many cases. However, there are situations in which

- we want to sort based on some other kind of comparison besides what < provides on built-in types, or

- we have a type `T` for which `operator<` is not defined or is defined in a different way from how we want to order `T` values for present purposes.

In such cases, we can use the three-argument version of `sort` and pass it a function object. Here's a simple case of defining a function object type and using an object of the type:

```
class IntGreater {
 public:
    bool operator()(int x, int y) const {return x > y;}
};

int x[10000];
... code to insert values in x[0], ..., x[9999]

// Sort x into ascending order:
sort(&x[0], &x[10000]);
...
// Sort x into descending order:
sort(&x[0], &x[10000], IntGreater());
```

Here class `IntGreater` defines a function object type, because it overloads the function call operator, `operator()`; and `IntGreater()` is an object of this type, constructed using the implicitly defined default constructor for the class. In the second call of `sort`, we pass `IntGreater()` to be used for comparisons. Since `sort` is coded to produce the elements in ascending order when using a < comparison operator, it instead produces descending order when using the > comparison operator supplied by `IntGreater()`.

8.2 *How Function Objects Differ from Function Pointers*

Passing a function object to an algorithm is similar to passing a pointer to a function, but there are some important differences. Since the function object has `operator()` overloaded, it is possible to

- pass function objects to algorithms at compile time, and

- increase efficiency, by inlining the corresponding call.

Although such costs may seem trivial, they do make a difference when the functions involved are very simple ones, such as integer additions or comparisons. STL's use of function objects rather than function pointers helps assure that we can program using generic algorithms in *all* situations, without worrying about losing efficiency.

8.3 *STL-Provided Function Objects*

STL provides a dozen or so function object types for the most common cases. In fact, we didn't need to define the `IntGreater` type; there's already a function object type (called `greater<T>`) for this purpose in the library, so we could have just used `greater<int>` instead of defining `IntGreater`. However, there are likely to be many cases that come up in programming with STL in which we need to define new function object types. The programs in Part II contain some specific examples. In the reference guide in Part III, Chapter 21 details the function objects STL provides.

CHAPTER 9   *Container Adaptors*

Adaptors are STL components that can be used to change the interface of another component. They are defined as template classes that take a component type as a parameter. STL provides *container adaptors, iterator adaptors,* and *function adaptors.* We'll look at these in turn in this and the next two chapters.

To see the advantages of a mechanism for adapting interfaces, let's first look at the problem of providing basic data structures like stacks and queues.

A *stack* is a simpler kind of container than vector, list, or deque; any one of these containers could be used as a stack, in the sense that each supports the operations one does on a stack:

- insertion at one end (push, with push_back);

- deletion from the same end (pop, with pop_back);

- retrieving the value at that end (top, with back); and

- testing for the stack being empty (with empty or size).

Besides these points, another important property of the stack type is the fact that it presents *only a very limited interface.* No other operations besides the basic stack operators are provided.

This is an important point to note because although we might choose to use a list, say, as the current implementation of a stack, we may want the ability to switch, at some later time, to a different implementation of stack operations. So unless we restrict the interface, it is difficult to ensure that we don't inadvertently start using the current implementation in nonstack-like ways.

The usual solution adopted in C++ container class libraries is to define a stack type as a class, StackAsList, with a private member holding a list object, and to define public functions push, pop, top, and empty in terms of list operations. Then none of the other list operations is available on stack objects, which is just what we want.

However, since in some situations it's better to use a vector instead of a list to represent a stack, such libraries may also provide a StackAsVector class. The same approach is used with other containers, resulting in a proliferation of classes such as QueueAsVector, QueueAsList, QueueAsDoubleList, PriorityQueueAsVector, PriorityQueueAsList, and so on.

In STL this kind of proliferation is completely avoided by the use of *container adaptors*. STL provides container adaptors to produce `stack`, `queue`, and `priority_queue` containers out of its other sequence containers.

9.1 *Stack Container Adaptor*

The `stack` container adaptor can be applied to a `vector`, `list`, or `deque`:

- `stack< vector<T> >` is a stack of `T` with a vector implementation;

- `stack< list<T> >` is a stack of `T` with a list implementation;

- `stack< deque<T> >` is a stack of `T` with a deque implementation.

The stack adaptor can be applied to any container that supports the `empty`, `size`, `push_back`, `pop_back`, and `back` operations. Each of `vector<T>`, `list<T>`, and `deque<T>` does provide these operations, so each can be made into a stack. In fact, if we define some *new* container class `C<T>` that supports these operations, we can also adapt it to serve as a stack, with `stack< C<T> >`.

9.2 *Queue Container Adaptor*

A *queue* differs from a stack in that elements are inserted on one end but removed from the *opposite* end. This is often called first-in, first-out (FIFO) service, in contrast to the last-in, first-out (LIFO) service a stack provides.

STL provides a `queue` container adaptor that can be applied to any container that supports the `empty`, `size`, `front`, `back`, `push_back`, and `pop_front` operations. These operations are supported by `list` and `deque`, implying that we can construct queues out of these containers:

- `queue< list<T> >` is a queue of `T` with a `list` implementation;

- `queue< deque<T> >` is a queue of `T` with a `deque` implementation.

The operations `queue` provides are called `empty`, `size`, `front`, `back`, `push`, and `pop`.

Note that the `queue` adapter cannot be applied to `vector`, because `vector` does not support `pop_front`. Why was `pop_front` omitted from the interface of `vector`? `Pop_front` could easily be programmed on vectors as `v.erase(v.begin())`, but that kind of operation on vectors should be avoided because it's very inefficient for long vectors—since all of the elements after the first position must be shifted over to fill the hole, it is a linear time operation.

By providing `pop_front` in `list` and `deque`, where it can be done in constant time, and omitting it from `vector`, where it would require linear time, STL makes it easy to get efficient implementations of queues and difficult to get an inefficient one.

9.3 *Priority Queue Container Adaptor*

A *priority queue* is a type of sequence in which the element immediately available for retrieval is the largest of those in the sequence, for some particular way of ordering the elements. The STL `priority_queue` adaptor converts

- any container `C<T>` that provides a random access iterator type and the `empty`, `size`, `push_back`, `pop_back`, and `front` operations, and .

- a comparison function object, `comp`,

into a priority queue that uses `comp` for comparisons when making the largest element available for retrieval.

Both `vector<T>` and `deque<T>` provide random access iterators and the necessary operations, so we could have, for example,

- `priority_queue< vector<int>, less<int> >`, a type of priority queues of `int`s with a `vector` implementation and using the built-in `<` operation defined for `int`s, and

- `priority_queue< deque<float>, greater<float> >`, a type of priority queues of `float`s with a `deque` implementation and using the `>` operation on `float`s for comparisons.

Since `>` is used instead of `<` in the second example, the element available for retrieval is actually the *smallest* element rather than the largest.

CHAPTER 10   *Iterator Adaptors*

Iterator adaptors are STL components that can be used to change the interface of an iterator component. Two kinds of iterator adaptors are defined in STL: *reverse iterators* and *insert iterators*.

10.1 *Reverse Iterators*

STL's `reverse_bidirectional_iterator` adaptor transforms a given bidirectional iterator into one in which the traversal direction is reversed. The transformed iterator has the same interface as the original. Correspondingly, there is also a `reverse_iterator` adaptor that can be applied to any random access iterator. These adaptors are defined by template classes that take an iterator type as a parameter. In most cases, though, it is not necessary to use these adaptors directly, since each of the STL container types provides two reverse iterator types (which are predefined with the aid of one of the adaptors):

- `reverse_iterator`, a mutable iterator type; and

- `const_reverse_iterator`, a constant iterator type.

Each container type `C<T>` also provides member functions called `rbegin` and `rend` such that if, for example, `C1` is an object of type `C<T>`, the loop

```
C<T>::reverse_iterator r;
for (r = C1.rbegin(); r != C1.rend(); ++r) {
   ... perform some computation with *r
}
```

iterates through the contents of `C<T>` in the reverse of the order given by the usual loop:

```
C<T>::iterator i;
for (i = C1.begin(); i != C1.end(); ++i) {
   ... perform some computation with *i
}
```

When reverse iterators are passed to a generic algorithm, they make the algorithm "see in reverse" the container's sequence of elements. Otherwise, all computations proceed as with normal iterators. For example, if

```
sort(vector1.begin(), vector1.end())
```

sorts a vector `vector1` into ascending order, then

```
sort(vector1.rbegin(), vector1.rend())
```

sorts it into ascending order as seen by looking at the elements in reverse order. The result is therefore in descending order when observed in the usual order.

10.2 Insert Iterators

An *insert iterator* puts an algorithm into "insert mode" rather than its usual "overwrite mode." This means that instead of `*i = ...` causing the object at position `i` to be *overwritten*, `*i = ...` causes an *insertion* into that position (using one of the container's insertion member functions). STL provides three iterator adaptors, which are defined as template functions that take a container as a parameter. The `back_inserter` adaptor causes the container's `push_back` member function to be used; `front_inserter` causes the container's `push_front` member function to be used; and `inserter` causes the container's `insert` member function to be used.

Such insertions force the container to expand the space currently allocated for it, unlike assignments, which must have space for their results already available. For example, the following code will fail because there is no space in `vector1` into which `copy`'s assignments can store their results:

```
vector<int> vector1; // vector1 is empty.
deque<int> deque1(200, 1);   // deque1 holds 200 1's.
...
copy(deque1.begin(), deque1.end(), vector1.begin());// ERROR
```

During the copying, a run-time error will occur when doing

```
*(vector1.begin()) = *(deque1.begin())
```

But with `back_inserter`, `copy` will work because `vector1`'s `push_back` function is used, causing storage for `vector1` to be expanded as necessary:

```
copy(deque1.begin(), deque1.end(), back_inserter(vector1));
```

Back_inserter can be used with vector, list, and deque container types, since they all provide a push_back member function. This adaptor takes any container C1 that has a push_back function and produces an iterator type whose * and = operators are defined so that the code

```
*i = x
```

executes as though

```
C1.push_back(x)
```

were performed instead.

Similarly, front_inserter causes insertions at the front of a container. It can be used with list and deque containers, since they provide a push_front function:

```
int array1[100];
list<int> list1;
... code to assign values to array1[0], ..., array1[99]

copy(&array1[0], &array1[100], front_inserter(list1));
```

The elements of array1 will appear at the front of list1 (in the reverse of their order in array1).

No push_front member function is provided by vector since it would have to be a linear time operation (just as we saw with pop_front in the discussion of container adaptors in Chapter 9).

The most general insert iterator adaptor is inserter, which allows insertions at any point in a container's current sequence of elements, as indicated by an iterator argument:

```
copy(&array1[0], &array1[100],
     inserter(list1, list1.begin()+1));
```

In this case, the elements of array1 would be inserted after the first element of list1 and would be in the same order as in array1 (that is, the iterator is incremented with ++ after each insertion so that it moves over the element just inserted).

The inserter adaptor uses a container's insert member function, insert(iterator, value); since all of STL's container types provide such a function, `inserter` can be applied to any type of container (including sorted associative containers).

You'll see several more examples of the use of insert iterators in the example programs in Part II.

CHAPTER 11

Function Adaptors

We've seen how many generic STL algorithms can take a function object as an argument and perform differently depending on the argument. Both function objects and iterators can be viewed as "algorithm adaptors."

Just as iterator adaptors help us construct a wider variety of iterators to use with generic algorithms, *function adaptors* help us construct a wider variety of function objects. Using function adaptors is often easier than directly constructing a new function object type with a struct or class definition. STL provides three categories of function adaptors: *negators*, *binders*, and *adaptors for pointers to functions*. These adaptors are defined by template functions that take a function object or a function as a parameter.

11.1 Negators

A *negator* is a kind of function adaptor used to reverse the sense of predicate function objects. There are two negator adaptors, `not1` and `not2`. For example,

```
where = find_if(&array1[0], &array1[1000],
                not1(bind2nd(greater<int>(), 200)));
```

searches for the first integer in `array1` that is *not* greater than 200 (i.e., $<= 200$). In general, `not1` takes a unary predicate object p and returns a unary predicate object defining the function

```
bool operator()(const T& x) { return !(p(x)); }
```

where T is the type of p's argument.[1]

The `not2` function adaptor takes a binary predicate object p and returns a binary predicate defining the function

---

1. In this case we could also have obtained the same function object using another STL-provided function object, `less_equal<T>`:
   ```
   where = find_if(x,x+1000,bind2nd(less_equal<int>,200));
   ```

```
bool operator()(const T& x, const U& y)
    { return !(p(x, y)); }
```

where `T` and `U` are the first and second argument types of `p`, respectively.

11.2 *Binders*

A *binder* is a kind of function adaptor used to convert binary function objects into unary function objects by binding an argument to some particular value. For example,

```
int array1[1000];
... code to initialize array1[0], ..., array1[999]
int* where = find_if(&array1[0], &array1[1000],
                bind2nd(greater<int>(), 200));
```

finds the first integer in `array1` that is greater than `200`. The `find_if` algorithm is similar to `find`, but instead of a value to search for it takes a unary predicate function object `p` (that is, a function object that encapsulates a one-argument function that returns a `bool` value):

```
find_if(first, last, p)
```

returns an iterator pointing to the first position in the range from `first` to `last` for which `p` returns true, or `last` if no such position exists. In the above example, we construct the predicate for our search by starting with `greater<int>()`, a function object that defines a binary function

```
bool operator()(int x, int y) { return x > y; }
```

By applying `bind2nd` to this function object and `200`, we produce a function object that defines a unary function

```
bool operator()(int x) { return x > 200; }
```

just as if we had programmed another function object type

```
struct Greater200 : unary_function<int, bool> {
    bool operator()(int x) {return x > 200; }
};
```

directly. Function adaptor `bind1st` can be used in a similar way to bind the first argument of a binary function object. More examples of the use of both binders and negators appear in Part II of this book.

11.3 *Adaptors for Pointers to Functions*

Adaptors for pointers to functions are provided to allow pointers to unary and binary functions to work with the other function adaptors provided in the library. These adaptors may also be useful by themselves in avoiding one form of "code bloat" (see Section 1.3.5 on page 12) as we show by example in this section.

Although function objects can always be used in place of the older, less efficient technique of passing a pointer to a function, there are times when pointers to functions should still be used. Suppose, for example, that within the same program we need to use two different sets that differ only in the comparison functions passed to them:

```
set<string, less<string> > set1;
set<string, greater<string> > set2;
```

The problem with this is that the compiler is likely to duplicate most or all of the code that implements sets, even though most of it is identical in the two instances.[2]

To avoid such duplication, we can instead work with a *single* instance of `set` by using an adaptor for pointers to functions:

```
set<string,
    pointer_to_binary_function<const string&,
                               const string&,
                               bool> >
```

Here, for the type of comparison function to be used in maintaining sorted order in the set, we use an adaptor for pointers to binary functions. When constructing sets of this type, we supply an instance of this adaptor type created from a particular pointer to a binary function using `ptr_fun`, as in the following program.

---

2. Some STL providers have alleviated much of the problem with `set` and the other sorted associative containers (which have larger implementations than the sequence containers) by restructuring their defining classes so that only the code that interacts with the comparison function is duplicated in different instances. To date, however, this has not been done with the HP reference implementation.

Example 11-1 Illustrating the use of an adaptor for pointers to functions.

```cpp
#include <set.h>
#include <bstring.h>

bool less1(const string& x, const string& y)
{
  return x < y;
}

bool greater1(const string& x, const string& y)
{
  return x > y;
}

int main()
{
  typedef
    set<string,
        pointer_to_binary_function<const string&,
                                    const string&, bool> >
    set_type1;

  set_type1 set1(ptr_fun(less1));

  set1.insert("the");
  set1.insert("quick");
  set1.insert("brown");
  set1.insert("fox");

  set_type1::iterator i;
  for (i = set1.begin(); i != set1.end(); ++i)
    cout << *i << " ";
  cout << endl;

  set_type1 set2(ptr_fun(greater1));

  set2.insert("the");
  set2.insert("quick");
  set2.insert("brown");
  set2.insert("fox");

  for (i = set2.begin(); i != set2.end(); ++i)
    cout << *i << " ";
```

```
   cout << endl;
}
```

Output from Example 11-1:
```
brown fox quick the

the quick fox brown
```

In this example there is only one instance of the `set` type, `set_type1`. The program constructs two `set_type1` objects: `set1`, which uses `ptr_fun(less1)` for its comparison object; and `set2`, which uses `ptr_fun(greater1)`. Because of the extra level of indirection involved with pointers to functions, programs such as this will run slightly slower than the corresponding programs with separate instances of `set`, but with a considerable savings in executable file size.

PART II
Putting It Together: Example Programs

In this part, we solve some simple but nontrivial programming problems using STL components.

CHAPTER 12 *A Program for Searching a Dictionary*

In Part I all of our examples were small ones designed just to illustrate individual STL components. Now, in Part II, we'll look at some slightly larger examples, ones that simultaneously demonstrate several STL components. In Chapters 12 to 15 we explore variations on the theme of searching a dictionary for anagrams (words that can be formed by transposing the letters of a given word). In these chapters we repeatedly tackle the same or similar problems using different approaches, including (in Chapter 13) combining STL components with user-defined types. Chapter 16 gives a small example of defining a new iterator type and using it with existing STL components. The example program in Chapter 17 illustrates issues of combining STL with object-oriented programming.

12.1 *Finding Anagrams of a Given Word*

Let's start with the problem of finding, in a given dictionary, all the anagrams of a given word. We'll develop a program that reads a dictionary from a file, then repeatedly accepts a word (or arbitrary string of letters) from the standard input stream, looks up all permutations of its letters in the dictionary, and outputs those words it finds. Here's an example of how we might interact with the program (all user input is underlined):

```
Anagram finding program:
finds all words in a dictionary that can
be formed with the letters of a given word.

First, enter the name of the file containing
the dictionary: diction

Reading the dictionary ...
The dictionary contains 20159 words.

Now type a word (or any string of letters),
and I'll see if it has any anagrams: rseuce
```

```
      cereus
      recuse
      rescue
      secure

Ready for another word: crtae

      caret
      carte
      cater
      crate
      trace

Ready for another word: nbgie

      begin
      being
      binge

Ready for another word: nadeirga

      drainage
      gardenia

Ready for another word: grinch

   Sorry, none found.

Ready for another word: gonar

      argon
      groan
      organ

Ready for another word:
```

The exact results will, of course, depend on the dictionary. The 20,159-word dictionary used in this example is available with the source code for all examples in this book, as described in Appendix B.

Here is the complete program, which we'll explain in detail in the rest of the chapter.

Example 12-1 Program to find all anagrams of a given word, using a dictionary read from a file.

```
#include <iterator.h>
#include <algo.h>
#include <vector.h>
#include <fstream.h>
#include <bstring.h>

int main()
{
  cout << "Anagram finding program:\n"
    << "finds all words in a dictionary that can\n"
    << "be formed with the letters of a given word.\n\n"
    << "First, enter the name of the file containing\n"
    << "the dictionary: " << flush;

  string dictionary_name;
  cin >> dictionary_name;

  ifstream ifs(dictionary_name.c_str());
  cout << "\nReading the dictionary ..." << flush;

  // Copy words from dictionary file to a vector:
  typedef istream_iterator<string, ptrdiff_t>
          string_input;
  vector<string> dictionary;
  copy(string_input(ifs), string_input(),
      back_inserter(dictionary));

  cout << "\nThe dictionary contains "
    << dictionary.size() << " words.\n\n";

  cout << "Now type a word (or any string of letters),\n"
    << "and I'll see if it has any anagrams: " << flush;

  // For each input word, check if it has any
  // anagrams in the dictionary:
  for (string_input j(cin); j != string_input(); ++j) {

    // Put the input string into a vector so it
    // can be sorted.
    vector<char> word = *j;
```

```
   // Start with letters of word in alphabetical order:
   sort(word.begin(), word.end());

   // Search dictionary for all permutations of word:
   bool found_one = false;
   do {
     if (binary_search(dictionary.begin(),
                       dictionary.end(),
                       string(word))) {
       cout << "\n  " << string(word) << flush;
       found_one = true;
     }
   } while (next_permutation(word.begin(), word.end()));

   if (!found_one)
     cout << "\n  Sorry, none found.";
   cout << "\n\nReady for another word: " << flush;
  }
}
```

12.2 *Interacting with the Standard I/O Streams*

In this program we read the name of the file as a string, using the ANSI/ISO (Draft) Standard `string` class:

```
   string dictionary_name;
   cin >> dictionary_name;
```

We then prepare to read the dictionary from a file using an `ifstream`. We use the `string` class member function `c_str` to get the C-style `const char*` character string the `ifstream` constructor expects:

```
   ifstream ifs(dictionary_name.c_str());
```

Then we copy the dictionary file into a `vector` container using the generic `copy` algorithm and the `back_inserter` iterator adaptor to insert the words of the dictionary one by one at the end of the vector. For use here and later in the program, we define the type `string_input` as an istream iterator type:

```
   typedef istream_iterator<string, ptrdiff_t>
          string_input;
```

When the dictionary has been read in, we report its size. The program is now ready to accept letter strings from the user and look them up. The look-ups are conducted using the generic `binary_search` algorithm, which requires the dictionary to be in alphabetical order. It's assumed here that the dictionary file was already in alphabetical order.[1]

Input of the candidate words (or arbitrary letter-strings) is controlled by an istream iterator `j`, set up for traversing the standard `cin` input stream until an end-of-stream indicator is hit:

```
for (string_input j(cin); j != string_input(); ++j) {
    . . .
}
```

In the body of this loop, we generate all permutations of the letters of the given word and search the dictionary for each one. We use repeated calls of the generic `next_permutation` algorithm to generate the permutations. The initial letter string given to `next_permutation` should be the one in which the letters appear in alphabetical order. The candidate word is in `*j`. Although we would like to sort its characters as they appear in `(*j).c_str()`, that is disallowed because `c_str` returns `const char*`, and the `const` qualifier prevents any modifications. So instead, we put the characters into a vector, using a `string`-to-`vector<char>` conversion provided by the `string` class,

```
vector<char> word = *j;
```

and then use the generic `sort` algorithm to sort this vector:

```
// Start with letters of word in alphabetical order:
sort(word.begin(), word.end());
```

The sorted `word` is the first permutation of the letters that the program will look for in the dictionary. So, for example, if the letters in `word` are `gonar`, after sorting `word` will contain `agnor`.

12.3 *Searching the Dictionary*

The inner loop tests each permutation for membership in the dictionary:

---

1. If not, the `sort` algorithm could be used to sort it by inserting the line
   `sort(dictionary.begin(), dictionary.end());`
   before the message to the user.

```
bool found_one = false;
do {
   if (binary_search(dictionary.begin(),
                     dictionary.end(),
                     string(word))) {
      cout << "\n  " << string(word) << flush;
      found_one = true;
   }
} while (next_permutation(word.begin(), word.end()));
```

The generic `binary_search` algorithm returns `true` if it finds the current candidate word in the dictionary, `false` otherwise.[2] The time for this search is proportional to the logarithm of the size of the dictionary.

If `word` is found in the dictionary, we send this permutation of the original letter sequence to the standard output stream.

12.4 *Generating Permutations*

The generic `next_permutation` algorithm is then used to change `word` into the next permutation of its characters, where "next" means the one that follows in the lexicographical ordering of all permutations. (That's why we sorted `word` initially, so we would start with the first permutation in this ordering.)

For example, with the letters `agnor`, the permutations in lexicographical order are `agnor, agnro, agonr, agorn, angor, angro, . . . , argon, . . . , groan, . . . , organ, . . . , ronga`. (The total number is 5! = 120.)

If the last permutation in lexicographical order hasn't been reached, `next_permutation` puts the next permutation into `word` and returns `true`; otherwise it reverts `word` back to the first permutation in lexicographical order—the sorted one, that is—and returns `false`, terminating the inner loop.[3]

---

2. As noted in Chapter 5, STL provides three other generic algorithms based on binary searching: `lower_bound`, `upper_bound`, and `equal_range`. These algorithms return iterators that pinpoint the position or range of positions that contain values equal to the given value. They all run in logarithmic time.

3. Alex Stepanov points out that, given this behavior of `next_permutation`, we could have a very brief sorting algorithm:
   ```
   template <class BidirectionalIterator>
   void brief_sort(BidirectionalIterator first,
                   BidirectionalIterator last)
   { while (next_permutation(first, last)); }
   ```
   Brief textually, however anything but brief in the time it takes (worse than proportional to *n!*). This algorithm is *not* in the library.

12.5 How Fast Is It?

This program is reasonably fast for short strings, but note that the number of permutations of a string of length n is $n!$, so it takes quite long when n is greater than 8 or so. Although we don't revisit this look-up program per se in the following chapters, it could be reprogrammed for much faster operation using the approach taken in those chapters. (Exercise for the reader!)

CHAPTER 13   *A Program for Finding All Anagram Groups*

The program developed in this chapter, like the program of Chapter 12, uses a dictionary, but the operations on the dictionary are more elaborate. The program searches the dictionary for all "anagram groups," that is, groups of words that are permutations of each other, like `caret`, `carte`, `cater`, `crate`, `trace`.

In most of our previous examples, all of the types were either built-in C++ types or types provided by the STL library. In the present example, we use library components with a type we define.

13.1 *Finding Anagram Groups*

The main idea of the program is to create an internal dictionary vector containing *pairs* of strings. These pairs of strings are set up as follows:

- The second member of a pair holds a word w from the dictionary file.

- The first member holds the string that results from sorting the letters of w into alphabetical order.

When these pairs are sorted using their first members as keys, all of the words that are anagrams come together in consecutive positions of the vector. (Actually, the pairs containing those words come together.) For example, if the dictionary file contains the words

```
argon cater cereus groan maker organ
secure trace
```

then the vector of pairs will initially contain the words shown in the following table:

first	second
agnor	argon
acert	cater
ceersu	cereus
agnor	groan
aekmr	maker
agnor	organ
ceersu	secure
acert	trace

After sorting on the first members of these pairs it will contain these words:

first	second
acert	cater
acert	trace
agnor	argon
agnor	groan
agnor	organ
aekmr	maker
ceersu	cereus
ceersu	secure

Thus, anagram groups like `argon`, `groan`, and `organ` come together. The program can then make a single pass through the dictionary to find groups of pairs that agree in their first member and output the list of their second members as an anagram group. Singletons like

first	second
aekmr	maker

will be ignored.

13.2 *Defining a Data Structure to Work with STL*

To implement this approach, we first define a data structure for holding pairs of strings. We want to be able to sort the characters of the first member of this pair, but as we noted in Chapter 12, this can't be done to the characters stored in a standard `string` object. So instead we store the string in the first member as a vector of characters, to which `sort` can be applied.

```
struct PS : pair<vector<char>, string> {
  PS() : pair<vector<char>,string>(vector<char>(), string())
    { }

  PS(const string& s) : pair<vector<char>, string>(s, s) {
    sort(first.begin(), first.end());
  }

  operator string() const { return second; }
};
```

This defines type `PS` as a struct derived from `pair<vector<char>, string>`, using the STL `pair` template class (described in Section 1.3.1 on page 6). In general, if `p` is a `pair<T1, T2>` object, `p.first` refers to one member of the pair, of type `T1`, and `p.second` refers to the other, of type `T2`. The second constructor takes a string argument and stores the string itself in the `second` member but converts it to a vector to store in the `first` member (using an implicit type conversion defined by the `string` class). This constructor serves as a type conversion from `string` to `PS`, and `operator string()` provides a type conversion from `PS` to `string`. The presence of these type conversions will allow us to use the generic `copy` algorithm to copy strings from an input string into a vector of `PS` objects, and from the vector to an output stream.

We could use type `pair<vector<char>, string>` itself, instead of defining the `PS` structure as above. But then we would not be able to define the type conversions needed in order to use `copy`, and we would have to code the I/O with explicit loops.

13.3 *Creating Function Objects for Comparisons*

In order to use STL components to do operations like sorting and searching `PS` objects, we also need to create two function objects—`firstLess` and `firstEqual`—to communicate to the components how we want to compare two `PS` objects.

```
struct FirstLess : binary_function<PS, PS, bool> {
  bool operator()(const PS& p, const PS& q) const
  {
    return p.first < q.first;
  }
} firstLess;
```

Thus, when `firstLess` is passed to algorithms such as `sort` or `binary_search`, it makes them base comparisons of PS objects on comparisons of their `first` members. Since the type of the `first` members of PS objects is `vector<char>`, the algorithms will use the < operator defined on vector objects. This is lexicographical ordering, which in the case of `vector<char>` is precisely the normal alphabetical ordering we want.

In the same way, we define a function object `firstEqual` to handle equality of PS objects.

```
struct FirstEqual : binary_function<PS, PS, bool> {
  bool operator()(const PS& p, const PS& q) const
  {
    return p.first == q.first;
  }
} firstEqual;
```

13.4 The Complete Anagram Group Finding Program

We present the full program here and then explain the details of its operation in the remainder of this chapter.

Example 13-1 Find all anagram groups in a dictionary, and print them to standard output stream.

```
#include <iterator.h>
#include <algo.h>
#include <vector.h>
#include <fstream.h>
#include <bstring.h>
#include "ps.h" // Definitions of PS, firstLess, firstEqual

int main() {
  cout << "Anagram group finding program:\n"
    << "finds all anagram groups in a dictionary.\n\n"
    << "First, enter the name of the file containing\n"
    << "the dictionary: " << flush;
```

```
string dictionary_name;
cin >> dictionary_name;

ifstream ifs(dictionary_name.c_str());
cout << "\nReading the dictionary ..." << flush;

// Copy words from dictionary file to
// a vector of PS objects:
typedef istream_iterator<string, ptrdiff_t>
        string_input;
vector<PS> word_pairs;
copy(string_input(ifs), string_input(),
     back_inserter(word_pairs));

cout << "\nSearching " << word_pairs.size()
  << " words for anagram groups..." << flush;

// Sort word_pairs, using the first member of
// each pair as a basis for comparison. This
// brings all anagram groups together:
sort(word_pairs.begin(), word_pairs.end(), firstLess);

// Output all of the anagram groups:
cout << "\n\nThe anagram groups are: " << endl;
vector<PS>::const_iterator j = word_pairs.begin(),
                           finis = word_pairs.end();
while (true) {
  // Make j point to the next anagram
  // group, or to the end of the vector:
  j = adjacent_find(j, finis, firstEqual);
  if (j == finis) break;

  // Find the end of the anagram group that begins at j:
  vector<PS>::const_iterator k =
    find_if(j + 1, finis,
      not1(bind1st(firstEqual, *j)));

  // Output the anagram group in positions j to k:
  cout << endl << "   ";
  copy(j, k, ostream_iterator<string>(cout, " "));
  cout << endl;
```

```
            // Prepare to continue search at position k:
            j = k;
        }
    }
}
```

13.5 *Reading the Dictionary into a Vector of PS Objects*

The first part of the program is very similar to that of the program in Chapter 12: we read in the dictionary from a file and store it into a vector. However, instead of just storing each string read in, we store a PS object constructed from the string. The conversion from string to PS happens implicitly during the copy operation:

```
    // Copy words from dictionary file to
    // a vector of PS objects:
    typedef istream_iterator<string, ptrdiff_t>
            string_input;
    vector<PS> word_pairs;
    copy(string_input(ifs), string_input(),
        back_inserter(word_pairs));
```

As part of the definition of the PS(const string&) constructor, the first member of the object is sorted, putting the letters in the vector in alphabetical order. Thus, the word_pairs vector starts out with the structure shown in the first table in Section 13.1.

13.6 *Using a Comparison Object to Sort Word Pairs*

The next step of the algorithm is to use the function object firstLess to tell the generic sort algorithm how to order the PS objects based on the first member of every pair:

```
    sort(word_pairs.begin(), word_pairs.end(), firstLess);
```

This sort operation rearranges the vector element pairs such that all of the pairs containing words that are anagrams come together in consecutive positions of the vector. At this point, the word_pairs vector has the structure shown in the second table in Section 13.1.

13.7 Using an Equality Predicate Object to Search for Adjacent Equal Elements

Finally, we prepare to output the anagram groups by setting up constant iterators pointing to the beginning and end of the vector:

```
vector<PS>::const_iterator j = word_pairs.begin(),
                      finis = word_pairs.end();
```

In the loop that follows, we use iterator `j` to scan the vector, looking for the beginning of an anagram group. We first use `adjacent_find`, a generic search algorithm.

```
j = adjacent_find(j, finis, firstEqual);
```

This advances `j` to the first position in `word_pairs` such that `firstEqual(*j, *(j+1))` is `true`; if no such adjacent values are in the range, then `finis` is returned.

If the end of the dictionary has been reached, the loop and the program both terminate:

```
if (j == finis) break;
```

Otherwise, we need to search from the position `j+1` onward for the pair whose first element is not equal to the first element of the pair pointed to by `j`. The details of how this is done are presented in the next section.

13.8 Using a Function Adaptor to Obtain a Predicate Object

We could conduct the necessary search with the generic `find` algorithm, except that we want to consider the search successful when we find a value *not equal* to a given value, rather than equal to it. So we use `find_if`, the version of `find` that takes a predicate object. Since we don't already have a suitable predicate object available to pass to `find_if`, we use a couple of function adaptors to manufacture one out of `firstEqual`.

We first apply `bind1st` to `firstEqual` and the value `*j` to produce a function object that takes a single argument `x` and returns true if `*j == x`, false otherwise.

The resulting predicate function object is the opposite of the sense needed, so we apply to it another function adaptor, `not1`. The result is a predicate function object that returns `true` if `*j != x`, and `false` otherwise, which is precisely what we need:

```
vector<PS>::const_iterator k =
    find_if(j + 1, finis,
             not1(bind1st(firstEqual, *j)));
```

13.9 *Copying the Anagram Group to the Output Stream*

Thus the iterator j returned by `adjacent_find` and the iterator k returned by `find_if` delimit the range of word pairs containing words that are anagrams in their second components, and we use

```
copy(j, k, ostream_iterator<string>(cout, " "));
```

to put them on the standard output stream. Note that during the `copy` operation there is an *implicit conversion* of a PS word pair to a `string`: when a PS object is converted to a `string`, its second element is returned.

Finally, we advance j to k to continue looking for the next anagram group.

13.10 *Output of the Anagram Program*

Here is the output of this program when given the dictionary in the `diction` file available with the source code (see Appendix B).

Output from Example 13-1:
```
Anagram group finding program:
finds all anagram groups in a dictionary.

First, enter the name of the file containing
the dictionary: diction

Reading the dictionary ...

Searching 20159 words for anagram groups...

The anagram groups are:

  hasn't shan't

  drawback backward
```

bacterial calibrate

cabaret abreact

bandpass passband

abroad aboard

banal nabla

balsa basal

saccade cascade

coagulate catalogue

ascertain sectarian

activate cavitate

vacuolate autoclave

caveat vacate

charisma archaism

maniac caiman

caviar variac

scalar lascar rascal sacral

causal casual

drainage gardenia

emanate manatee

and so on. The program finds a total of 865 anagram groups in this 20,159-word dictionary.

CHAPTER 14

A Better Anagram Program: Using the List and Map Containers

One problem we might have with the anagram finder we developed in Chapter 13 is that the output is a bit unorganized; we might like to see the anagram groups in order of maximum size first. In this chapter we extend the program so that it does organize its output in this way, and in the process we'll illustrate the use of both another of the sequence containers, list, and one of the sorted associative containers, map.

14.1 A Data Structure Holding Pairs of Iterators

In this program we create another data structure using the template class pair. This data structure is called PPS, and its objects hold pairs of iterators that refer to PS structures (which we developed in the last chapter).

```
typedef vector<PS>::const_iterator PSi;

struct PPS : pair<PSi, PSi> {
  PPS() : pair<PSi, PSi>(PSi(), PSi()) { }
  PPS(PSi p, PSi q) : pair<PSi, PSi>(p, q) { }
};
```

A PPS iterator pair will be used to delimit a range of dictionary entries whose second members are the words of an anagram group; for example:

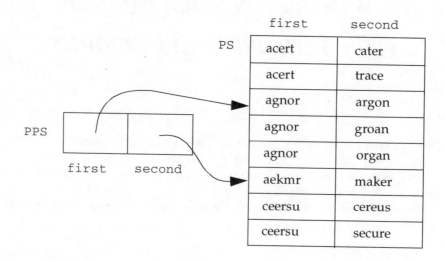

Note that this diagram shows the second iterator in a PPS structure pointing to the position *past the end* of the positions with equal words, in keeping with the standard convention for STL iterator ranges.

14.2 *Storing Information in a Map of Lists*

Now, after sorting the dictionary vector to get the anagram groups together, we scan it as before, but instead of outputting each anagram group as we find it, we save its range in a PPS structure. To make it easy to output the groups according to their size, we save all of the ranges of a given size s in a list of PPS structures, and we store that list as the value associated with s in a map,

```
typedef map<int, list<PPS>, greater<int> > map_1;
map_1 groups;
```

That is, for a given integer group size s, groups[s] will hold a list of PPS objects, and the map is organized so that iterating through it from groups.begin() to groups.end() produces the entries in order from largest to smallest (to get smallest-to-largest order we would have used less<int> as the function type passed to map).

So, when we generate a PPS(j, k) object, we just have to insert it into the list groups[k-j], since k-j is the size of the range (and therefore of the anagram group):

```
if (k-j > 1)
  groups[k-j].push_back(PPS(j,k));
```

14.3 *Outputting the Anagram Groups in Order of Size*

Once the whole vector of pairs has been scanned, we iterate through the groups map as follows:

```
map_1::const_iterator m;
for (m = groups.begin(); m != groups.end(); ++m) {

  cout << "\n\nAnagram groups of size "
    << (*m).first << ":\n";

  list<PPS>::const_iterator l;
  for (l = (*m).second.begin();
      l != (*m).second.end(); ++l) {
    cout << "\n   ";
    j = (*l).first;  // beginning of the anagram group
    k = (*l).second; // end of the anagram group
    copy(j, k, ostream_iterator<string>(cout, " "));
    cout << endl;
  }
  cout << endl;
}
```

The size of group `m` is given by `(*m).first`, and `(*m).second` is the corresponding entry, a `list<PPS>` object. With the inner for loop, we iterate over the elements of the list. Each list entry `*l` is a pair whose first and second members are `vector<PS>` iterators giving a range in the `pairs` vector of entries that represents an anagram group, so we just have to copy those entries to the output stream. Again, during the copy there is an implicit conversion of pairs to strings.

14.4 *A Better Anagram Program*

Putting all this together, we have the following example program.

Example 14-1 Finding all anagram groups in order of decreasing size.
```
#include <iterator.h>
#include <algo.h>
#include <vector.h>
#include <map.h>
```

```cpp
#include <list.h>
#include <fstream.h>
#include <bstring.h>
#include "ps.h" // Definitions of PS, firstLess, firstEqual

typedef vector<PS>::const_iterator PSi;

struct PPS : pair<PSi, PSi> {
  PPS() : pair<PSi, PSi>(PSi(), PSi()) { }
  PPS(PSi p, PSi q) : pair<PSi, PSi>(p, q) { }
};

int main() {
  cout << "Anagram group finding program:\n"
    << "finds all anagram groups in a dictionary.\n\n"
    << "First, enter the name of the file containing\n"
    << "the dictionary: " << flush;

  string dictionary_name;
  cin >> dictionary_name;

  ifstream ifs(dictionary_name.c_str());
  cout << "\nReading the dictionary ..." << flush;

  // Copy words from dictionary file to
  // a vector of PS objects:
  typedef istream_iterator<string, ptrdiff_t>
          string_input;
  vector<PS> word_pairs;
  copy(string_input(ifs), string_input(),
      back_inserter(word_pairs));

  cout << "\nSearching " << word_pairs.size()
    << " words for anagram groups..." << flush;

  // Sort word_pairs, using the first member of
  // each pair as a basis for comparison. This
  // brings all anagram groups together:
  sort(word_pairs.begin(), word_pairs.end(), firstLess);

  // Set up the map from anagram group sizes to lists of
  // groups of that size.
  typedef map<int, list<PPS>, greater<int> > map_1;
```

```
map_1 groups;

// Find all of the anagram groups and save their
// positions in the groups map.
cout << "\n\nThe anagram groups are: " << endl;
PSi j = word_pairs.begin(), finis = word_pairs.end(), k;
while (true) {
  // Make j point to the next anagram
  // group, or to the end of the vector:
  j = adjacent_find(j, finis, firstEqual);
  if (j == finis) break;

  // Find the end of the anagram group that begins at j:
  k = find_if(j + 1, finis,
          not1(bind1st(firstEqual, *j)));

  if (k-j > 1)
    // Save the positions j and k delimiting the anagram
    // group in the list of groups of size k-j:
    groups[k-j].push_back(PPS(j, k));

  // Prepare to continue search at position k:
  j = k;
}

// Iterate through the groups map to output the anagram
// groups in order of decreasing size:
map_1::const_iterator m;
for (m = groups.begin(); m != groups.end(); ++m) {

  cout << "\n\nAnagram groups of size "
    << (*m).first << ":\n";

  list<PPS>::const_iterator l;
  for (l = (*m).second.begin();
       l != (*m).second.end(); ++l) {
    cout << "\n    ";
    j = (*l).first;  // Beginning of the anagram group
    k = (*l).second; // End of the anagram group
    copy(j, k, ostream_iterator<string>(cout, " "));
    cout << endl;
  }
```

```
        cout << endl;
    }
}
```

14.5 Output of the Program

When this program is applied to the 20,159-word dictionary available with the source code (see Appendix B), the first part of the output is as follows:

Output from Example 14-1:
```
Anagram group finding program:
finds all anagram groups in a dictionary.

First, enter the name of the file containing
the dictionary: diction

Reading the dictionary ...
Searching 20159 words for anagram groups...

The anagram groups are:


Anagram groups of size 5:

    crate carte cater caret trace



Anagram groups of size 4:

    scalar lascar rascal sacral

    bate beat beta abet

    glare lager large regal

    mantle mantel mental lament

    peal pale leap plea

    leapt plate pleat petal

    slate steal stale least
```

```
        mane name mean amen

        mate team tame meat

        pare pear reap rape

        tea ate eat eta

        cereus recuse rescue secure

        edit tide tied diet

        vile live evil veil

        item mite emit time

        rinse siren resin risen

        stripe sprite esprit priest

Anagram groups of size 3:

        abed bead bade

        bread debar beard

        brad bard drab

        brae bare bear

        garb grab brag

        tuba tabu abut

        came mace acme

        cavern carven craven

        secant stance ascent

        avocet octave vocate
```

```
care acre race

infarct frantic infract

gander danger garden
```

and so on. In this dictionary the program finds a total of 79 anagram groups of size 3 and 862 of size 2.

14.6 *Why Use a Map Container?*

Looking back over this example, what were the advantages of using a map to associate lists of word groups with integer sizes? It would appear that we could have just used a small array or vector, since we aren't likely to have very large groups of anagrams, even with a large dictionary (the maximum size is 5 with the `dic-tion` file). The key advantages of maps are as follows:

1. *No size dependence:* With an array, we would have had to worry about how big it should be (is 20 big enough?), and no matter how big we make it, someone may come along with an anomalous dictionary with larger groups of anagrams (for example, one in which a word is simply repeated many times).

2. *Automatic expansion:* Using a `vector`, with its expansion capability, would help to avoid the above problem with arrays, but not entirely automatically. Whenever we found a group larger than the current vector size, we would have to expand the vector to that size and initialize the new entries to empty lists.

By using a map, we avoid these problems completely.

CHAPTER 15

A Faster Anagram Program: Using Multimaps

Often when we first start thinking about implementing some application, we are not sure which of several possible approaches would be the most efficient. As we pointed out in Chapter 6, one of the great advantages of building our implementations with STL is that it is possible to try different data structures and algorithms in our implementations without making drastic changes to our code. In this chapter we will illustrate this point by modifying our anagram group finding program once more. Our goal this time is not to enhance the output, as it was in Chapter 14, but to see if a different way of storing the dictionary makes the program any faster (it will turn out that it does).

15.1 *Finding Anagram Groups, Version 3*

The pair-of-strings data structure, PS, used in the anagram programs of the preceding two chapters provides a way to associate a string s with another string that results from sorting the letters of s. Let's now look at another way to make such associations using a multimap, one of the STL sorted associative containers. Since these containers are designed for efficient handling of such associations, it seems worth exploring whether using one in our anagram finding application might be more efficient than storing the PS objects in a vector.

A multimap allows us to store multiple keys of a given type Key and to efficiently retrieve values of another type T based on the stored Key. In the program developed in this chapter, both Key and T will be the string type. We will make an entry into the multimap for each word in the dictionary as follows:

- we use the letter-sorted version of the word as the *key*, and

- the original word as the associated *value*.

This is essentially the same approach as with the vector of PS objects used in Chapters 13 and 14, but with a multimap the entries are automatically kept in sorted order, so *there is no need to explicitly sort them* as we did with the vector. The iterator type provided by a multimap takes us through the entries according to their sorted order, so carrying out the search for anagram groups is very similar to the way we did it in the previous chapters using a vector.

Sorting the dictionary according to the first members of the PS objects is the main part of the computation that might be made faster. Why do we suspect it might be faster to use a multimap than a vector? Putting objects into a vector and sorting the vector can be one of the most efficient sorting methods, but only if the objects are small enough to be easily moved around in the vector. With large objects, it is more efficient to work with pointers, which are smaller than the objects. Although the PS objects are not particularly large, they could be large enough that sorting methods based on pointer manipulations would be faster than ones based on moving the objects. Since multimaps (and the other STL sorted associative containers) do achieve sorted order using pointer manipulations, it is worth exploring whether they can speed up the sorting required in our anagram program.

We now present the entire program, followed by details about key points in the implementation.[1]

Example 15-1 Finding all anagram groups in a given dictionary of words.

```
#include <iterator.h>
#include <algo.h>
#include <map.h>
#include <multimap.h>
#include <list.h>
#include <fstream.h>
#include <bstring.h>
#include <assert.h>

typedef multimap<string, string, less<string> > multimap_1;

typedef multimap_1::value_type PS;

typedef multimap_1::const_iterator PSi;

struct PPS : pair<PSi, PSi> {
  PPS() : pair<PSi, PSi>(PSi(), PSi()) { }
  PPS(PSi p, PSi q) : pair<PSi, PSi>(p, q) { }
};

int main() {
  cout << "Anagram group finding program:\n"
    << "finds all anagram groups in a dictionary.\n\n"
    << "First, enter the name of the file containing\n"
    << "the dictionary: " << flush;
```

---

1. With some compilers, this program may not compile as shown, because of a compiler bug. The last section of this chapter discusses the problem and presents a work-around.

```
string dictionary_name;
cin >> dictionary_name;

ifstream ifs(dictionary_name.c_str());
cout << "\nReading the dictionary ..." << flush;

// Copy words from dictionary file to
// a multimap:
typedef istream_iterator<string, ptrdiff_t>
        string_input;
multimap_1 word_pairs;

for (string_input in(ifs); in != string_input(); ++in) {
  vector<char> vstring = *in;
  sort(vstring.begin(), vstring.end());
  word_pairs.insert(PS(string(vstring), *in));
}

cout << "\nSearching " << word_pairs.size()
  << " words for anagram groups..." << flush;

// Set up the map from anagram group sizes to lists of
// groups of that size.
typedef map<int, list<PPS>, greater<int> > map_1;
map_1 groups;

// Find all of the anagram groups and save their
// positions in the groups map.
cout << "\n\nThe anagram groups are: " << endl;
PSi j = word_pairs.begin(), finis = word_pairs.end(), k;
while (true) {
  // Make j point to the next anagram
  // group, or to the end of the multimap:
  j = adjacent_find(j, finis,
                    not2(word_pairs.value_comp()));
  if (j == finis) break;

  // Find the end of the anagram group that begins at j:
  k = find_if(j, finis,
              bind1st(word_pairs.value_comp(), *j));

  multimap_1::size_type n = 0;
```

```
      distance(j, k, n);
      if (n > 1)
        // Save the positions j and k delimiting the anagram
        // group in the list of groups of size n:
        groups[n].push_back(PPS(j, k));

      // Prepare to continue search at position k:
      j = k;
    }

  // Iterate through the groups map to output the anagram
  // groups in order of decreasing size:
  map_1::const_iterator m;
  for (m = groups.begin(); m != groups.end(); ++m) {

    cout << "\n\nAnagram groups of size "
      << (*m).first << ":\n";

    list<PPS>::const_iterator l;
    for (l = (*m).second.begin();
        l != (*m).second.end(); ++l) {
      cout << "\n     ";
      j = (*l).first;  // Beginning of the anagram group
      k = (*l).second; // End of the anagram group
      for (; j != k; ++j)
        cout << (*j).second << " ";
      cout << endl;
    }
    cout << endl;
  }
}
```

15.2 Declaration of the Multimap

In the declaration

```
typedef multimap<string, string, less<string> > multimap_1;
```

we define `multimap_1` as a type abbreviation for a type of multimap whose types `Key` and `T` are both strings, and whose entries are ordered according to the usual less-than ordering of the keys. The type of the entries in a `multimap_1` container is

```
pair<const string, string>
```

and this type is given by `multimap_1::value_type`. In the next declaration we use this type to define another type abbreviation, `PS`, to be used later in the program:

```
typedef multimap_1::value_type PS;
```

This `PS` type is similar to the `PS` type defined in the previous chapter, but this time we do not have to define any conversions between `PS` objects and `string`s, or any function objects for comparing `PS` objects. Instead, we can use facilities that are provided automatically by the `multimap` type.

15.3 Reading the Dictionary into the Multimap

In the first phase of the program, after creating an empty multimap `word_pairs`, we read each string from the input stream and create a sorted version of it in a `vector<char> vstring`. We then insert an entry in multimap `word_pairs` with `string(vstring)` as the key and the original string as the associated value. The code that carries out the reading, sorting, and inserting is

```
for (string_input in(ifs); in != string_input(); ++in) {
    vector<char> vstring = *in;
    sort(vstring.begin(), vstring.end());
    word_pairs.insert(PS(string(vstring), *in));
}
```

As in previous versions of the anagram program, we put the string into a vector in order to sort it, since string objects do not allow their storage to be modified. In the previous versions we stored the sorted vector of characters itself as the first member of the pair stored in the dictionary. Here we convert the sorted vector back to a string by means of `string(vstring)` and use this string as the key for the multimap entry. We could have set up the multimap to store the character vector.

15.4 Finding the Anagram Groups in the Multimap

Next we set up the `groups` map as in the previous version:

```
typedef map<int, list<PPS>, greater<int> > map_1;
```

```
map_1 groups;
```

and prepare to iterate through the `word_pairs` multimap finding all of the groups of adjacent entries with equal keys.

```
PSi j = word_pairs.begin(), finis = word_pairs.end(), k;
```

The above declaration sets up iteration through the multimap entries in the order corresponding to the comparison function supplied in the definition of `multimap_1`, in this case `less<string>`.

In the while loop that follows the initialization, the basic strategy used is the same as in previous versions of the anagram program; in fact, we could have programmed the loop almost identically if we had defined a function object similar to `firstEqual` for comparing `PS` objects.

With multimaps, however, we can take advantage of the `value_comp` member function, which provides a function object for comparing entries based on comparison of their keys using the given key comparison object, `less<string>`. This function is used *in constructing the predicate*, which, when passed to the STL `adjacent_find` function, allows us to determine the next anagram group.

The goal is to determine a predicate that allows us to find the next multimap entry that is *greater* than the previous entry. This is done by taking advantage of the following fact: in the multimap, for any two adjacent entries u and v, either u is less than v or u is equal to v. Hence, by searching for adjacent entries u and v such that u is *not* less than v, we can find the first ones that are equal.

Since the `word_pairs.value_comp()` predicate object returns true for operands u and v such that u is less than v, all we need to do is negate it using function adaptor `not2` to obtain the predicate object we need to pass to `adjacent_find`:

```
j = adjacent_find(j, finis,
                    not2(word_pairs.value_comp()));
```

This call to `adjacent_find` locates the beginning of a run of entries that are equal in their keys. As in the previous versions, `find_if` can be used to locate the end of the run, this time constructing the predicate object using `word_pairs` and `bind1st`:

```
k = find_if(j, finis,
              bind1st(word_pairs.value_comp(), *j));
```

As in the version in Chapter 14, we then compute the distance from the beginning position `j` and the ending position `k`, and save this pair of iterators for later output. In Chapter 14 we could compute this distance as `k - j`, but that was possible only because `j` and `k` were random access iterators, for which the `-` operator is provided. Here j and k are bidirectional iterators, and thus the – operator is not available. Instead, we call the generic `distance` function:

```
multimap_1::size_type n = 0;
distance(j, k, n);
if (n > 1)
   // Save the positions j and k delimiting the anagram
   // group in the list of groups of size n:
   groups[n].push_back(PPS(j, k));
```

The `distance` function takes linear time and is generally to be avoided, but it is available for special cases such as this, in which we expect the searches to be short.

15.5 *Outputting the Anagram Groups in Order of Size*

This phase of the program is quite similar to the way we did it in Chapter 14. The only difference is that now we cannot use `copy` to place the PS objects on the output stream, since we don't have a type conversion from our current PS objects to strings. So instead we use a for loop:

```
j = (*l).first;  // Beginning of the anagram group
k = (*l).second; // End of the anagram group
for (; j != k; ++j)
   cout << (*j).second << " ";
```

15.6 *Output of the Program*

The output of this version of the anagram group finding program is the same as that from the previous version given in Chapter 14.

15.7 *How Fast Is It?*

Timings of this version of the program show it to be about 30% faster than the version of Chapter 14. The second and third phases of the program may be slightly slower in the new version (because iteration with multimap iterators is slower than with vector iterators), so the speed gain comes in the first phase where the internal dictionary is stored in a multimap, with sorting occurring implicitly, rather than in a vector, which has to be sorted explicitly.

15.8 *Note on a Compiler Problem*

With some compilers, Example 15-1 may produce compile-time errors. The problem occurs with compilers that, in some circumstances, attempt to compile a template function even though the program contains no call of the function. In this case the problem is with the type definition and declaration:

```
typedef multimap_1::const_iterator PSi;

struct PPS : pair<PSi, PSi> {
  PPS() : pair<PSi, PSi>(PSi(), PSi()) { }
  PPS(PSi p, PSi q) : pair<PSi, PSi>(p, q) { }
};
```

The <pair.h> header contains the following template function definition for the < operator:

```
template <class T1, class T2>
inline bool operator<(const pair<T1, T2>& x,
                      const pair<T1, T2>& y) {
    return x.first < y.first ||
           (!(y.first < x.first) && x.second < y.second);
}
```

This definition requires a < operator to be defined for types T1 and T2, which in this case are `multimap_1::const_iterator` (type PSi as it's named in the `typedef`). But since multimap iterators are bidirectional and not random access, the < operator is not defined on them. In Example 15-1, this shouldn't matter, because the program never uses operator < on PPS objects. There's no need for the compiler to attempt to compile the instance

```
    operator<(const pair<PPS, PPS>&, const pair<PPS, PPS>&)
```

but some compilers do so anyway. This is a compiler bug, which you will have to work around.

The obvious solution is to provide a definition of the < operator for objects of type PSi, but we need to be careful how we define it. Since it's not actually called in our program, we might think it doesn't matter how it's defined. We could thus use a simple, but incorrect, definition like

```
bool operator<(const PSi& x, const PSi& y) { return true; }
```

This would be okay in our program, but in general it would be a bad idea to introduce such incorrect definitions into programs, because later someone might introduce modifications to the program that use this < operator, without being aware that it was incorrectly defined.

Any definition that tries to compute this < operator correctly will be inefficient, taking linear time. So we suggest a definition that tells the operator to abort the program if it is ever called, for example,

```
// Work-around for compiler bug: this is not called in this
// program, but is defined to give a warning and
// abort if it ever is.
bool operator<(const PSi& x, const PSi& y)
{
  cout << "Program attempted to use operator< on multiset "
    << "iterators; aborting." << endl;
  exit(1);
  return false;
}
```

This provides a definition of the operator that satisfies the compiler but also makes it clear that it is a definition that isn't, and shouldn't be, used.

CHAPTER 16 *Defining an Iterator Class*

As we hope the examples of the preceding chapters have shown, one of the most attractive features of STL is the way its component interfaces are designed, allowing algorithms and data structures to be fitted together in a myriad of different ways.

This structure not only provides a huge amount of functionality relative to the size of the library source code, it is also the reason that STL is better suited than other software libraries to be the basis for developing more extensive and more specialized libraries. Of course, most STL users will probably not become developers of major new extensions, but many will at some point have occasion to develop simple new components. In this chapter we'll go through a small exercise of developing such a component, an iterator adaptor that is useful for debugging or optimizing programs that use iterators.

16.1 *A New Kind of Iterator: Counting Iterator*

We define a new kind of iterator called a "counting iterator," which does just what a normal iterator does, plus keeping track of how many operations, such as ++ operations, are done on the iterator. Upon request, this counting iterator can print out the count(s) it has accumulated thereby providing usage statistics. Consider the following code (we'll write the contents of the file counting.h below):

Example 16-1   Demonstrating a counting iterator class.
```
#include <iostream.h>
#include <algo.h>
#include <bstring.h>
#include "counting.h"

int main()
{
    int x[] = {12, 4, 3, 7, 17, 9, 11, 6};
    counting_iterator<int*, int> i(x, "Curly"),
                                 j(x, "Moe"),
                                 end(x+8, "Larry");
```

```
cout << "Traversing array x\n"
    << "  from i (Curly) to end (Larry)\n";
while (i != end) {
   cout << *i << endl;
   ++i;
}

cout << "After the traversal:\n";
i.report();
end.report();

cout << "Assigning j (Moe) to i (Curly)."
    << endl;
i = j;

cout << "Searching the array\n"
    << "  from i (Moe) to end (Larry)\n"
    << "  using find\n";
counting_iterator<int*, int> k =
   find(i, end, 9);

cout << "After the find:\n";
k.report();
i.report();
end.report();
}
```

In this program the calls of the `report` member function are supposed to print the identity of the iterator in terms of the name given to it in the constructor call, the version number (initially 1, and incremented each time a copy is made of the iterator), and the number of ++ operations that have been done on the iterator. For example the first call, `i.report()`, should print

```
Iterator Curly, v. 1, reporting 8 ++ operations
```

because in the while loop ++i is executed 8 times.

To make this work, we must define `counting_iterator` as a class whose objects behave as iterators, but which also keep track of how many times ++ has been performed on them. In fact, to do the job completely, we may have to define several classes, one corresponding to each of the iterator categories (input, output, forward, bidirectional, random access).

For the sake of brevity, we restrict our attention to one of these, the *forward* iterator category. That is, we provide an iterator adaptor that converts any forward iterator (i.e., one that provides at least the operations of a forward iterator, but it could provide more) into a forward iterator that traverses a sequence in just the same way as the original iterator, while also keeping track of how many times ++ operations are applied to it. This new iterator also has a `report` member function capable of displaying its accumulated statistics.

16.2   A Counting Iterator Class

Here is the class definition:

Example 16-2   Definition of `counting_iterator` **(file** `counting.h`**).**

```
#include <iostream.h>
#include <bstring.h>

template <class ForwardIterator, class T>
class counting_iterator {
private:
    ForwardIterator current;
    int plus_count;
    string name;
    int version;
public:
    counting_iterator(ForwardIterator first,
                      const string& n)
        : current(first),
          plus_count(0),
          name(n),
          version(1) { }

    counting_iterator(const
            counting_iterator<ForwardIterator, T>& other)
        : current(other.current),
          plus_count(other.plus_count),
          name(other.name),
          version(other.version + 1)
      // copy constructor
    {
            cout << "copying " << name
                 << ", new version is "
                 << version << endl;
    }
```

```
T& operator*()
  // dereference
{
    return *current;
}

bool operator==(const
   counting_iterator<ForwardIterator, T>& other) const
  // test for equality
{
    return current == other.current;
}

bool operator!=(const
   counting_iterator<ForwardIterator, T>& other)
      const
  // test for inequality
{
    return current != other.current;
}

counting_iterator<ForwardIterator, T>& operator++()
 // prefix ++
{
    ++current;
    ++plus_count;
    return *this;
}

counting_iterator<ForwardIterator, T> operator++(int)
  // postfix ++
{
    counting_iterator<ForwardIterator, T> tmp = *this;
    ++(*this);
    return tmp;
}

void report() const
  // Display statistics on standard
  // output stream.
{
    cout << "Iterator " << name
         << ", v. " << version
```

```
                            << ", reporting  " << plus_count
                            << "  ++ operations " << endl;

      }
};
```

This class definition begins with the declaration of the private data members needed to keep track of the state of the iterator (`current`), the number of times `++` has been applied to it (`plus_count`), and the name and version number used to identify the iterator in the copy constructor and report function.

The copy constructor copies these data members, except that `version` is incremented, and reports the name and new version number on the standard output stream. Having a "talking copy constructor" like this can aid greatly in understanding where and how many times iterator objects are being copied.

Note that `==`, `!=`, and both prefix and postfix versions of `++` are provided, according to the STL requirements on forward iterators (see Section 18.3 on page 248). Note also how the postfix `++` is simply defined in terms of the prefix version.

With this definition of `counting_iterator` in `counting.h`, here is the complete output of the sample program given at the beginning of the chapter:

Output from Example 16-1:
```
Traversing array x
   from i (Curly) to end (Larry)
12
4
3
7
17
9
11
6
After the traversal:
Iterator Curly, v. 1, reporting  8  ++ operations
Iterator Larry, v. 1, reporting  0  ++ operations
Assigning j (Moe) to i (Curly).
Searching the array
   from i (Moe) to end (Larry)
   using find
Copying Moe, new version is 2
Copying Larry, new version is 2
Copying Moe, new version is 3
After the find:
Iterator Moe, v. 3, reporting  5  ++ operations
Iterator Moe, v. 1, reporting  0  ++ operations
Iterator Larry, v. 1, reporting  0  ++ operations
```

Note that calling the `find` function causes i and end to be copied (because the iterator parameters to `find` are value parameters), and the final value of the copy of i (Moe, version 2) is copied when returning the result in k (Moe, version 3).

Since we defined `counting_iterator` as an *iterator adaptor* (i.e., it has an iterator class as a template parameter), we can use it to convert the iterator type associated with any of the STL container classes into a counting iterator. For example, to declare a counting iterator i usable with `list<char>`, we can say:

```
counting_iterator<list<char>::iterator, char> i;
```

As we have defined it, `counting_iterator` produces iterators of the forward category only (it would more properly be called `forward_counting_iterator`). Thus the iterators it produces cannot be used with STL algorithms that require bidirectional or random access iterators, but defining counting iterator adaptors for these categories is a straightforward exercise (if you are interested in trying this exercise, see Sections 18.4 on page 249 and 18.5 on page 250 for discussion of the requirements on iterators of these categories).

In summary, an iterator adaptor such as `counting_iterator` can confirm or reveal a great deal of information about the way an STL generic algorithm or user code uses iterators, and such information can be very useful in debugging or optimizing programs. We hope this example also illustrates some of the main issues in defining other kinds of iterator adaptors or other new software components that are compatible with STL.

CHAPTER 17

Combining STL with Object-Oriented Programming

Many people's initial reaction to STL is, "But it's not object-oriented!" It's true that STL makes little use of class inheritance and none at all of virtual functions, two of the hallmarks of C++ object-oriented programming.[1] But STL gives up little in omitting use of these language features. Through its innovative use of templates and framework of fine-grained, interchangeable components, STL achieves most of the flexibility that one ordinarily finds in programs that make heavy use of inheritance and virtual functions, while gaining a great deal in terms of efficiency.

Nevertheless, there remain valid reasons for using derived classes and virtual functions in some settings, and it is quite possible to combine these techniques with STL to good advantage. Two reasons to do so are as follows:

- **Having containers that hold objects of different types.** We may need to store objects of different types in a single container; this is known as *heterogeneous storage*, versus the *homogeneous storage* directly provided by STL's template container classes.

- **Avoiding code bloat.** Even if we only need homogeneous storage in any one container, we may need many different instances of the same container type, leading to the problem of "code bloat." For example, having list<int>, list<string>, list<vector<int> >, and so on, in the same program results in several slightly different copies of the list class code present in our executable file.[2]

---

1. The other two language features that are usually included among those considered essential for full-blown object oriented programming are data abstraction (encapsulation) and polymorphism, both of which *are* heavily ingrained in STL.

2. In theory, compilers could do "code sharing" in many cases. For example, if sizeof(T1) == sizeof(T2), then most of the code for list<T1> and list<T2> could be shared, since most of it is independent of the type of elements stored. But current production C++ compilers seem to make little or no use of code sharing.

In this chapter we show, in terms of a simple example, how STL components and generic programming techniques can be combined with class inheritance and virtual functions to achieve one or both of these goals, at some cost in efficiency and compile-time checking.

17.1 Using Inheritance and Virtual Functions

The example is based on the "shapes" example from Section 6.4 of Ref. 14. This is a simple program for drawing geometric shapes on a screen, used to illustrate object-oriented programming techniques. It consists of

- a screen manager: low-level routines and data structures defining the screen; it knows about points and straight lines only;

- a shape library: a set of definitions of general shapes, such as rectangles and circles, and standard routines for manipulating them; and

- an application program: a set of application-specific definitions and code using them.

The shape library organizes the different shapes it supports into a simple class hierarchy, consisting of a shape base class and derived line and rectangle classes. Operations for drawing and moving shapes are defined as virtual functions in class shape and are given specific meanings for each derived shape in their respective derived classes. This organization allows all shapes to be drawn or moved via the interface provided by class shape. It also happens to allow objects of different types (rectangles and lines) to be stored in the same container, since they can be stored using shape* pointers.

The details of the screen manager and shapes library can be found in Ref. 14, Section 6.4. The header files screen.h and shapes.h and corresponding implementation files screen.cpp and shapes.cpp are replicated in Appendix A. The exact details are not particularly important for this discussion, but the key point is that draw and move are defined as virtual functions in shape, so that application-level functions (such as stacking one shape over another) written in terms of draw and move will work for all shapes. For example, since draw is a virtual function, when we apply it to a shape object that is a rectangle, the function that is used is the draw defined within the derived rectangle class, and similarly for line or other derived classes that might be added.

The application program in Ref. 14 is an extremely simple one that merely draws a stylized "face" and moves it around. In our adaptation of the example, we define an STL vector<shape*> and show how to manipulate specific shapes in a vector of this type with a combination of (nonvirtual) STL vector member function calls, STL generic algorithm calls, and shape virtual function calls.

Example 17-1 Combining STL components with inheritance and virtual functions.

```
#include "shape.h"
#include <vector.h>
#include <algo.h>

class myshape : public rectangle {
 /* Define a new shape, a simple "face," derived from
    rectangle.
  */
  line* l_eye;
  line* r_eye;
  line* mouth;
 public:
  myshape(point, point);
  void draw();
  void move(int, int);
};

myshape::myshape(point a, point b) : rectangle(a,b)
{
   int ll = neast().x - swest().x+1;
   int hh = neast().y - swest().y+1;
   l_eye =
     new line(point(swest().x+2,swest().y+hh*3/4),2);
   r_eye =
     new line(point(swest().x+ll-4,swest().y+hh*3/4),2);
   mouth =
     new line(point(swest().x+2,swest().y+hh/4),ll-4);
}

void myshape::draw()
   // Draw it by drawing the rectangle and a point for the
   // "nose"; the eye and mouth objects are refreshed
   // separately by the shape_refresh function.
{
   rectangle::draw();
   int a = (swest().x + neast().x)/2;
   int b = (swest().y + neast().y)/2;
   put_point(point(a,b));
}

void myshape::move(int a, int b)
```

```
      // Move it by moving the base rectangle and secondary
      // objects.
  {
    rectangle::move(a,b);
    l_eye->move(a,b);
    r_eye->move(a,b);
    mouth->move(a,b);
  }


  // Beginning of definitions added in order to use STL
  // with shape classes.

  struct CompWestX : binary_function<shape*, shape*, bool> {

    bool operator()(shape* p, shape* q) const
      // Compare shapes based on the x-coordinate of
      // west point. The west function is virtual in the
      // shape class, so the comparison is made based on
      // how it is defined for a more specific shape.
    {
      return p->west().x < q->west().x;
    }
  } compWestX;

  void outputWestX (const vector<shape*>& vs)
      // Output the x-coordinate of the west point of each
      // shape in vs.
  {
    vector<shape*>::const_iterator i;
    for (i = vs.begin(); i != vs.end(); ++i)
      cout << "The x-coordinate of the west point of shape "
           << i - vs.begin() << " is " << (*i)->west().x
      << endl;
  }


  // End of definitions added in order to use STL.

  int main()
  {
  // First part is same as in Stroustrup's book.
    screen_init();
    shape* p1 = new rectangle(point(0,0),point(10,10));
    shape* p2 = new line(point(0,15),17);
```

```
    shape* p3 = new myshape(point(15,10),point(27,18));
    shape_refresh();
    p3->move(-10,-10);
    stack(p2,p3);
    stack(p1,p2);
    shape_refresh();

// This part is added as a tiny example of use of STL
// along with code that uses a class hierarchy and
// virtual functions. First put points into an STL vector.
    vector<shape*> vs;
    vs.push_back(p1);
    vs.push_back(p2);
    vs.push_back(p3);

// Use STL-provided iterator to move all points
// horizontally 20 units.
    vector<shape*>::iterator i;
    for (i = vs.begin(); i != vs.end(); ++i)
      (*(*i)).move(20, 0);
    shape_refresh();

// Demonstrate use of STL generic sorting algorithm with
// objects in a class hierarchy.
    outputWestX(vs);
    cout << "Sorting the shapes according to the "
         << "x-coordinate of their west points." << endl;
    sort(vs.begin(), vs.end(), compWestX);
    cout << "After sorting:" << endl;
    outputWestX(vs);
    screen_destroy();
}
```

Output from Example 17-1:
First, the different shapes are output in their original positions:

```
                        * * * * * * * * * * * *
                        *                     *
                        *   * *       * *     *
* * * * * * * * * * * * * *                   *
                        *          *          *
                        *                     *
                        *   * * * * * * * *   *
                        *                     *
* * * * * * * * * *     * * * * * * * * * * * *
*                 *
*                 *
*                 *
*                 *
*                 *
*                 *
*                 *
*                 *
*                 *
* * * * * * * * * *
```

Then these shapes are moved around to form:

```
        * * * * * * * * * *
        *                 *
        *                 *
        *                 *
        *                 *
        *                 *
        *                 *
        *                 *
        *                 *
        *                 *
        * * * * * * * * * *
    * * * * * * * * * * * * * *
      * * * * * * * * * * * *
      *                     *
      *   * *       * *     *
      *                     *
      *          *          *
      *                     *
      *   * * * * * * * *    *
      *                     *
      * * * * * * * * * * * *
```

These shapes are all moved over 20 spaces by putting them in a vector and traversing the vector, moving each shape it contains.

```
            * * * * * * * * * *
            *                 *
            *                 *
            *                 *
            *                 *
            *                 *
            *                 *
            *                 *
            *                 *
            *                 *
            * * * * * * * * * *
        * * * * * * * * * * * * * * * * *
          * * * * * * * * * * * *
          *                     *
          *  * *         * *    *
          *                     *
          *            *        *
          *                     *
          *  * * * * * * * *    *
          *                     *
          * * * * * * * * * * * *
```

The last part shows the west point x-coordinates of each shape in the vector, before and after sorting with STL's generic `sort` algorithm:

```
The x-coordinate of the west point of shape 0 is 26
The x-coordinate of the west point of shape 1 is 23
The x-coordinate of the west point of shape 2 is 25
Sorting the shapes according to the x-coordinate of their
west points.
After sorting:
The x-coordinate of the west point of shape 0 is 23
The x-coordinate of the west point of shape 1 is 25
The x-coordinate of the west point of shape 2 is 26
```

17.2 *Avoiding "Code Bloat" from Container Instances*

The `vector<shape*>` type introduced in Example 17-1 allows different shapes (rectangles, lines, etc.) to be stored in the same container. In some cases we might not have any need for this kind of heterogeneous storage, but we might need several different vector instances, each holding some specific shape, such as

```
vector<rectangle> vr;
vector<line> vl, vl2;
vector<circle> vc;
vector<myshape> ms1, ms2, ms3;
etc.
```

The problem this introduces is that the compiler may insert a separate copy of the vector class code for each instance of `vector`, resulting in an unacceptably large executable file. One way to avoid this "code bloat" is to use `vector<shape*>` as the type of all shape vectors we declare:

```
vector<shape*> vr;
vector<shape*> vl, vl2;
vector<shape*> vc;
vector<shape*> ms1, ms2, ms3;
etc.
```

Then only one copy of the `vector` code will be included in the executable file. What we give up is some of the type checking that the compiler was able to do using the first set of declarations, and some run-time speed (due to the extra level of indirection involved in calling virtual functions).

Of course this only works if the types of objects we want to store in containers are all derived from the same base class. If not, we would have to try to reorganize them into such an arrangement.

As a final note, these techniques can be applied to help avoid code bloat that arises from instances of *any* template class, not just STL container classes. The amount of reduction in executable file size will depend on how much of the class implementation is independent of the exact type of its template parameters. With container-defining template classes there is typically more independence than with other kinds of template classes. See also Section 11.3 on page 187 for other techniques of avoiding code bloat that arises from template classes or functions.

PART III   STL Reference Guide

Part III describes all STL components, including some details not mentioned in Parts I or II. Look here for the complete description of any component.

CHAPTER 18 *Iterator Reference Guide*

This chapter begins Part III, the STL Reference Guide. Consult this guide for complete details on all STL components. This guide does not contain examples, but examples and tutorial descriptions of almost all components can be located in Parts I and II by consulting the entry for the component in the Index at the back of the book. The present chapter is a reference guide to STL iterator components, including

- the requirements that must be satisfied by a class or a built in type to be used as an iterator of a particular iterator category (input iterators, output iterators, forward iterators, bidirectional iterators, or random access iterators);

- stream iterator classes, for using generic algorithms with input streams or output streams;

- iterator adaptors (reverse iterators and insert iterators).

The following terminology is used in the statement of iterator requirements.

Value type. Iterators are objects that have `operator*` returning a value of some class or built-in type T called the *value type* of the iterator.

Distance type. For every iterator type for which equality is defined, there is a corresponding signed integral type called the *distance type* of the iterator.

Past-the-end values. Just as a regular pointer to an array guarantees that there is a valid pointer value pointing past the last element of the array, so for any iterator type there is an iterator value that points past the last element of a corresponding container. These values are called *past-the-end* values.

Dereferenceable values. Values of the iterator for which `operator*` is defined are called *dereferenceable*. STL components never assume that past-the-end values are dereferenceable.

Singular values. Iterators might also have *singular* values that are not associated with any container. For example, after the declaration of an uninitialized pointer x (as with `int* x`), x should always be assumed to have a singular value of a pointer. Results of most expressions are undefined for singular values. The only exception is an assignment of a nonsingular value to an iterator that holds a singular value. In this case the singular value is overwritten the same way as any other value. Dereferenceable and past-the-end values are always nonsingular.

Reachability. An iterator j is called *reachable* from an iterator i if and only if there is a finite sequence of applications of `operator++` to i that makes i == j. If j is reachable from i, they refer to the same container.

Ranges. All of the library's algorithmic templates that operate on containers have interfaces that use ranges. A *range* is a pair of iterators that serve as beginning and end markers for a computation. A range [i, i) is an empty range; in general, a range [i, j) consists of the iterators obtained by starting with i and applying `operator++` until j is reached, but does not include j. Range [i, j) is *valid* if and only if j is reachable from i. The result of the application of the algorithms in the library to invalid ranges is undefined.

Mutable versus constant. Iterators can be *mutable* or *constant* depending on whether the result of `operator*` behaves as a reference or as a reference to a constant. Constant iterators do not satisfy the requirements for output iterators.

For all iterator operations that are required in each category, the computing time requirement is *constant time* (amortized). For this reason, in this chapter we will not mention computing times separately in any of the following sections on requirements.

18.1 *Input Iterator Requirements*

As Stepanov and Lee stress in Ref. 12, it is important to state the requirements on the components as generally as possible. For example, instead of saying "class X must define a member function `operator++()`," we say "for any object x of type X, ++x is defined." (We leave open the possibility that X is a built-in type and that the operator is globally defined rather than a class member function.)

In this and the following four requirements sections in this chapter, for each iterator type X we will assume that

- a and b denote values of type X,

- n denotes a value of the distance type for X,

- r denotes a value of X&,

- t denotes a value type T, and

- u, tmp, and m denote identifiers.

A class or a built-in type X satisfies the requirements of an input iterator for the value type T if and only if the following expressions are defined and meet the requirements specified for them:

X(a)   The copy constructor, which makes X(a) == a. A destructor is assumed.

X u(a);   Results in u == a.

X u = a;   Results in u == a.

a == b   The return type must be convertible to bool, and == must be an equivalence relation.

a != b   The return type must be convertible to bool, and the result must be the same as !(a == b).

*a   The return type must be convertible to T. It is assumed that a is dereferenceable. If a == b, then it must be the case that *a == *b.

++r   The return type must be convertible to const X&. It is assumed that r is dereferenceable. The result is that r is dereferenceable or r is the past-the-end value of the container, and &r == &++r.

r++   The return type must be convertible to const X&. The result must be the same as that of { X tmp = r; ++r; return tmp; }.

*++r   The return type must be convertible to T.

*r++   The return type must be convertible to T.

For input iterators, a == b does *not* imply ++a == ++b. The main consequence is that algorithms on input iterators should be *single-pass* algorithms; i.e., they should never attempt to copy the value of an iterator and use it to pass through the same position twice. Furthermore, value type T is *not* required to be a reference type, so algorithms on input iterators should not attempt to assign through them. (Forward iterators remove these restrictions.)

18.2 *Output Iterator Requirements*

A class or a built-in type X satisfies the requirements of an output iterator for the value type T if and only if the following expressions are defined and meet the requirements specified for them:

X(a)   *a = t is equivalent to *X(a) = t. Further, a destructor is assumed in this case.

X u(a);   The result is that u is a copy of a. Note, however, that equality and inequality are not necessarily defined, and algorithms should not attempt to use output iterators to pass through a position twice (i.e., should be single-pass).

X u = a;   Same as above.

*a = t   t is assigned through the iterator to the position to which a refers. The result of this operation is not used.

++r   The return type must be convertible to const X&. It is assumed that r is dereferenceable on the left-hand side of an assignment. The result is that either r is dereferenceable on the left-hand side of an assignment or r is the past-the-end value of the container, and &r == &++r.

r++   The return type must be convertible to const X&. The result must be the same as that of { X tmp = r; ++r; return tmp; }.

*++r   The return type must be convertible to T.

*r++   The return type must be convertible to T.

The only valid use of operator* on output iterators is on the left-hand side of an assignment statement. As with input iterators, algorithms that use output iterators should be single-pass. Equality and inequality operators might not be defined. Algorithms that use output iterators can be used with ostreams as the destination for placing data via the ostream_iterator class as well as with insert iterators and insert pointers.

18.3 *Forward Iterator Requirements*

A class or a built-in type X satisfies the requirements of a forward iterator for the value type T if and only if the following expressions are defined and meet the requirements specified for them:

X u;   The resulting value of u might be singular. A destructor is assumed.

`X()`	`X()` might be a singular value.
`X(a)`	The result must satisfy `a == X(a)`.
`X u(a);`	The result must satisfy `u == a`.
`X u = a;`	The result must satisfy `u == a`.
`a == b`	The return type must be convertible to `bool`, and `==` must be an equivalence relation.
`a != b`	The return type must be convertible to `bool`, and the result must be the same as `!(a == b)`.
`r = a`	The return type is `X&`, and the result must satisfy `r == a`.
`*a`	The return type must be convertible to `T`. It is assumed that `a` is dereferenceable. If `a == b`, then it must be that `*a == *b`. If `X` is mutable, `*a = t` is valid.
`++r`	The return type must be convertible to `X&`. It is assumed that `r` is dereferenceable, and the result is that `r` either is dereferenceable or is the past-the-end value, and `&r == &++r`. Moreover, `r == s` and `r` is dereferenceable imply `++r == ++s`.
`r++`	The return type must be convertible to `const X&`. The result must be the same as that of `{ X tmp = r; ++r; return tmp; }`.
`*++r`	The return type must be convertible to `T`.
`*r++`	The return type must be convertible to `T`.

The condition that `a == b` implies `++a == ++b` (which is not true for input or output iterators), along with the removal of the restrictions on the number of the assignments through the iterator (which applies to output iterators), allows the use of multipass, one-directional algorithms with forward iterators.

18.4 *Bidirectional Iterator Requirements*

A class or a built-in type `X` satisfies the requirements of a bidirectional iterator for the value type `T` if and only if the following expressions are defined and meet the requirements specified for them, in addition to the requirements that are described in the previous section for forward iterators:

`--r`	The return type must be convertible to `const X&`. It is assumed that there exists `s` such that `r == ++s`; then `--r` refers to the same position as `s`. Also `--r` is dereferenceable and `&r == &--r`. Both of the

following properties must hold: `--(++r) == r`, and if `--r == --s,` then `r == s`.

r--
: The return type must be convertible to `const X&`. The result must be the same as that of `{ X tmp = r; --r; return tmp; }`.

*r--
: The return type must be convertible to `T`.

18.5 *Random Access Iterator Requirements*

A class or a built-in type `X` satisfies the requirements of a random access iterator for the value type `T` if and only if the following expressions are defined and meet the requirements specified for them, in addition to the requirements of a bidirectional iterator type:

r += n
: The return type must be `X&`. The result must be the same as would be computed by

```
{ Distance m = n;
  if (m >= 0)
    while (m--) ++r;
  else
    while (m++) --r;
  return r; }
```

but is computed in constant time.

a + n
: The return type must be `X`. The result must be the same as would be computed by `{ X tmp = a; return tmp += n; }`.

n + a
: Same as above.

r -= n
: The return type must be `X&`. The result must be the same as would be computed by `r += -n`.

a - n
: The return type must be `X`. The result must be the same as would be computed by `{ X tmp = a; return tmp -= n; }`.

b - a
: The return type must be `Distance`. It is assumed that there exists a value `n` of the type `Distance` such that `a + n == b`; the result returned is `n`.

a[n]
: The return type must be convertible to `T`. The result is `*(a + n)`.

a < b
: The return type must be convertible to `bool`, and `<` must be a total ordering relation.

a > b   The return type must be convertible to `bool`, and > must be a total ordering relation opposite to <.

a >= b   The return type is convertible to `bool`, and the result must be the same as `!(a < b)`.

a <= b   The return type is convertible to `bool`, and the result must be the same as `!(b < a)`.

18.6 *Istream Iterators*

The library provides *stream iterators*, defined by template classes, to allow algorithms to work directly with input/output streams. The `istream_iterator` class defines input iterator types, and the `ostream_iterator` class defines output iterator types. For example, the following code fragment:

```
istream_iterator<int> end_of_stream;
partial_sum_copy(istream_iterator<int>(cin),
                 end_of_stream,
                 ostream_iterator<int>(cout, "\n"));
```

reads a file containing integers from the input stream `cin` and sends the partial sums to `cout`, separated by newline characters.

This section is a reference guide for `istream_iterator`s, which are used to read values from the input stream for which they are constructed. Section 18.7 covers `ostream_iterator`s, which are used to write values into the output stream for which they are constructed.

18.6.1 Files

```
#include <iterator.h>
```

18.6.2 Class Declaration

```
template <class T, class Distance = ptrdiff_t>
class istream_iterator : input_iterator<T, Distance>;
```

18.6.3 Description

An `istream_iterator<T>` reads (using `operator>>`) successive elements of type `T` from the input stream for which it was constructed. Each time ++ is used on a constructed `istream_iterator<T>` object, the iterator reads and stores a value of type `T`. The end-of-stream value is reached when `operator void*()` on the stream returns `false`. In this case, the iterator becomes equal to the *end-of-*

stream iterator value. This end-of-stream value can only be constructed using the constructor with no arguments: `istream_iterator<T>()`. Two end-of-stream iterators are always equal. An end-of-stream iterator is not equal to a non-end-of-stream iterator. Two non-end-of-stream iterators are equal when they are constructed from the same stream.

One can only use `istream_iterators` to read values; it is impossible to store anything into a position to which an `istream_iterator` value refers.

The main peculiarity of istream iterators is the fact that `++` operators are not equality-preserving; that is, `i == j` does not guarantee that `++i == ++j`. Every time `++` is used, a new value is read from the associated istream. The practical consequence of this fact is that istream iterators can only be used with single-pass algorithms.

18.6.4 Constructors

```
istream_iterator()
```

Constructs the end-of-stream iterator value. Note that two end-of-stream iterators are always equal.

```
istream_iterator(istream& s)
```

Constructs an `istream_iterator<T>` object that reads values from the input stream `s`.

```
istream_iterator(const istream_iterator<T, Distance>& x)
```

Copy constructor.

```
~istream_iterator()
```

Destructor.

18.6.5 Public Member Functions

```
const T& operator*() const
```

Dereferencing operator. By returning a reference to const `T`, it ensures that it cannot be used to write values to the input stream for which the iterator is constructed.

```
istream_iterator<T, Distance>& operator++()
```

This operator reads and stores a value of `T` each time it is called.

```
istream_iterator <T, Distance> operator++(int)
```

This operator reads and stores x values of T each time it is called.

18.6.6   Comparison Operations

```
template <class T, class Distance>
bool operator==(const istream_iterator<T,Distance>& x,
                const istream_iterator<T,Distance>& y)
```

Equality operator. Two end-of-stream iterators are always equal. An end-of-stream iterator is not equal to a non-end-of-stream iterator. Two non-end-of-stream iterators are equal when they are constructed from the same stream.

18.7   Ostream Iterators

18.7.1   Files

```
#include <iterator.h>
```

18.7.2   Class Declaration

```
template <class T>
class ostream_iterator : public output_iterator;
```

18.7.3   Description

An `ostream_iterator<T>` object writes (using `operator<<`) successive elements onto the output stream for which it was constructed. If it is constructed with `char*` as a constructor argument, then this *delimiter* string is written to the stream after each T value is written.

It is not possible to *read* a value with an output iterator. It can only be used to *write* values to an output stream for which it is constructed.

18.7.4   Constructors

```
ostream_iterator(ostream& s)
```

Constructs an iterator that can be used to write to the output stream s.

```
ostream_iterator(ostream& s, const char* delimiter)
```

Constructs an iterator that can be used to write to the output stream s. The character string `delimiter` is written out after every value (of type T) written to s.

```
ostream_iterator(const ostream_iterator<T>& x)
```

Copy constructor.

```
~ostream_iterator()
```

Destructor.

18.7.5 Public Member Functions

```
ostream_iterator<T>& operator*()
```

Dereferencing operator. An assignment `*o = t` through an output iterator `o` causes `t` to be written to the output stream, and the stream pointer is advanced in preparation for the next write.

```
ostream_iterator<T>&
operator=(const ostream_iterator<T>& x)
```

Assignment operator. Replaces the current iterator with a copy of the iterator `x`.

```
ostream_iterator<T>& operator++()
ostream_iterator<T> operator++(int x)
```

These operators are present to allow ostream iterators to be used with algorithms that both assign through an output iterator and advance the iterator; they actually do nothing, since assignments through the iterator advance the stream pointer also.

18.8 *Reverse Bidirectional Iterators*

Bidirectional iterators and random access iterators have corresponding reverse iterator adaptors. These adaptors produce iterators that can be used for traversing a data structure in the opposite of the normal direction. To iterate through elements in some valid range `[i, j)` in reverse order, start with a reverse iterator initialized with `j` and increment it `j - i - 1` times with `++`. The elements traversed are those that would be obtained by initializing a normal iterator with `j - 1` and decrementing it `j - i - 1` times with `--`, namely those in positions

$$j - 1, j - 2, \ldots, i + 1, i.$$

Note that iterator i - 1 might not be defined (in fact, it isn't if i marks the beginning of some container) and so cannot serve as a "past-the-end" value for reverse iteration. This problem is solved by defining the dereference operator * on reverse iterators so that

$$\&*(\texttt{reverse\_iterator(i)}) \;==\; \&*(\texttt{i - 1}). \qquad (1)$$

This mapping allows the reverse iterator to use iterators j, j - 1, . . . , i + 1 as though they were j - 1, j - 2, . . . , i + 1, i, and iterator i is then available to use as the "past-the-end" value.

This section describes `reverse_bidirectional_iterator`, and the following section describes `reverse_iterator` (for reversing a random access iterator).

The `reverse_bidirectional_iterator` adaptor takes a bidirectional iterator and produces a new bidirectional iterator for traversal in the opposite direction.

18.8.1 Class Declaration

```
template <class BidirectionalIterator, class T,
          class Reference = T&, class Distance = ptrdiff_t>
class reverse_bidirectional_iterator :
    public bidirectional_iterator<T, Distance>;
```

In subsequent sections we assume the following type definition for the sake of brevity:

```
typedef
   reverse_bidirectional_iterator<BidirectionalIterator, T,
      Reference, Distance> self;
```

18.8.2 Constructors

```
reverse_bidirectional_iterator();
```

Default constructor, produces a singular value.

```
explicit
   reverse_bidirectional_iterator(BidirectionalIterator x);
```

Creates a reverse bidirectional iterator with current position specified by x, according to the relation (1). (The explicit keyword is a recent addition to C++ in the ANSI/ISO (Draft) Standard. It means that the constructor must be called explicitly; i.e., the compiler is not permitted to use it for implicit type conversions.)

18.8.3 Public Member Functions

```
BidirectionalIterator base();
```

Returns a bidirectional iterator to the current position (for which ++ and -- have the opposite meanings from those of this reverse bidirectional iterator).

```
Reference operator*();
```

Dereferencing operator, returns `*(base() - 1)`.

```
self& operator++();
```

Changes current position to `base() - 1` and returns the resulting iterator.

```
self operator++(int);
```

Changes current position to `base() - 1` but returns an iterator to the former position.

```
self& operator--();
```

Changes current position to `base() + 1` and returns the resulting iterator.

```
self operator--(int);
```

Changes current position to `base() + 1` but returns an iterator to the former position.

18.8.4 Equality Predicate

```
template <class BidirectionalIterator, class T,
    class Distance>
bool operator==(const self& x, const self& y);
```

Returns `(x.base() == y.base())`.

18.9 Reverse Iterators

The `reverse_iterator` adaptor takes a random access iterator and produces a new random access iterator for traversal in the opposite direction.

18.9.1 Class Declaration

```
template <class RandomAccessIterator, class T,
        class Reference = T&, class Distance = ptrdiff_t>
class reverse_iterator :
    public random_access_iterator<T, Distance>;
```

In subsequent sections we assume the following type definition for the sake of brevity:

```
typedef reverse_iterator<BidirectionalIterator, T,
                    Reference, Distance> self;
```

18.9.2 Constructor

```
reverse_iterator();
```

Default constructor, produces a singular value.

```
explicit reverse_iterator(RandomAccessIterator x);
```

Creates a reverse randomaccess iterator with current position specified by x, according to relation (1) on page 255.

18.9.3 Public Member Functions

```
RandomAccessIterator base();
```

Returns a random access iterator to the current position (for which ++ and -- have the opposite meanings from those of this reverse random access iterator).

```
Reference operator*();
```

Dereferencing operator, returns `*(base() - 1)`.

```
self& operator++();
```

Changes current position to `base() - 1` and returns the resulting iterator.

```
self operator++(int);
```

Changes current position to `base() - 1` but returns an iterator to the former position.

```
self& operator--();
```

Changes current position to `base()` + 1 and returns the resulting iterator.

```
self operator--(int);
```

Changes current position to `base()` + 1 but returns an iterator to the former position.

```
self operator+(Distance n) const;
```

Returns a reverse random access iterator to `base()` - n.

```
self& operator+=(Distance n);
```

Changes current position to `base()` - n and returns the resulting iterator.

```
self operator-(Distance n) const;
```

Returns a reverse random access iterator to `base()` + n.

```
self& operator-=(Distance n);
```

Changes current position to `base()` + n and returns the resulting iterator.

```
Reference operator[](Distance n);
```

Returns `*(*this + n)`.

```
template <class RandomAccessIterator, class T,
          class Reference, class Distance>
Distance operator-(const self& x, const self& y);
```

Returns `y.base()` - `x.base()`.

```
template <class RandomAccessIterator, class T,
          class Reference, class Distance>
self operator+(Distance n, const self& y);
```

Returns `y.base()` - `x.base()`.

18.9.4 Equality and Ordering Predicates

```
template <class RandomAccessIterator, class T,
          class Reference, class Distance>
bool operator==(const self& x, const self& y);
```

Returns `(x.base() == y.base())`.

```
template <class RandomAccessIterator, class T,
          class Reference, class Distance>
bool operator<(const self& x, const self& y);
```

Returns `(y.base() < x.base())`.

18.10 Back Insert Iterators

Insert iterator adaptors take a container (and in some cases an iterator into the container) and produce output iterators that convert assignments through the iterator into insertions instead. There are three types of insert iterator adaptors. One is `back_insert_iterator<Container>`, whose objects use the Container class's `push_back` member function to do the insertions. This class is described in this section, along with a template function `back_inserter`, which is usually more convenient to use than the class. The next section describes the corresponding components for using `push_front` to do the insertions, namely the `front_insert_iterator<Container>` class and `front_inserter` template function; and Section 18.12 describes the components for using `insert`, namely the `insert_iterator<Container>` class and `inserter` template function.

18.10.1 Class Declaration

```
template <class Container>
class back_insert_iterator : public output_iterator;
```

Container must be a type

- for which `Container::value_type` is a type, and

- that has a `push_back` member function that takes a single argument of type `Container::value_type`.

18.10.2 Constructors

```
explicit back_insert_iterator(Container& x);
```

Constructs an insert iterator i for converting assignments *i = value into use of x.push_back(value) instead.

18.10.3 Public Member Functions

```
back_insert_iterator<Container>&
  operator=(const Container::value_type& value);
```

Performs x.push_back(value), where x is the container the constructor associates with the iterator. Returns the iterator.

```
back_insert_iterator<Container>& operator*();
```

Returns the iterator itself (*this), so that an assignment *i = value uses the = operator just described rather than that of Container::value_type.

```
back_insert_iterator<Container>& operator++();
back_insert_iterator<Container> operator++(int);
```

These do nothing except return the iterator itself (*this).

18.10.4 Corresponding Template Function

```
template <class Container>
back_insert_iterator<Container> back_inserter(Container& x);
```

Returns back_insert_iterator<Container>(x). This function is provided just as a convenience.

18.11 *Front Insert Iterators*

18.11.1 Class Declaration

```
template <class Container>
class front_insert_iterator : public output_iterator;
```

Container must be a type

- for which Container::value_type is a type, and

- that has a `push_front` member function that takes a single argument of type `Container::value_type`.

18.11.2 Constructors

```
explicit front_insert_iterator(Container& x);
```

Constructs an insert iterator `i` for converting assignments `*i = value` into use of `x.push_front(value)` instead.

18.11.3 Public Member Functions

```
front_insert_iterator<Container>&
    operator=(const Container::value_type& value);
```

Performs `x.push_front(value)`, where `x` is the container the constructor associates with the iterator. Returns the iterator.

```
front_insert_iterator<Container>& operator*();
```

Returns the iterator itself (`*this`), so that an assignment `*i = value` uses the `=` operator just described rather than that of `Container::value_type`.

```
front_insert_iterator<Container>& operator++();
front_insert_iterator<Container> operator++(int);
```

These do nothing except return the iterator itself (`*this`).

18.11.4 Corresponding Template Function

```
template <class Container>
front_insert_iterator<Container>
    front_inserter(Container& x);
```

Returns `front_insert_iterator<Container>(x)`. This function is provided just as a convenience.

18.12 Insert Iterators

18.12.1 Class Declaration

```
template <class Container>
class insert_iterator : public output_iterator;
```

`Container` must be a type

- for which `Container::value_type` and `Container::value_type` are types, and

- that has an `insert` member function with interface

```
Container::iterator
  insert(Container::iterator,
         const Container::value_type&)
```

18.12.2 Constructors

```
insert_iterator(Container& x, Container::iterator i);
```

Constructs an insert iterator i for converting assignments `*i = value` into use of `x.insert(i, value)` instead.

18.12.3 Public Member Function

```
insert_iterator<Container>&
  operator=(const Container::value_type& value);
```

Performs `i = x.insert(i, value)`, where x is the container the constructor associates with the insert iterator, and i is the current value of the iterator passed to the constructor and updated as shown. Returns the insert iterator.

```
insert_iterator<Container>& operator*();
```

Returns the iterator itself (`*this`), so that an assignment `*i = value` uses the = operator just described rather than that of `Container::value_type`.

```
insert_iterator<Container>& operator++();
insert_iterator<Container> operator++(int);
```

These do nothing except return the iterator itself (`*this`).

18.12.4 Corresponding Template Function

```
template <class Container, class Iterator>
insert_iterator<Container>
  inserter(Container& x, Iterator i);
```

Returns `insert_iterator<Container>(x, i)`. This function is provided just as a convenience.

CHAPTER 19   *Container Reference Guide*

19.1 *Requirements*

19.1.1 Basic Design and Organization of STL Containers

STL containers are divided into two broad families: *sequence* containers and *sorted associative* containers.

Sequence containers include vectors, lists, and deques. These contain elements of a single type, organized in a strictly linear arrangement. Although only the three most basic sequence containers are provided, it is possible to construct other sequence containers efficiently using these basic containers through the use of *container adaptors,* which are STL classes that provide interface mappings. STL provides adaptors for stacks, queues, and priority queues.

The second STL container family consists of sorted associative containers, which include sets, multisets, maps, and multimaps. Associative containers allow for the fast retrieval of data based on keys. For example, a map allows a user to retrieve an object of type T based on a key of some other type, while sets allow for the fast retrieval of the keys themselves.

All of the STL containers have three important characteristics:

1. Every container allocates and manages its own storage.

2. Every container provides a minimal set of operations (as member functions) to access and maintain its storage. The provided set of member functions includes

- *Constructors and destructors:* these functions allow users to construct and destroy instances of the container. Most containers have several kinds of constructors.

- *Element access* member functions: these allow users to access the container elements. In most instances, the element access member functions do not change the container.

- *Insertion* member functions: these are used to insert elements into the container.

- *Erase* member functions: these are used to delete elements from the container.

3. Each container has an `allocator` object associated with it. This `allocator` object encapsulates information about the memory model currently being used and allows the classes to be portable across various platforms.

The same naming convention is used for the member functions of all containers, resulting in a uniform interface to all the classes. Some differences exist between sequence and associative container interfaces, which we examine after taking a look at the common components.

19.1.2   Common Members of All Containers

The public members of STL containers fall into a two-level hierarchy. The first level defines members that are common to *all* containers, while the second level contains two categories:

- members common to sequence containers (vectors, lists, deques);

- members common to associative containers (sets, maps, multisets, and multimaps).

The common members of all STL containers fall into two distinct categories: *type definitions* and *member functions*. We take a look at each in turn.

Common Type Definitions in All Containers. The common type definitions found in each STL container are presented below. It is assumed that X is a container class containing objects of type T; a and b are values of X; u is an identifier; and r is a value of X&.

`X::value_type`

> Type of values the container holds.

`X::reference`

> Type that can be used for storing into `X::value_type` objects. This type is usually `X::value_type&`.

`X::const_reference`

> Type that can be used for storing into constant `X::value_type` objects. This type is usually `const X::value_type&`.

`X::iterator`

> An iterator type for traversing the elements in x. It is either a random access iterator type (for vector or deque) or a bidirectional iterator type (for other containers).

`X::const_iterator`

> A iterator type for traversing the elements a constant container X. It is either a constant random access iterator type (for vector or deque) or a constant bidirectional iterator type (for other containers).

`X::reverse_iterator`

> An iterator type for reverse direction traversal of X .

`X::const_reverse_iterator`

> A constant iterator type for reverse direction traversal of X .

`X::difference_type`

> The type that can represent the difference between any two X iterator objects (varies with the memory model).

`X::size_type`

> The type that can represent the size of X (varies with the memory model).

Common Member Functions in All Containers. The common member functions required to be in each STL container are outlined below. In the descriptions, it is assumed that

- x is a container class containing objects of type T,
- a and b are values of X,
- u is an identifier, and
- r is a value of X&.

All of these operations take constant time unless otherwise noted.

`X()`

> The default constructor.

`X(a)`

> Constructor. Takes linear time.

`X u(a)`

> Copy constructor. Takes linear time.

`(&a)->~X()`

> Destructor. The destructor is applied to every element of a, and all the memory is returned. Takes linear time.

`a.begin()`

> Returns an `iterator` (`const_iterator` for constant a) that can be used to begin traversing all locations in the container.

`a.end()`

> Returns an `iterator` (`const_iterator` for constant a), that can be used in a comparison for ending traversal through the container.

`a.rbegin()`

> Returns a `reverse_iterator` (`const_reverse_iterator` for constant a) that can be used to begin traversing through all locations of the container in the reverse of the normal order.

`a.rend()`

> Returns a `reverse_iterator` (`const_reverse_iterator` for constant a) that can be used in a comparison for ending a reverse direction traversal through all locations in the container.

`a == b`

> Equality operation on containers of the same type. Returns `true` when the sequences of elements in a and b are elementwise equal (using `X::value_type::operator==`). Takes linear time.

`a != b`

> The opposite of the equality operation. Takes linear time.

`a.size()`

> Returns the number of elements in the container.

`a.max_size()`

> `size()` of the largest possible container.

`a.empty()`

> Returns `true` if the container is empty (i.e., if `a.size() == 0`).

`a < b`

> Compares two containers *lexicographically*. Takes linear time.

`a > b`

> Returns `true` if `b < a`, as defined above. Takes linear time.

`a <= b`

> Returns `true` if `!(a > b)`. Takes linear time.

`a >= b`

> Returns `true` if `!(a < b)`. Takes linear time.

`r = a`

> The assignment operator for containers. Takes linear time.

`a.swap(b)`

> Swaps two containers of the same type in constant time.

19.1.3 Sequence Container Requirements

All STL sequence containers define two constructors, three insert member functions, and two erase member functions in addition to the common types and member functions mentioned in the previous section.

The additional members are defined below. In the definitions, it is assumed that

- X is a sequence class (e.g., a vector, list, or deque),

- i and j satisfy input iterator requirements and [i,j) is a valid range,

- n is a value of X::size_type,

- p is a valid iterator to a,

- q, q1, and q2 are valid dereferenceable iterators to a, and [q1, q2) is a valid range, and

- t is a value of X::value_type.

```
X(n, t)
X a(n, t)
```

Constructs a sequence with n copies of t.

```
X(i, j)
X a(i, j)
```

Constructs a sequence equal to the contents of the range [i, j).

```
a.insert(p, t)
```

Inserts a copy of t before p. Returns an iterator pointing to the inserted copy.

```
a.insert(p, n, t)
```

Inserts n copies of t before p.

```
a.insert(p, i, j)
```

Inserts copies of elements in [i, j) before p.

```
a.erase(q)
```

Erases the element pointed to by q.

```
a.erase(q1, q2)
```

Erases the elements in the range [q1, q2).

19.1.4 Sorted Associative Container Requirements

STL provides four basic kinds of sorted associative containers: set, multiset, map, and multimap.

Before taking a detailed look at the type definitions and member functions provided by the associative containers, we need to define a few terms and explain some of the ideas behind the design.

Basic Design and Organization. All associative containers are parameterized on a type `Key` and an ordering relation `Compare` that induces a strict weak ordering on elements of type `Key`. In addition, `map` and `multimap` associate elements of an arbitrary type `T` with `Key` elements. An object of type `Compare` is called the *comparison object* of the container.

Equality of Keys. For sorted associative containers, *equivalence* of keys means the equivalence relation imposed by the comparison, and *not* the `operator==` on keys. Thus, two keys `k1` and `k2` are considered equivalent according to the comparison object `comp` if and only if

```
comp(k1, k2) == false && comp(k2, k1) == false.
```

Additional Definitions. The `set` and `map` containers support *unique* keys; they can store at most one element of each equivalence class of keys. `multiset` and `multimap` containers support *equivalent* keys; i.e., they can store multiple elements that have the same key equivalence class.

For `set` and `multiset`, the value type is the same as the key type; i.e., the values stored in sets and multisets are basically the keys themselves. For `map` and `multimap`, the value type is `pair<const Key, T>`; i.e., the elements stored in maps and multimaps are pairs whose first elements are `const Key` values and whose second elements are `T` values.

Finally, an `iterator` of a sorted associative container is of the bidirectional iterator category. `insert` operations do not affect the validity of iterators and references to the container, and `erase` operations only invalidate iterators and references to the erased elements.

Listed below are the type definitions and member functions defined by sorted associative containers in addition to the common container members outlined previously.

In all the definitions, we assume that

- `X` is a sorted associative container class,

- `a` is a value of `X`,

- `a_uniq` is a value of `X` when `X` supports unique keys, and `a_eq` is a value of `X` when `X` supports equivalent keys,

- `i` and `j` satisfy input iterator requirements and refer to elements of `value_type`, and `[i, j)` is a valid range,

- p is a valid iterator to a,

- q, q1, and q2 are valid dereferenceable iterators to a, and [q1, q2) is a valid range,

- t is a value of X::value_type, and

- k is a value of X::key_type.

19.1.5   Sorted Associative Container Types and Member Functions

X::key_type

> The type of keys, Key, with which X is instantiated.

X::key_compare

> The comparison object type, Compare, with which X is instantiated.

X::value_compare

> A type for comparing objects of X::value_type. This is the same as key_compare for set and multiset, while for map and multimap it is a type that compares pairs of Key and T values by comparing their keys using X::key_compare.

All of the operations below take constant time unless otherwise noted.

```
X()
X a;
```

> Constructs an empty container, using Compare() as a comparison object.

```
X(c)
X a(c)
```

> Constructs an empty container, using c as a comparison object.

```
X(i, j, c)
X a(i, j, c)
```

> Constructs an empty container, using c as a comparison object, and inserts elements from the range [i, j) in it. Takes $N \log N$ time in general, where N is the distance from i to j; linear if [i, j) is sorted with value_comp().

```
X(i, j)
X a(i, j)
```

Same as above, but uses `Compare()` as a comparison object.

```
a.key_comp()
```

Returns the comparison object, of type `X::key_compare`, out of which a was constructed.

```
a.value_comp()
```

Returns an object of type `X::value_compare` constructed out of the comparison object.

```
a_uniq.insert(t)
```

Inserts `t` if and only if there is no element in the container with key equivalent to the key of `t`. Returns a `pair<iterator,bool>` whose `bool` component indicates whether the insertion was made and whose `iterator` component points to the element with key equivalent to the key of `t`. Takes time logarithmic in the size of the container.

```
a_eq.insert(p, t)
```

Inserts `t` into the container and returns the iterator pointing to the newly inserted element.

```
a.insert(p, t)
```

Inserts `t` if and only if there is no element with key equivalent to the key of `t` in containers that support *unique* keys (i.e., sets and maps). Always inserts `t` in containers that support equivalent keys (i.e., multisets and multimaps). Iterator `p` is a hint pointing to where the insert should start to search. Takes time logarithmic in the size of the container in general, but amortized constant if `t` is inserted right after `p`.

```
a.insert(i, j)
```

Inserts the elements from the range `[i, j)` into the container. Takes $N \log N$ time in general, where N is the distance from `i` to `j`. Linear if `[i, j)` is sorted according to `value_comp()`.

`a.erase(k)`

> Erases all elements in the container with key equal to k. Returns the number of erased elements.

`a.erase(q)`

> Erases the element to which q points.

`a.erase(q1, q2)`

> Erases all the elements in the range `[q1, q2)`. Takes $O(\log(\texttt{size}() + N))$ time, where N is the distance from q1 to q2.

`a.find(k)`

> Returns an iterator pointing to an element with key equivalent to k, or `a.end()` if such an element is not found.

`a.count(k)`

> Returns the number of elements with keys equivalent to k.

`a.lower_bound(k)`

> Returns an iterator pointing to the first element with key not less than k.

`a.upper_bound(k)`

> Returns an iterator pointing to the first element with key greater than k.

`a.equal_range(k)`

> Returns a pair of iterators (constant iterators if a is constant), the first equal to `a.lower_bound(k)` and the second equal to `a.upper_bound(k)`.

19.2 *Organization of the Container Class Descriptions*

The remaining sections of this chapter describe the specific requirements for the three sequence containers (vector, list, deque) and sorted associative containers (set, multiset, map, multimap). Each of these container class descriptions contains the following subsections:

19.2.1 Files

This section shows the header file to be included in programs that use the class.

19.2.2 Class Declaration

The class name and template parameters are shown.

19.2.3 Description

This section describes the basic functionality of the class. It serves as a short introduction to the particular container being described.

19.2.4 Type Definitions

Explains the type definitions in the public interface of the class.

19.2.5 Constructors, Destructors and Related Functions

Contains descriptions of constructors and destructors in the class. Some classes also have other related functions that deal with allocation and deallocation issues, and these are explained wherever required.

19.2.6 Element Access Member Functions

Explains the functionality of all member functions that are used to access elements in the container.

19.2.7 Insert Member Functions

Explains all member functions that are used to insert elements into the container.

19.2.8 Erase Member Functions

Details all member functions that are used to erase elements from the container.

19.2.9 Additional Notes Section(s)

This section or sections contain details such as implementation dependencies, time complexity discussions for insert and erase member functions, memory model dependencies, etc. Any important information that is not included in the other sections is included in the notes sections.

19.3 Vector

19.3.1 Files

```
#include <vector.h>
```

19.3.2 Class Declaration

```
template <class T, class Allocator = allocator>
class vector;
```

We omit any further mention of the `Allocator` parameter.

19.3.3 Description

Vectors are containers that arrange elements of a given type in a strictly linear arrangement, and allow fast random access to any element (i.e., any element can be accessed in constant time).

Vectors allow constant time insertions and deletions at the end of the sequence. Inserting and/or deleting elements in the middle of a vector requires linear time. Further details of the time complexity of vector insertion can be found in the notes section.

19.3.4 Type Definitions

```
iterator
const_iterator
```

> `iterator` is a random access iterator type referring to T, and `const_iterator` is a constant random access iterator type referring to const T. It is guaranteed that there is a constructor for `const_iterator` out of `iterator`.

```
reference
const_reference
```

> `reference` is the type of locations of elements of the container (usually `T&` but more generally it is determined by the allocator type); and `const_reference` is a corresponding constant reference type.

```
size_type
```

> `size_type` is an unsigned integral type that can represent the size of any vector instance.

difference_type

>   A signed integral type that can represent the difference between any two
>   pointers to vector::iterator objects.

value_type

>   The type of values the vector holds. This is simply T.

reverse_iterator
const_reverse_iterator

>   Non-constant and constant reverse random access iterators.

19.3.5 Vector Constructors, Destructors and Related Functions

vector()

>   The default constructor, which constructs a vector of size zero.

explicit vector(size_type n, const T& value = T())

>   Constructs a vector of size n and initial izes all its elements with value. If the
>   second argument is not supplied, value is obtained with the default con-
>   structor, T(), for the element value type T.

vector(const vector<T>& x)

>   The vector copy constructor, which constructs a vector and initializes it with
>   copies of the elements of vector x.

template <class InputIterator>
vector(InputIterator first, InputIterator last)

>   Constructs a vector of size last - first and initializes it with copies of ele-
>   ments in the range [first, last), which must be a valid range of elements
>   of type T.
>
>   *Instead of the above constructor, STL versions for compilers that do not currently
>   support templated member functions should include the following constructor:*

vector(const T* first, const T* last)

>   Constructs a vector of size last - first and initializes it with copies of ele-
>   ments in the range [first, last).

```
vector<T>& operator=(const vector<T>& x)
```

The vector assignment operator. Replaces the contents of the current vector with a copy of the parameter vector x.

```
void reserve(size_type n)
```

This member function is a directive that informs the vector of a planned change in size, so storage can be managed accordingly. It does not change the size of the vector, and it takes time at most linear in the size of the vector. Reallocation happens at this point if and only if the current capacity is less than the argument of reserve (capacity is a vector member function that returns the size of the allocated storage in the vector). After a call to reserve, the capacity is greater than or equal to the argument of reserve if reallocation happens, and equal to the previous capacity otherwise.

Reallocation invalidates all the references, pointers, and iterators referring to the elements in the vector. It is guaranteed that no reallocation takes place during the insertions that happen after reserve takes place till the time when the size of the vector reaches the size specified by reserve.

```
~vector()
```

The vector destructor. Returns all allocated storage back to the free store.

```
void swap(vector<T>& x)
```

Swaps the contents of the current vector with those of the input vector x. The current vector replaces x and vice versa.

19.3.6 Comparison Operations

```
template <class T>
bool operator==(const vector<T>& x, const vector<T>& y)
```

Equality operation on vectors. Returns true if the sequences of elements in x and y are element-wise equal (using T::operator==). Takes linear time.

```
template <class T>
bool operator<(const vector<T>& x, const vector<T>& y)
```

Returns true if x is lexicographically less than y, false otherwise. Takes linear time.

19.3.7 Vector Element Access Member Functions

```
iterator begin()
const_iterator begin() const
```

Returns an `iterator` (`const_iterator` for constant vector) that can be used to begin traversing through the vector.

```
iterator end()
const_iterator end() const
```

Returns an `iterator` (`const_iterator` for constant vectors) that can be used in a comparison for ending traversal through the vector.

```
reverse_iterator rbegin()
const_reverse_iterator rbegin()
```

Returns a `reverse_iterator` (`const_reverse_iterator` for constant vectors) that can be used to begin traversing the vector in the reverse of the normal order.

```
reverse_iterator rend()
const_reverse_iterator rend()
```

Returns a `reverse_iterator` (`const_reverse_iterator` for constant vectors) that can be used in a comparison for ending reverse-direction traversal through the vector.

```
size_type size() const
```

Returns the number of elements currently stored in the vector.

```
size_type max_size() const
```

Returns the maximum possible size of the vector.

```
size_type capacity() const
```

Returns the largest number of elements that the vector can store without reallocation. See also the `reserve` member function.

```
bool empty() const
```

Returns `true` if the vector contains no elements (i.e., if `begin() == end()`), `false` otherwise.

```
reference operator[](size_type n)
const_reference operator[](size_type n) const
```

Returns the nth element from the beginning of the vector in constant time.

```
reference front()
const_reference front() const
```

Returns the first element of the vector; i.e., the element referred to which the iterator `begin()` refers. Undefined if the vector is empty.

```
reference back()
const_reference back() const
```

Returns the last element of the vector; i.e., the element referred to which the iterator `end() - 1` refers. Undefined if the vector is empty.

19.3.8 Vector Insert Member Functions

The time complexities of all insert member functions are described in the Notes subsection at the end of this section.

```
void push_back(const T& x)
```

Adds the element x at the end of the vector.

```
iterator insert(iterator position, const T& x = T())
```

Inserts the element x at the position in the vector referred to by `position`. Elements already in the vector are moved as required. The iterator returned refers to the position where the element was inserted.

```
void insert(iterator position, size_type n, const T& x)
```

Inserts n copies of the element x starting at the location to which `position` refers.

```
template <class InputIterator>
void insert(iterator position, InputIterator first,
            InputIterator last)
```

Copies of elements in the range [`first, last`) are inserted into the vector at the location to which `position` refers. [`first, last`) must be a valid range of elements of type T.

Instead of the above member, STL versions for compilers that do not currently support templated member functions should include the following member:

```
void insert(iterator position, const T* first,
            const T* last)
```

Copies of elements in the range [first, last) are inserted into the vector at the location to which position refers.

19.3.9   Vector Erase Member Functions

```
void pop_back()
```

Erases the last element of the vector. Undefined is the vector is empty.

```
void erase(iterator position)
```

Erases the element of the vector to which position refers. Undefined if the vector is empty.

```
void erase(iterator first, iterator last)
```

The iterators first and last are assumed to point into the vector, and all elements in the range [first, last) are erased from the vector.

19.3.10 Notes on Vector Insert and Erase Member Functions

Inserting a single element into a vector is linear in the distance from the insertion point to the end of the vector. The amortized complexity of inserting a single element at the end of a vector is constant (see Section 1.4.2 for a discussion of amortized complexity).

Insertion of multiple elements into a vector with a single call of the insert member function is linear in the sum of the number of elements plus the distance to the end of the vector. This means that it is much faster to insert many elements into the middle of a vector at once than to do the insertions one at a time.

All insert member functions cause reallocation if the new size is greater than the old capacity. If no reallocation happens, all the iterators and references before the insertion point remain valid.

erase invalidates all iterators and references after the point of the erase. The destructor of T is called for each erased element and the assignment operator of T is called the number of times equal to the number of elements in the vector *after* the erased elements.

19.4 Deque

19.4.1 Files

```
#include <deque.h>
```

19.4.2 Class Declaration

```
template <class T, class Allocator = allocator>
class deque;
```

We omit any further mention of the `Allocator` parameter.

19.4.3 Description

This class provides sequences that can be efficiently expanded in both directions: they allow constant time insertion and deletion of objects at either end. Like vectors, deques allow fast random access to any element (constant time).

19.4.4 Type Definitions

Same as for vectors (see Section 19.3.4 on page 274).

19.4.5 Deque Constructors, Destructors and Related Functions

```
deque()
```

> The default constructor. Constructs a deque with size zero.

```
explicit deque(size_type n, const T& value = T())
```

> Constructs a deque of size `n` and initializes all its elements with `value`. The default for `value` is set to `T()`, where `T()` is the default constructor of the type with which the deque is instantiated.

```
deque(const deque<T>& x)
```

> The deque copy constructor. Constructs a deque and initializes it with copies of the elements of deque `x`.

```
template <class InputIterator>
deque(InputIterator first, InputIterator last)
```

> Constructs a deque of size last - first and initializes it with copies of elements in the range [first, last), whichmust be a valid range of elements of type T.

> *Instead of the above constructor, STL versions for compilers that do not currently support templated member functions should include the following constructor:*

```
deque(const T* first, const T* last)
```

> Constructs a deque of size last - first and initializes it with copies of elements in the range [first, last).

```
deque<T>& operator=(const deque<T>& x)
```

> The deque assignment operator. Replaces the contents of the current deque with a copy of the parameter deque x.

```
~deque()
```

> The deque destructor. Returns all allocated storage back to the free store.

```
void swap(deque<T>& x)
```

> Swaps the contents of the current deque with those of the input deque x. The current deque replaces x, and vice versa.

19.4.6 Comparison Operations

```
template <class T>
bool operator==(const deque<T>& x, const deque<T>& y)
```

> Equality operation on deques. Returns true if the sequences of elements in x and y are elementwise equal (using T::operator==). Takes linear time.

```
template <class T>
bool operator<(const deque<T>& x, const deque<T>& y)
```

> Returns true if x is lexicographically less thany, false otherwise. Takes linear time.

19.4.7 Deque Element Access Member Functions

```
iterator begin()
const_iterator begin() const
```

Returns an `iterator` (`const_iterator` for constant deque) that can be used to begin traversing through all locations in the deque.

```
iterator end()
const_iterator end() const
```

Returns an `iterator` (`const_iterator` for constant deque) that can be used in a comparison for ending traversal through the deque.

```
reverse_iterator rbegin()
const_reverse_iterator rbegin() const
```

Returns a `reverse_iterator` (`const_reverse_iterator` for constant deques) that can be used to begin traversing all locations in the deque in the reverse of the normal order.

```
reverse_iterator rend()
const_reverse_iterator rend()
```

Returns a `reverse_iterator` (`const_reverse_iterator` for constant deques) that can be used in a comparison for ending reverse direction traversal through all locations in the deque.

```
size_type size() const
```

Returns the number of elements in the deque.

```
size_type max_size() const
```

Returns the maximum possible size of the deque.

```
bool empty() const
```

Returns `true` if the deque contains no elements (i.e., if `begin()` == `end()`), `false` otherwise.

```
reference operator[](size_type n)
const_reference operator[](size_type n) const
```

Allows constant time access to the nth element of the deque. Undefined if the vector is empty.

```
reference front()
const_reference front() const
```

Returns the first element of the deque; i.e., the element to which the iterator `begin()` refers. Undefined if the vector is empty.

```
reference back()
const_reference back() const
```

Returns the last element of the deque; i.e., the element to which the iterator `end() - 1` refers. Undefined if the vector is empty.

19.4.8 Deque Insert Member Functions

```
void push_front(const T& x)
```

Adds the element x at the beginning of the deque.

```
void push_back(const T& x)
```

Adds the element x at the end of the deque.

```
iterator insert(iterator position, const T& x = T())
```

Inserts the element x at the location in the deque to which `position` refers. The iterator returned refers to the position that contains the inserted element.

```
void insert(iterator position, size_type n,
            const T& x)
```

Inserts n copies of the element x starting at the location to which `position` refers.

```
template <class InputIterator>
void insert(iterator position, InputIterator first,
            InputIterator last)
```

Copies of elements in the range [first, last) are inserted into the deque at the location to which position refers. [first, last) must be a valid range of elements of type T.

Instead of the above member, STL versions for compilers that do not currently support templated member functions should include the following member:

```
void insert(iterator position, const T* first,
            const T* last)
```

Copies of elements in the range [first, last) are inserted into the deque at the location to which position refers.

19.4.9 Deque Erase Member Functions

```
void pop_front()
```

Erases the first element of the deque. Undefined if the deque is empty.

```
void pop_back()
```

Erases the last element of the deque. Undefined if the deque is empty.

```
void erase(iterator position)
```

Erases the element of the deque pointed to by position.

```
void erase(iterator first, iterator last)
```

The iterators first and last are assumed to point into the deque, and all elements in the range [first, last) are erased from the deque.

19.4.10 Complexity of Deque Insertion

Deques are specially optimized for insertion of single elements at either the beginning or the end of the data structure. Such insertions always take constant time and cause a single call to the copy constructor of T, where T is the type of the inserted object.

If an element is inserted into the middle of the deque, then in the worst case the time taken is linear in the *minimum* of the distance from the insertion point to the beginning of the deque and the distance from the insertion point to the end of the deque.

The `insert`, `push_front`, and `push_back` member functions invalidate all the iterators and references to the deque.

19.4.11 Notes on Deque Erase Member Functions

The `erase`, `pop_front`, and `pop_back` member functions invalidate all the iterators and references to the deque. The number of calls to the destructor (of the erased type `T`) is the same as the number of elements erased, but the number of calls to the assignment operator of `T` is equal to the minimum of the number of elements before the erased elements and the number of elements after the erased elements.

19.5 List

19.5.1 Files

```
#include <list.h>
```

19.5.2 Class Declaration

```
template <class T, class Allocator = allocator>
class list;
```

We omit any further mention of the `Allocator` parameter.

19.5.3 Description

This class implements the sequence abstraction as a linked list. All lists are "doubly linked" and may be traversed in either direction.

Lists should be used in preference to other sequence abstractions when there are frequent insertions and deletions in the middle of sequences. As with all STL containers, storage management is handled automatically.

Unlike vectors or deques, lists are not random access data structures. For this reason, some STL generic algorithms such as `sort`, `random_shuffle`, and so forth, cannot operate on lists. The list class provides its own `sort` member function.

Besides `sort`, lists also include some other special member functions for splicing two lists, reversing lists, making all list elements unique, and merging two lists. All of these special member functions are discussed in Section 19.5.10.

19.5.4   Type Definitions

```
iterator
const_iterator
```

> `iterator` is a bidirectional iterator referring to `T`. `const_iterator` is a constant bidirectional iterator referring to `const T`. It is guaranteed that there is a constructor for `const_iterator` out of `iterator`.

```
reference
const_reference
```

> `reference` is the type of locations in the container (usually `T&`, but more generally it is determined by the allocator type); and `const_reference` is a corresponding constant reference type.

```
size_type
```

> An unsigned integral type that can represent the size of any list instance.

```
difference_type
```

> A signed integral type that can represent the difference between any two `list::iterator` objects.

```
value_type
```

> The type `T` of values the list holds.

```
reverse_iterator
const_reverse_iterator
```

> Nonconstant and constant reverse bidirectional iterator types.

19.5.5   List Constructors, Destructors, and Related Functions

```
list()
```

> The default constructor. Constructs an empty list.

```
explicit list(size_type n, const T& value = T())
```

> Constructs a list of size n and initializes all its elements with `value`.

```
list(const list<T>& x)
```

> The list copy constructor. Constructs a list and initializes it with copies of the elements of list x.

```
template <class InputIterator>
list(InputIterator first, InputIterator last)
```

> Constructs a list of size last - first and initializes it with copies of elements in the range [first, last), which must be a valid range of elements of type T.

> *Instead of the above constructor, STL versions for compilers that do not currently support templated member functions should include the following constructor:*

```
list(const T* first, const T* last)
```

> Constructs a list of size last - first and initializes it with copies of elements in the range [first, last).

```
list<T>& operator=(const list<T>& x)
```

> The list assignment operator. Replaces the contents of the current list with a copy of list x.

```
~list()
```

> The list destructor. Returns all allocated storage back to the free storage list.

```
void swap(list<T>& x)
```

> Swaps the contents of the current list with those of the input list x. The current list replaces x, and vice versa.

19.5.6 Comparison Operations

```
template <class T>
bool operator==(const list<T>& x, const list<T>& y)
```

> Equality operation on lists. Returns true if the sequences of elements in x and y are elementwise equal (using T::operator==). Takes linear time.

```
template <class T>
bool operator<(const list<T>& x, const list<T>& y)
```

> Returns `true` if x is lexicographically less than y, `false` otherwise. Takes linear time. See Section 20.31 on page 353 for the definition of lexicographical comparison.

19.5.7   List Element Access Member Functions

```
iterator begin()
const_iterator begin() const
```

> Returns an `iterator` (`const_iterator` for constant list) that can be used to begin traversing through the list.

```
iterator end()
const_iterator end() const
```

> Returns an `iterator` (`const_iterator` for constant list) that can be used in a comparison for ending traversal through the list.

```
reverse_iterator rbegin()
const_reverse_iterator rbegin() const
```

> Returns a `reverse_iterator` (`const_reverse_iterator` for constant lists) that can be used to begin traversing the list in the reverse of the normal order.

```
reverse_iterator rend()
const_reverse_iterator rend() const
```

> Returns a `reverse_iterator` (`const_reverse_iterator` for constant lists) that can be used in a comparison for ending reverse direction traversal through the list.

```
size_type size() const
```

> Returns the number of elements currently stored in the list.

```
size_type max_size() const
```

> Returns the maximum possible size of the list.

```
bool empty() const
```

Returns `true` if the list contains no elements (i.e., if `begin() == end()`), `false` otherwise.

```
reference front()
const_reference front() const
```

Returns the first element of the list; i.e., the element pointed to by the iterator `begin()`. Undefined if the list is empty.

```
reference back()
const_reference back() const
```

Returns the last element of the list; i.e., the element pointed to by the iterator `end() - 1`. Undefined if the list is empty.

19.5.8 List Insert Member Functions

```
void push_front(const T& x)
```

Inserts the element x at the beginning of the list.

```
void push_back(const T& x)
```

Inserts the element x at the end of the list.

```
iterator insert(iterator position, const T& x = T())
```

Inserts the element x at the position in the list to which `position` points. The iterator returned points to the position that contains the inserted element.

```
void insert(iterator position, size_type n,
            const T& x)
```

Inserts n copies of the element x starting at the position to which iterator `position` is pointing.

```
template <class InputIterator>
void insert(iterator position, InputIterator first,
            InputIterator last)
```

Copies of elements in the range `[first, last)` are inserted into the vector at the position to which `position` refers. `[first, last)` must be a valid range of elements of type T.

Instead of the above member, STL versions for compilers that do not currently support templated member functions should include the following member:

```
void insert(iterator position, const T* first,
            const T* last)
```

Copies of elements in the range [first, last) are inserted into the vector at the position to which position refers.

19.5.9   List Erase Member Functions

```
void pop_front()
```

Erases the first element of the list. Undefined if the list is empty.

```
void pop_back()
```

Erases the last element of the list. Undefined if the list is empty.

```
void erase(iterator position)
```

Erases the element of the list to which the iterator position points. Undefined if the list is empty

```
void erase(iterator first, iterator last)
```

The iterators first and last are assumed to point into the list, and all elements in the range [first, last) are erased from the list.

19.5.10 Special List Operations: splice, merge, reverse, sort

```
void splice(iterator position, list<T>& x)
```

Inserts the contents of list x before position and removes all elements from x. The operation takes constant time. Essentially, the contents of x are transferred into the current list.

```
void splice(iterator position, list<T>& x, iterator i)
```

Inserts the element pointed to by iterator i in list x before position and removes the element from x. It takes constant time. i is assumed to be a valid iterator in the list x.

```
void splice(iterator position, list<T>& x,
            iterator first, iterator last)
```

Inserts the elements in the range [first, last) in list x before position and removes the elements from list x. The operation takes time proportional to last - first, unless &x == this; in that case, constant time. The range [first, last) is assumed to be a valid range in x, and position must not be in [first, last).

```
void remove(const T& value)
```

Erases all elements in the list that are equal to value, using T::operator==. The relative order of other elements is not affected. The entire list is traversed exactly once.

```
template <class Predicate>
void remove_if(Predicate pred)
```

Erases all elements in the list such that satisfy pred; i.e., all x for which pred(x) returns true. The relative order of other elements is not affected. The entire list is traversed exactly once.

The above member function is not present in STL versions for compilers that do not currently support templated member functions.

```
void unique()
```

Erases all but the first element from every consecutive group of equal elements in the list. Exactly size() - 1 applications of T::operator== are done. This function is most useful when the list is sorted, so that all elements that are equal appear in consecutive positions. In that case, each element in the resulting list is unique.

```
template <class BinaryPredicate>
void unique(BinaryPredicate binary_pred)
```

Erases all but the first element from every consecutive group of elements in the list such that binary_pred returns true when applied to a pair of the elements. Exactly size() - 1 applications of binary_pred are done.

The above member function is not present in STL versions for compilers that do not currently support templated member functions.

```
void merge(list<T>& x)
```

This function merges the argument list x into the current list. It is assumed that both lists are sorted according to the operator< of type T. The merge is stable; i.e., for equivalent elements in the two lists, the elements from the current list always precede the elements from the argument list x. x is empty after the merge. At most size() + x.size() - 1 comparisons are done.

```
template <class Compare>
void merge(list<T>& x, Compare comp)
```

This function merges the argument list x into the current list. It is assumed that both lists are sorted according to the comparison object comp. The merge is stable; i.e., for equivalent elements in the two lists, the elements from the current list always precede the elements from the argument list x. x becomes empty after the merge. At most size() + x.size() - 1 comparisons are done.

The above member function is not present in STL versions for compilers that do not currently support templated member functions.

```
void reverse()
```

Reverses the order of the elements in the list. It takes linear time.

```
void sort()
```

Sorts the list according to the operator< of type T. The sort is stable; i.e., the relative order of equivalent elements is preserved. $O(N \log N)$ comparisons are done, where N is the size of the list.

```
template <class Compare>
void sort(Compare comp)
```

Sorts the list using the ordering determined by the comp function object. The sort is stable; i.e., the relative order of equivalent elements is preserved. $O(N \log N)$ comparisons are done, where N is the size of the list.

The above member function is not present in STL versions for compilers that do not currently support templated member functions.

19.5.11 Notes on List Insert Member Functions

List insert operations do not affect the validity of iterators and references to other elements of the list. Insertion of a single element of type T into a list takes constant time and makes only one call to the copy constructor of T. Insertion of multiple elements into a list is linear in the number of elements inserted, and the number of calls to the copy constructor of T is exactly equal to the number of elements inserted.

19.5.12 Notes on List Erase Member Functions

erase invalidates only the iterators and references to the erased elements. Erasing a single element of type T is a constant time operation, with a single call to the destructor of T. Erasing a range in a list takes time linear in the size of the range, and the number of calls to the destructor of type T is exactly equal to the size of the range.

19.6 Set

19.6.1 Files

```
#include <set.h>
```

19.6.2 Class Declaration

```
template <class Key, class Compare = less<Key>,
          class Allocator = allocator>
class set;
```

We omit any further mention of the Allocator parameter.

19.6.3 Description

A set<Key, Compare> stores unique elements of type Key and allows for the retrieval of the elements themselves. All elements in the set are ordered by the ordering relation Compare, which must induce a strict weak ordering on the elements. (See Section 20.23 on page 340.)

As with all STL containers, the set container only allocates storage and provides a minimal set of operations (such as insert, erase, find, count, etc.). The set class does not itself provide operations for union, intersection, difference, etc. These operations are handled by generic algorithms in STL. (See Section 20.28 on page 348.)

19.6.4   Type Definitions

`key_type`

> The type of the keys, `Key`, with which the set is instantiated.

`value_type`

> Same as `key_type`.

`reference`
`const_reference`

> `reference` is a constant reference type of locations in the container (usually `const Key&`, but more generally it is determined by the allocator type); and `const_reference` is the same type.

`key_compare`

> The comparison object type, `Compare`, with which the set is instantiated. This type is used to order the keys in the set.

`value_compare`

> This is the type of the ordering relation used to order the values stored in the set. It is the same as `key_compare`, since the type of a value stored in a set is the same as the type of the key.

`iterator`
`const_iterator`

> `iterator` is a constant bidirectional iterator referring to `const value_type`. `const_iterator` is the same type as `iterator`.

`size_type`

> `size_type` is an unsigned integral type that can represent the size of any set instance.

`difference_type`

> A signed integral type that can represent the difference between any two `set::iterator` objects.

```
reverse_iterator
const_reverse_iterator
```

These are the same constant reverse bidirectional iterator type.

19.6.5   Set Constructors, Destructors, and Related Functions

```
set(const Compare& comp = Compare())
```

The default constructor. Constructs an empty set and stores the comparison object `comp` for ordering the elements.

```
set(const set<Key, Compare>& x)
```

The set copy constructor. Constructs a set and initializes it with copies of the elements of set x.

```
template <class InputIterator>
set(InputIterator first, InputIterator last,
    const Compare& comp = Compare())
```

Constructs an empty set and inserts copies of elements in the range [`first`, `last`), which must be a valid range of elements of type `value_type`, i.e., `Key`. The comparison object `comp` is used to order the elements of the set.

Instead of the above constructor, STL versions for compilers that do not currently support templated member functions should include the following constructor:

```
set(const value_type* first, const value_type* last,
    const Compare& comp = Compare())
```

Constructs an empty set and initializes it with copies of elements in the range [`first`, `last`). The ordering relation `comp` is used to order the elements of the set.

```
set<Key, Compare>& operator=(const set<Key, Compare>& x)
```

The set assignment operator. Replaces the contents of the current set with a copy of set x.

```
void swap(set<Key, Compare>& x)
```

Swaps the contents of the current set with those of set x.

```
~set()
```

The set destructor. Returns all allocated storage back to the free store.

19.6.6   Comparison Operations

```
template <class Key, class T, class Compare>
bool operator==(const set<Key, T, Compare>& x,
                const set<Key, T, Compare>& y)
```

Equality operation on sets. Returns `true` if the sequences of elements in x and y are elementwise equal (using `T::operator==`). Takes linear time.

```
template <class Key, class T, class Compare>
bool operator<(const set<Key, T, Compare>& x,
               const set<Key, T, Compare>& y)
```

Returns `true` if x is lexicographically less than y, `false` otherwise. Takes linear time.

19.6.7   Set Element Access Member Functions

```
key_compare key_comp() const
```

This function returns the comparison object of the set.

```
value_compare value_comp() const
```

Returns an object of type `value_compare` constructed out of the comparison object. For sets, this is the same as the comparison object of the set.

```
iterator begin() const
```

Returns a constant iterator that can be used to begin traversing through all locations in the set.

```
iterator end() const
```

Returns a constant iterator that can be used in a comparison for ending traversal through the set.

```
reverse_iterator rbegin()
```

Returns a constant reverse iterator that can be used to begin traversing all locations in the set in the reverse of the normal order.

```
reverse_iterator rend()
```

Returns a constant reverse iterator that can be used in a comparison for ending reverse direction traversal through all locations in the set.

```
bool empty() const
```

Returns `true` if the set is empty, `false` otherwise.

```
size_type size() const
```

Returns the number of elements in the set.

```
size_type max_size() const
```

Returns the maximum possible size of the set. The maximum size is simply the total number of elements of type `Key` that can be represented in the memory model used.

19.6.8   Set Insert Member Functions

```
iterator insert(iterator position, const value_type& x)
```

Inserts the element x into the set if x is not already present in the set. The iterator `position` is a hint, indicating where the `insert` function should start to search. The search is necessary since sets are ordered containers. The insertion takes $O(\log N)$ time, where N is the number of elements in the set, but is amortized constant if x is inserted right after `position`.

```
pair<iterator, bool> insert(const value_type& x)
```

Inserts the element x into the set if x is not already present in the set. The returned value is a `pair`, whose `bool` component indicates whether the insertion has taken place, and whose `iterator` component points to the just inserted element in the set if the insertion takes place, otherwise to the element x already present. The insertion takes $O(\log N)$ time, where N is the number of elements in the set.

```
template <class InputIterator>
void insert(InputIterator first, InputIterator last)
```

Copies of elements in the range [`first`, `last`) are inserted into the set. [`first`, `last`) must be a valid range of elements of type `value_type`, i.e., `Key`. In general, the time taken for these insertions is $O(d \log(N + d))$, where N

is the size of the set and d is the distance from `first` to `last`. The time is linear if the range [`first`, `last`) is sorted according to the ordering relation `value_comp()`.

Instead of the above member function, STL versions for compilers that do not currently support templated member functions should include the following member:

```
void insert(const value_type* first,
            const value_type* last)
```

Copies of elements in the range [`first`, `last`) are inserted into the set.

19.6.9 Set Erase Member Functions

```
void erase(iterator position)
```

Erases the set element pointed to by `position`. The time taken is amortized constant.

```
size_type erase(const key_type& x)
```

Erases the set element equivalent to `x`, if present. Returns the number of erased elements, which is 1 if `x` is present in the set, and 0 otherwise. Takes $O(\log N)$ time, where N is the size of the set.

```
void erase(iterator first, iterator last)
```

The iterators `first` and `last` are assumed to point into the set, and all elements in the range [`first`, `last`) are erased from the set. The time taken is $O(d + \log N)$, where N is the size of the set and d is the distance from `first` to `last`.

19.6.10 Special Set Operations

```
iterator find(const key_type& x) const
```

Searches for the element `x` in the set. If `x` is found, the function returns the iterator pointing to it. Otherwise, `end()` is returned. Takes $O(\log N)$ time, where N is the size of the set.

```
size_type count(const key_type& x) const
```

Returns the number of elements in the set that are equal to `x`. If `x` is present in the set, this number is 1; otherwise, it is 0. Takes $O(\log N)$ time, where N is the size of of the set.

```
iterator lower_bound(const key_type& x) const
```

> Returns an iterator pointing to the first set element that is not less than x. If all elements in the multiset are less than x, then `end()` is returned. Since set elements are not repeated, the returned iterator points to x itself if x is present in the set. Takes $O(\log N)$ time, where N is the size of of the set.

```
iterator upper_bound(const key_type& x) const
```

> The `upper_bound` function returns an iterator to the first set element greater than x. If no element in the multiset is greater than x, then `end()` is returned. Takes $O(\log N)$ time, where N is the size of of the set.

```
pair<iterator,iterator> equal_range(const key_type& x) const
```

> This function returns the pair (`lower_bound(x)`, `upper_bound(x)`). Takes $O(\log N)$ time, where N is the size of of the set.

19.7 *Multiset*

19.7.1 Files

```
#include <multiset.h>
```

19.7.2 Class Declaration

```
template <class Key, class Compare = less<Key>,
          class Allocator = allocator>
class multiset;
```

We omit any further mention of the `Allocator` parameter.

19.7.3 Description

A multiset is an sorted associative container that can store multiple copies of the same key. As with sets, all elements in the multiset are ordered by the ordering relation `Compare`, which induces a strict weak ordering on the elements.

Multisets are necessary because we sometimes need to store elements, all of which are alike in most ways but which differ only in certain known characteristics. For example, a set of cars sorted by the make of the car would be a multiset, since there could be several cars in the set with the same manufacturer, but different in other aspects, such as engine capacity, price, and so on.

The interface of the multiset class is exactly the same as that of the set class. The only difference is that multisets possibly contain multiple values of the same key value. As a result, some of the member functions also have slightly different semantics.

19.7.4   Type Definitions

Same as for the `set` class. (See Section 19.6.4.)

19.7.5   Multiset Constructors, Destructors, and Related Functions

```
multiset(const Compare& comp = Compare())
```

The default constructor. Constructs an empty multiset and stores the comparison object `comp` for ordering the elements.

```
multiset(const multiset<Key, Compare>& x)
```

The multiset copy constructor. Constructs a multiset and initializes it with copies of the elements of multiset x.

```
template <class InputIterator>
multiset(InputIterator first, InputIterator last,
    const Compare& comp = Compare())
```

Constructs an empty multiset and inserts copies of elements in the range `[first, last)`, which must be a valid range of elements of type `value_type`, i.e., `Key`. The comparison object `comp` is used to order the elements of the multiset.

Instead of the above constructor, STL versions for compilers that do not currently support templated member functions should include the following constructor:

```
multiset(const value_type* first, const value_type* last,
    const Compare& comp = Compare())
```

Constructs an empty multiset and inserts copies of elements in the range `[first, last)`. The ordering relation `comp` is used to order the elements of the multiset.

```
multiset<Key, Compare>&
operator=(const multiset<Key, Compare>& x)
```

The multiset assignment operator. Replaces the contents of the current multiset with a copy of multiset x.

```
void swap(multiset<Key, Compare>& x)
```

Swaps the contents of the current multiset with those of multiset x.

```
~multiset()
```

The multiset destructor. Returns all allocated storage back to the free store.

19.7.6   Comparison Operations

```
template <class Key, class T, class Compare>
bool operator==(const multiset<Key, T, Compare>& x,
               const multiset<Key, T, Compare>& y)
```

Equality operation on multisets. Returns true if the sequences of elements in x and y are elementwise equal (using T::operator==). Takes linear time.

```
template <class Key, class T, class Compare>
bool operator<(const multiset<Key, T, Compare>& x,
              const multiset<Key, T, Compare>& y)
```

Returns true if x is lexicographically less than y, false otherwise. Takes linear time.

19.7.7   Multiset Element Access Member Functions

```
key_compare key_comp() const
```

This function returns the comparison object of the multiset.

```
value_compare value_comp() const
```

Same function as key_comp.

```
iterator begin() const
```

Returns a constant iterator that can be used to begin traversing through all locations in the multiset.

```
iterator end() const
```

Returns a constant iterator that can be used in a comparison for ending traversal through the multiset.

`reverse_iterator rbegin()`

Returns a constant reverse iterator that can be used to begin traversing all locations in the multiset in the reverse of the normal order.

`reverse_iterator rend()`

Returns a constant reverse iterator that can be used in a comparison for ending reverse direction traversal through all locations in the multiset.

`bool empty() const`

Returns `true` if the multiset is empty, `false` otherwise.

`size_type size() const`

Returns the number of elements in the multiset.

`size_type max_size() const`

Returns the maximum possible size of the multiset.

19.7.8 Multiset Insert Member Functions

`iterator insert(iterator position, const value_type& x)`

Inserts the element x into the multiset. The iterator `position` is a hint, indicating where the `insert` function should start to search. Returns an iterator pointing to the newly inserted element. Takes $O(\log N)$ time in general, where N is the number of elements in the multiset, but is amortized constant if x is inserted right after the iterator `position`.

`iterator insert(const value_type& x)`

Inserts the element x into the multiset and returns an iterator pointing to the newly inserted element. Takes $O(\log N)$ time, where N is the number of elements in the multiset.

```
template <class InputIterator>
void insert(InputIterator first, InputIterator last)
```

[first, last) must be a valid range of elements of type Key. Copies of elements in the range [first, last) are inserted into the multiset. In general, the time taken for these insertions is $O(d \log(N + d))$, where N is the size of the set and d is the distance from first to last. The time is linear if the range [first, last) is sorted according to the ordering relation value_comp().

Instead of the above member function, STL versions for compilers that do not currently support templated member functions should include the following member:

```
void insert(const value_type* first,
            const value_type* last)
```

Copies of elements in the range [first, last) are inserted into the multiset.

19.7.9   Multiset Erase Member Functions

```
void erase(iterator position)
```

Erases the multiset element pointedto by position. The time taken is amortized constant. Note that this function erases only a single element, possibly leaving other elements in the multiset with keys equivalent to *position. The time taken is amortized constant.

```
size_type erase(const key_type& x)
```

Erases all elements equivalent to x from the multiset. Returns the number of erased elements. In general, this function takes time proportional to $d \log(N + d)$, where N is the size of the set and d is the number of elements with key equivalent to x.

```
void erase(iterator first, iterator last)
```

The iterators first and last are assumed to point into the multiset, and all elements in the range [first, last) are erased from the multiset. Takes $O(d + \log N)$ time, where N is the size of the multiset and d is the distance from first to last.

19.7.10 Special Multiset Operations

```
iterator find(const key_type& x) const
```

Searches for the element x in the multiset. If x is found, the function returns an iterator pointing to it. Otherwise, end() is returned. Takes $O(\log N)$ time, where N is the size of the multiset.

```
size_type count(const key_type& x) const
```

Returns the number of elements in the multiset that are equivalent to x. Takes $O(\log N)$ time, where N is the size of the multiset.

```
iterator lower_bound(const key_type& x) const
```

Returns an iterator pointing to the first multiset element that is not less than x. If all elements in the multiset are less than x, then end() is returned. Takes $O(\log N)$ time, where N is the size of the multiset.

```
iterator upper_bound(const key_type& x) const
```

Returns an iterator to the first multiset element whose key is greater than x. If no element is greater than x, then end() is returned. Takes $O(\log N)$ time, where N is the size of the multiset.

```
pair<iterator,iterator> equal_range(const key_type& x) const
```

This function returns the pair (lower_bound(x), upper_bound(x)). Takes $O(\log N)$ time, where N is the size of of the set.

19.8 Map

19.8.1 Files

```
#include <map.h>
```

19.8.2 Class Declaration

```
template <class Key, class T, class Compare = less<Key>,
          class Allocator = allocator>
class map;
```

We omit any further mention of the Allocator parameter.

19.8.3   Description

A map is a sorted associative container that supports unique keys of a given type Key, and provides for fast retrieval of values of another type T based on the stored keys. As in all other STL sorted associative containers, the ordering relation Compare is used to order the elements of the map.

Elements are stored in maps as pairs in which each Key has an associated value of type T. Since maps store only unique keys, each map contains at most one Key, T pair for each Key value. It is not possible to associate more than one value with a single key.

19.8.4   Type Definitions

key_type

The type Key of the keys in the map.

value_type

The type of the values stored in the map, pair<const Key, T>. The first member of this pair is declared const so that it is not possible to change the key using a nonconstant iterator or reference (it is possible to change the second member, the associated value of type T).

key_compare

This is the comparison object type, Compare, with which the map is instantiated. It is used to order keys in the map.

value_compare

A type of comparison objects for comparing objects of map::value_type (i.e., objects of type pair<const Key, T>), by comparing their keys using map::key_compare.

iterator
const_iterator

iterator is a bidirectional iterator referring to value_type. const_iterator is a constant bidirectional iterator referring to const value_type. It is guaranteed that there is a constructor for const_iterator out of iterator.

```
reference
const_reference
```

reference is the type of locations of values stored in the map (usually pair<const Key&, T>&, but more generally it is determined by the allocator type) that can be used for storing into map::value_type objects. const_reference is the corresponding constant reference type.

```
size_type
```

size_type is an unsigned integral type that can represent the size of any map instance.

```
difference_type
```

A signed integral type that can represent the difference between any two map::iterator objects.

```
reverse_iterator
const_reverse_iterator
```

Constant and nonconstant reverse bidirectional iterator types.

19.8.5 Map Constructors, Destructors, and Related Functions

```
explicit map(const Compare& comp = Compare())
```

The default constructor. Constructs an empty map and stores the comparison object comp for ordering the elements.

```
map(const map<Key, T, Compare>& x)
```

The map copy constructor. Constructs a map and initializes it with copies of the elements of map x.

```
template <class InputIterator>
map(InputIterator first, InputIterator last,
    const Compare& comp = Compare())
```

Constructs an empty map and inserts copies of elements in the range [first, last). The comparison object comp is used to order the elements of the map.

Instead of the above constuctor, STL versions for compilers that do not currently support templated member functions should include the following constructor:

```
map(const value_type* first, const value_type* last,
    const Compare& comp = Compare())
```

Constructs an empty map and initializes it with copies of elements in the range [first, last]. The comparison object comp is used to order the elements of the map.

```
map<Key, T, Compare>& operator=(const map<Key, Compare>& x)
```

The map assignment operator. Replaces the contents of the current map with a copy of map x.

```
void swap(map<Key, T, Compare>& x)
```

Swaps the contents of the current map with those of the map x The current map replaces x, and vice versa.

```
~map()
```

The map destructor. Returns all allocated storage back to the free store.

19.8.6 Comparison Operations

```
template <class Key, class T, class Compare>
bool operator==(const map<Key, T, Compare>& x,
                const map<Key, T, Compare>& y)
```

Equality operation on maps. Returns true if the sequences of elements in x and y are elementwise equal (using T::operator==). Takes linear time..

```
template <class Key, class T, class Compare>
bool operator<(const map<Key, T, Compare>& x,
               const map<Key, T, Compare>& y)
```

Returns true if x is lexicographically less than y, false otherwise . Takes linear time.

19.8.7 Map Element Access Member Functions

```
key_compare key_comp() const
```

Returns the comparison object of the map.

```
value_compare value_comp() const
```

Returns an object of type `value_compare` constructed out of the comparison object. The returned object compares pairs in the map by comparing their keys using `key_comp()`.

```
iterator begin()
const_iterator begin() const
```

Returns an `iterator` (`const_iterator` for a constant map) that can be used to begin traversing through all locations in the map.

```
iterator end()
const_iterator end() const
```

Returns an `iterator` (`const_iterator` for a constant map) that can be used in a comparison for ending traversal through the map.

```
reverse_iterator rbegin()
const_reverse_iterator rbegin() const
```

Returns a `reverse_iterator` (`const_reverse_iterator` for constant maps) that can be used to begin traversing all locations in the map in the reverse of the normal order.

```
reverse_iterator rend()
const_reverse_iterator rend() const
```

Returns a `reverse_iterator` (`const_reverse_iterator` for constant maps) that can be used in a comparison for ending reverse direction traversal through all locations in the map.

```
bool empty() const
```

Returns `true` if the map is empty, `false` otherwise.

```
size_type size() const
```

Returns the number of elements in the map.

```
size_type max_size() const
```

Returns the maximum possible size of the map.

```
T& operator[](const key_type& x)
const T& operator[](const key_type& x) const
```

Returns a reference to the type T value associated with the key x. In the case of a constant map, a constant reference to it is returned. The map-subscripting operator is different from the subscripting operator of vectors and deques in that if the map contains no element of type T associated with key x, then the pair (x, T()) is inserted into the map.

19.8.8   Map Insert Member Functions

```
iterator insert(iterator position, const value_type& x)
```

Inserts the value x into the map if no element already present in the map has an equivalent key. The iterator position is a hint, indicating where to start to search. This insertion takes $O(\log N)$ time in general, where N is the number of elements in the set, but takes amortized constant time if x is inserted right after the iterator position.

```
pair<iterator, bool> insert(const value_type& x)
```

Inserts the value x into the map if no element already present in the map has an equivalent key. The returned value is a pair, whose bool component indicates whether the insertion has taken place, and whose iterator component points to the just inserted value in the map if the insertion takes place, otherwise to the value x already present. Note that the type of x is pair<const Key, T>, not Key. The function takes $O(\log N)$ time, where N is the number of elements in the set.

```
template <class InputIterator>
void insert(InputIterator first, InputIterator last)
```

Copies of elements in the range [first, last) are inserted into the map. [first, last) must be a valid range of elements of type value_type, i.e., pair<Key, T>. In general, the time taken for these insertions is $O(d \log(N + d))$, where N is the size of the map and d is the distance from first to last. The time is linear if the range [first, last) is sorted according to the ordering relation value_comp().

Instead of the above member function, STL versions for compilers that do not currently support templated member functions should include the following member:

```
void insert(const value_type* first,
            const value_type* last)
```

Copies of elements in the range [first, last) are inserted into the map.

19.8.9   Map Erase Member Functions

```
void erase(iterator position)
```

Erases the map element pointed to by the iterator position. The time taken is amortized constant.

```
size_type erase(const key_type& x)
```

Erases the map element with key equivalent to x, if present. Returns the number of erased elements, which is 1 if there is an element with key equivalent to x, and 0 otherwise. Takes $O(\log N)$ time, where N is the size of the map.

```
void erase(iterator first, iterator last)
```

The iterators first and last are assumed to point into the map, and all elements in the range [first, last) are erased from the map. The time taken is $O(d + \log N)$, where N is the size of the map and d is the distance from first to last.

19.8.10 Special Map Operations

```
iterator find(const key_type& x)
const_iterator find(const key_type& x) const
```

Searches the map for an element with key equivalent to x. If such an element is found, the function returns the iterator (const_iterator for constant maps) pointing to it. Otherwise, end() is returned. Takes $O(\log N)$ time, where N is the size of the map.

```
size_type count(const key_type& x) const
```

Returns the number of elements in the map with key equivalent to x. This number is 1 or 0.

```
iterator lower_bound(const key_type& x)
const_iterator lower_bound(const key_type& x) const
```

>   Returns an iterator (const_iterator for constant maps) pointing to the
>   first map element whose key is not less than x. If the map contains an element
>   with key not less than x, then the returned iterator points to this element. If
>   the keys of all elements in the map are less than x, end() is returned. Takes
> $O(\log N)$ time, where N is the size of the map.

```
iterator upper_bound(const key_type& x)
const_iterator upper_bound(const key_type& x) const
```

>   Returns an iterator (const_iterator for constant maps) to the first map
>   element whose key is greater than x. If no element has a key greater than x,
>   end() is returned. Takes $O(\log N)$ time, where N is the size of the map.

```
pair<iterator, iterator> equal_range(const key_type& x)
pair<const_iterator, const_iterator>
        equal_range(const key_type& x) const
```

>   Returns the pair (lower_bound(x), upper_bound(x)). Takes $O(\log N)$
>   time, where N is the size of the map.

19.9 *Multimap*

19.9.1 Files

```
#include <multimap.h>
```

19.9.2 Class Declaration

```
template <class Key, class T, class Compare = less<Key>,
        class Allocator = allocator>
class multimap;
```

We omit any further mention of the Allocator parameter.

19.9.3 Description

A multimap is an associative container that stores multiple equivalent keys of a
given type Key and allows efficient retrieval of values of another type T based on
the stored Key. As in all other STL associative containers, the ordering relation
Compare is used to order the elements of the map. Elements are stored in multimaps as pairs in which each Key has an associated value of type T.

19.9.4   Type Definitions

Same as for the map class. (See Section 19.8.4.)

19.9.5   Multimap Constructors, Destructors and Related Functions

```
explicit multimap(const Compare& comp = Compare())
```

The default constructor. Constructs an empty multimap and stores the comparison object comp for ordering the elements.

```
multimap(const multimap<Key, T, Compare>& x)
```

The multimap copy constructor. Constructs a multimap and initializes it with copiesof the elements of multimap x.

```
template <class InputIterator>
multimap(InputIterator first, InputIterator last,
         const Compare& comp = Compare())
```

Constructs an empty multimap and inserts copies of elements in the range [first, last). The comparison object comp is used to order the elements of the multimap.

Instead of the above constructor, STL versions for compilers that do not currently support templated member functions should include the following constructor:

```
multimap(const value_type* first, const value_type* last,
         const Compare& comp = Compare())
```

Constructs an empty multimap and initializes it with copies of elements in the range [first, last). The comparison object comp is used to order the elements of the multimap.

```
multimap<Key, T, Compare>&
  operator=(const multimap<Key, Compare>& x)
```

The multimap assignment operator. Replaces the contents of the current multimap with a copy of multimap x.

```
void swap(multimap<Key, T, Compare>& x)
```

Swaps the contents of the current multimap with those of the multimap x. The current multimap replaces x, and vice versa.

```
~multimap()
```

The multimap destructor. Returns all allocated storage back to the free store.

19.9.6 Comparison Operations

```
template <class Key, class T, class Compare>
bool operator==(const multimap<Key, T, Compare>& x,
                const multimap<Key, T, Compare>& y)
```

Equality operation on multimaps. Returns `true` if the sequences of elements in x and y are elementwise equal (using `T::operator==`). Takes linear time.

```
template <class Key, class T, class T, Compare>
bool operator<(const multimap<Key, T, Compare>& x,
               const multimap<Key, T, Compare>& y)
```

Returns `true` if x is lexicographically less than y, `false` otherwise. Takes linear time.

19.9.7 Multimap Element Access Member Functions

```
key_compare key_comp() const
```

Returns the comparison object of the multimap.

```
value_compare value_comp() const
```

Returns an object of type `value_compare` constructed out of the comparison object. The returned object compares pairs in the multimap by comparing their keys using `key_comp()`.

```
iterator begin()
const_iterator begin() const
```

Returns an `iterator` (`const_iterator` for a constant multimap) that can be used to begin traversing through all locations in the multimap.

```
iterator end()
const_iterator end() const
```

Returns an `iterator` (`const_iterator` for a constant multimap) that can be used in a comparison for ending traversal through the multimap.

```
reverse_iterator rbegin()
const_reverse_iterator rbegin() const
```

Returns a `reverse_iterator` (`const_reverse_iterator` for constant multimaps) that can be used to begin traversing all locations in the multimap in the reverse of the normal order.

```
reverse_iterator rend()
const_reverse_iterator rend() const
```

Returns a `reverse_iterator` (`const_reverse_iterator` for constant multimaps) that can be used in a comparison for ending reverse direction traversal through all locations in the multimap.

```
bool empty() const
```

Returns `true` if the multimap is empty, `false` otherwise.

```
size_type size() const
```

Returns the number of elements in the multimap.

```
size_type max_size() const
```

Returns the maximum possible size of the multimap.

19.9.8   Multimap Insert Member Functions

```
iterator insert(iterator position, const value_type& x)
```

Inserts the value `x` into the multimap. Note that the type of `x` is `pair<const Key, T>`. The iterator `position` is a hint, indicating where the `insert` function should start to search to do the insert. The insertion takes $O(\log N)$ time in general, where N is the number of elements in the multimap, but is amortized constant if `x` is inserted right after the iterator `position`.

```
iterator insert(const value_type& x)
```

Inserts the value `x` into the multimap and returns the iterator pointing to the newly inserted value. Note that the type of `x` is `pair<const Key, T>`. The insertion takes $O(\log N)$ time, where N is the number of elements in the multimap.

```
template <class InputIterator>
void insert(InputIterator first, InputIterator last)
```

Copies of elements in the range [first, last) are inserted into the multi-map. [first, last) must be a valid range of elements of type value_type, i.e., pair<Key, T>. In general, the time taken for these insertions is $O(d \log(N + d))$, where N is the size of the multimap and d is the distance from first to last. The time is linear if the range [first, last) is sorted according to the ordering relation value_comp().

Instead of the above member function, STL versions for compilers that do not currently support templated member functions should include the following member:

```
void insert(const value_type* first, const value_type* last)
```

Copies of elements in the range [first, last) are inserted into the multi-map.

19.9.9 Multimap Erase Member Functions

```
void erase(iterator position)
```

Erases the multimap element pointed to by the iterator position. The time taken is amortized constant.

```
size_type erase(const key_type& x)
```

Erases all multimap elements with key equivalent to x. Returns the number of erased elements. In general, this function takes time proportional to $d \log(N + d)$, where N is the size of the set and d is the number of elements with key equivalent to x.

```
void erase(iterator first, iterator last)
```

The iterators first and last are assumed to point into the multimap, and all elements in the range [first, last) are erased from the multimap. Takes $O(d + \log N)$ time, where N is the size of the multiset and d is the distance from first to last.

19.9.10 Special Multimap Operations

```
iterator find(const key_type& x)
const_iterator find(const key_type& x) const
```

Searches the multimap for an element with key equivalent to x. If such an element is found, the function returns the `iterator` (`const_iterator` for constant multimaps) pointing to it. Otherwise `end()` is returned. Takes $O(\log N)$ time, where N is the size of the multimap.

```
size_type count(const key_type& x) const
```

Returns the number of elements in the multimap with key equivalent to x.

```
iterator lower_bound(const key_type& x)
const_iterator lower_bound(const key_type& x) const
```

Returns an `iterator` (`const_iterator` for constant multimaps) pointing to the first multimap element whose key is not less than x. If the multimap contains an element with key not less than x, then the returned iterator points to this element. If the keys of all elements in the multimap are less than x, `end()` is returned. Takes $O(\log N)$ time, where N is the size of the multimap.

```
iterator upper_bound(const key_type& x)
const_iterator upper_bound(const key_type& x) const
```

Returns an `iterator` (`const_iterator` for constant multimaps) to the first multimap element whose key is greater than x. If no element has a key greater than x, `end()` is returned. Takes $O(\log N)$ time, where N is the size of the multimap.

```
pair<iterator, iterator> equal_range(const key_type& x)
pair<const_iterator, const_iterator>
      equal_range(const key_type& x) const
```

Returns the pair (`lower_bound(x)`, `upper_bound(x)`). Takes $O(\log N)$ time, where N is the size of the multimap.

19.10 Stack Container Adaptor

19.10.1 Files

```
#include <stack.h>
```

19.10.2 Class Declaration

```
template <class Container> class stack;
```

19.10.3 Description

A stack is a data structure that allows the following operations: *inserting* at one end, *deleting* from the same end, *retrieving* the value at the same end, and testing for *emptiness*. Thus, stacks provide a "last-in, first-out" service. The element deleted or retrieved is always the last one inserted.

STL provides a `stack` container adapter, which can be used to implement a stack with any container that supports the following operations on sequences: `back`, `push_back`, and `pop_back`. In particular, vectors, lists, and deques can be used to implement stacks; for example,

- `stack<vector<char> >` is a stack of characters with an underlying vector implementation;

- `stack<list<int> >` is a stack of integers with an underlying list implementation;

- `stack<deque<float> >` is a stack of floats with an underlying deque implementation.

The difference between `stack` and these sequence abstractions is that `stack` has a much more restricted interface, one that disallows any operations on its objects other than the usual stack operations.

19.10.4 Public Member Functions

```
bool empty() const
```

Returns `true` if the stack is empty, `false` otherwise.

```
size_type size() const
```

Returns the number of elements in the stack.

```
void push(const value_type& x)
```

Inserts the value x at the top of the stack.

```
void pop()
```

Removes the element at the top of the stack. Undefined if the stack is empty.

```
value_type& top()
const value_type& top() const
```

Returns the element most recently pushed on the stack. The stack remains unchanged.

19.10.5 Comparison Operations

```
template <class Container>
bool operator==(const stack<Container>& x,
                const stack<Container>& y)
```

Equality operation on stacks. Returns `true` if the sequences of elements in x and y are elementwise equal (using `T::operator==`). Takes linear time.

```
template <class Container>
bool operator<(const stack<Container>& x,
               const stack<Container>& y)
```

Returns `true` if x is lexicographically less than y, `false` otherwise. Takes linear time.

19.11 *Queue Container Adaptor*

19.11.1 Files

```
#include <stack.h>
```

19.11.2 Class Declaration

```
template <class Container> class queue;
```

19.11.3 Description

A queue is a data structure in which elements are inserted at one end and removed from the opposite end. The order of removal is the same as the order of insertion (first-in, first-out).

STL provides a `queue` container adapter, which can be used to implement a queue with any sequence container that supports the following operations: `empty`, `size`, `front`, `back`, `push_back`, and `pop_front`. In particular, lists and deques can be used to implement queues; for example:

- `queue<list<int> >` is a queue of integers with an underlying list implementation;

- `queue<deque<float> >` is a queue of floats with an underlying deque implementation.

Note that vectors cannot be used with the `queue` adaptor, since they do not provide a `pop_front` function. This function is not provided for vectors because it would be inefficient for long vectors.

19.11.4 Public Member Functions

`bool empty() const`

> Returns `true` if the queue is empty, `false` otherwise.

`size_type size() const`

> Returns the number of elements in the queue.

`void push(const value_type& x)`

> Inserts the element x at the end of the queue.

`void pop()`

> Removes the element at the front of the queue.

`value_type& front()`
`const value_type& front() const`

> Returns the element at the front of the queue. The queue remains unchanged.

`value_type& back()`
`const value_type& back() const`

> Returns the element at the end of the queue. This is the element that was last inserted into the queue. The queue remains unchanged.

19.11.5 Comparison Operations

```
template <class Container>
bool operator==(const queue<Container>& x,
                const queue<container>& y)
```

> Equality operation on queues. Returns `true` if the sequences of elements in x and y are elementwise equal (using `T::operator==`). Takes linear time.

```
template <class Container>
bool operator<(const queue<Container>& x,
               const queue<Container>& y)
```

Returns true if x is lexicographically less than y, false otherwise. Takes linear time.

19.12 Priority Queue Container Adaptor

19.12.1 Files

```
#include <stack.h>
```

19.12.2 Class Declaration

```
template <class Container>
class priority_queue;
```

19.12.3 Description

A priority queue is a container in which the element immediately available for retrieval is the largest of those in the container, for some particular way of ordering the elements.

STL provides a priority_queue container adapter, which can be used to implement a priority_queue with any container that supports the following operations: empty, size, front, push_back, and pop_back. In particular, vectors and deques can be used with the priority_queue adaptor.

Note that since a priority_queue involves an ordering on it elements, a comparison function object comp needs to be supplied. For example:

- priority_queue<vector<int>, less<int> > is a priority queue of integers with a vector implementation, using the built-in < operation for integers to compare the objects.

- priority_queue<deque<float>, greater<float> > is a priority queue of floats with a deque implementation, using the > operation on floats for comparisons. Note that since > is used instead of <, the element available for retrieval at any time is actually the *smallest* element rather than the largest.

19.12.4 Constructors

```
explicit priority_queue(const Compare& comp = Compare())
```

Constructs an empty priority queue and stores the comparison function object comp for ordering the elements.

```
template <class InputIterator>
priority_queue(InputIterator first, InputIterator last,
    const Compare& comp = Compare())
```

Constructs an empty priority queue and inserts copies of elements in the range [first, last). The comparison object comp is used to order the elements of the priority queue.

Instead of the above constructor, STL versions for compilers that do not currently support templated member functions should include the following constructor:

```
priority_queue(const value_type* first,
               const value_type* last,
               const Compare& comp = Compare())
```

Constructs a priority queue whose elements are copies of elements in the range [first, last), using comp to order the elements.

19.12.5 Public Member Functions

```
bool empty() const
```

Returns true if the priority queue is empty, false otherwise.

```
size_type size() const
```

Returns the number of elements in the priority queue.

```
value_type& top()
const value_type& top() const
```

Returns the element with the highest priority from the priority queue. The priority queue remains unchanged.

```
void push(const value_type& x)
```

Inserts the element x in the priority queue.

```
void pop()
```

Removes the element with the highest priority from the priority queue.

19.12.6 Comparison Operations

Equality and less-than operations are not provided for priority queues.

CHAPTER 20

Generic Algorithm
Reference Guide

The STL generic algorithms can be divided into four main categories:

1. nonmutating sequence algorithms;

2. mutating sequence operations;

3. sorting-related operations;

4. generalized numeric algorithms.

All of the library algorithms are *generic*, in the sense that they can operate on a variety of containers. The algorithms are not directly parameterized in terms of containers. Instead, they are parameterized by *iterator types*. This allows the algorithms to work with user-defined data structures, as long as these containers have iterator types satisfying the assumptions on the algorithms. The semantic descriptions of the algorithms are thus written in terms of iterator types and iterator objects.

The header file for all of the STL generic algorithms is `<algo.h>`.

20.1 *Organization of the Algorithm Descriptions*

Within the main categories, we divide the algorithm descriptions into sections, grouping together in each section all algorithms with similar purpose and semantics. Each of these algorithm sections is divided into three parts: **Prototypes**, **Description**, and **Time Complexity**.

20.1.1 Prototypes

This part shows the function prototypes for all algorithms described in the section. In most sections there are several algorithms with the same name, distinguished by their parameter types (function overloading). The most frequent case of this overloading is functions that have predicate versions. These take a function object that returns a `bool` value, and they use that predicate in place of an operator, such as `==` or `<`.

In a few cases there are two functions that have the same basic purpose (such as `find` and its predicate version `find_if` in Section 20.4, or `fill` and `fill_n` in Section 20.15) and thus might have been given the same name. The name difference is necessary since they could not be distinguished by their parameter types. See also Chapter 5, especially Section 5.1, for further discussion of algorithm names.

One of the most crucial parts of the specification of STL generic algorithms is the requirements on its iterator parameters. This information is given here implicitly, and usually without discussion in the **Description** section, by the naming convention used for template parameters that are supposed to be iterator types. The names used (InputIterator, OutputIterator, ForwardIterator, BidirectionalIterator, and RandomAccessIterator) correspond to the classification of iterator types into five categories. See also Chapter 4, especially Section 4.6.

20.1.2 Description

Under this heading we describe the semantics of each algorithm in the group, always in terms of the parameter names and types used in the **Prototypes**. Our description includes the effect (if any) of the algorithm on its parameters, and the return value (if any).

Almost all STL generic algorithms take at least two iterator parameters that define a *range* of elements in some container (some take two more defining another range, or one more defining the beginning of another range). For definition and discussion of the range concept and notation, see Chapter 4, page 49, and Chapter 18, page 246.

Some of the predicate versions of algorithms need the predicate function objects passed to them to have certain semantic properties. In particular, all of the sorting-related algorithms assume that the comparison function objects passed to them define *strict weak orderings*. This term is defined in the overview section for that category, Section 20.23 on page 340; see also Section 5.4.

No examples are given in this chapter, but Chapter 5 has examples of most of the STL generic algorithms. Consult the Index also for pointers to examples in other chapters.

20.1.3 Time Complexity

In this part bounds on the computing time for each algorithm are given. The terminology and notation (big-Oh notation) used in these descriptions are discussed in Chapter 1, Section 4. In many cases more precise bounds are given on the number of applications of operators or function objects used by the algorithm.

20.2 Nonmutating Sequence Algorithm Overview

Nonmutating sequence algorithms are those that do not directly modify the containers on which they operate. There are seven subcategories of algorithms in this category:

- `for_each` applies a given function to each element;

- `find` does a linear search;

- `adjacent_find` does a linear search for adjacent equal elements;

- `count` computes the number of occurrences of a given value;

- `mismatch` scans two sequences to find the first position where they disagree;

- `equal` scans two sequences checking for elementwise equality;

- `search` scans a sequence for a match with another sequence.

Each of these algorithms, except `for_each`, has two versions: one that uses `==` for comparisons, and a predicate version, which uses a predicate function object for comparisons. There are no semantic requirements on the predicate objects, although if they do not define an equality relation, the use of the word "equality" in the stating the results of the algorithms should be reinterpreted in light of this fact. For example, the description of `adjacent_find` in Section 20.5 uses the term "consecutive duplicate" and describes it as "an element equal to the element immediately following it in the range." With the predicate version, "consecutive duplicate" should be interpreted as "consecutive elements x and y such that `binary_pred(x, y) == true`." This formulation is meaningful even if `binary_pred` does not define an equality relation.

20.3 For Each

20.3.1 Prototype

```
template <class InputIterator, class Function>
Function for_each(InputIterator first,
                  InputIterator last, Function f);
```

20.3.2 Description

The `for_each` algorithm applies the function `f` to each element in the range `[first, last)`.

The function `f` is applied to the result of dereferencing every iterator in the range `[first, last)`. It is assumed that `f` does not apply any nonconstant function through the dereferenced iterator. `f` is applied exactly `last - first` times. If `f` returns a result, the result is ignored.

20.3.3 Time Complexity

Linear. If N is the size of `[first, last)`, then exactly N applications of `f` are made.

20.4 Find

20.4.1 Prototypes

```
template <class InputIterator, class T>
InputIterator find(InputIterator first,
                   InputIterator last, const T& value);

template <class InputIterator, class Predicate>
InputIterator find_if(InputIterator first,
                      InputIterator last, Predicate pred);
```

20.4.2 Description

The first version of the algorithm traverses the range `[first, last)` and returns the first iterator `i` such that `*i == value`. The second version returns the first iterator `i` such that `pred(*i) == true`. In either case, if such an iterator is not found, then the iterator `last` is returned.

20.4.3 Time Complexity

Linear. The number of applications of `!=` (or pred, for `find_if`) is the size of the range `[first, last)`.

20.5 Adjacent Find

20.5.1 Prototypes

```
template <class ForwardIterator>
ForwardIterator adjacent_find(ForwardIterator first,
```

```
                            ForwardIterator last);

template <class ForwardIterator, class BinaryPredicate>
ForwardIterator adjacent_find(ForwardIterator first,
                              ForwardIterator last,
                              BinaryPredicate binary_pred);
```

20.5.2   Description

The `adjacent_find` algorithm returns an iterator i referring to the first consecutive duplicate element in the range [first, last), or last if there is no such element. A consecutive duplicate is an element equal to the element immediately following it in the range.

Comparisons are done using == in the first version of the algorithm and a function object `binary_pred` in the second version.

20.5.3   Time Complexity

Linear. The number of comparisons done is the size of the range [first, i).

20.6   *Count*

20.6.1   Prototypes

```
template <class InputIterator, class T, class Size>
void count(InputIterator first, InputIterator last,
           const T& value, Size& n);

template <class InputIterator, class Predicate, class Size>
void count_if(InputIterator first, InputIterator last,
              Predicate pred, Size& n);
```

20.6.2   Description

The `count` algorithm adds to n the number of elements in the range [first, last) that are equal to value. Using a reference parameter, rather than returning the number, is necessary since the size type for the result cannot otherwise be deduced from built-in iterator types, such as int*.

The `count_if` algorithm adds to n the number of iterators in the range [first, last) for which pred(*i) == true.

20.6.3   Time Complexity

Linear. The number of comparisons done is the size of the range [first, last).

20.7 Mismatch

20.7.1 Prototypes

```
template <class InputIterator1, class InputIterator2>
pair<InputIterator1, InputIterator2>
   mismatch(InputIterator1 first1, InputIterator1 last1,
            InputIterator2 first2);

template <class InputIterator1, class InputIterator2,
          class BinaryPredicate>
pair<InputIterator1, InputIterator2>
   mismatch(InputIterator1 first1, InputIterator1 last1,
            InputIterator2 first2,
            BinaryPredicate binary_pred);
```

20.7.2 Description

mismatch compares corresponding pairs of elements from two ranges and returns the first mismatched pair.

The algorithm finds the first position at which a value in the range [first1, last1) disagrees with the value in the range starting at first2. It returns a pair of iterators i and j which satisfy the following conditions:

- i points into the range [first1, last1);

- j points into the range beginning at first2;

- i and j are both equidistant from the beginning of their corresponding ranges;

- !(*i == *j), or binary_pred(i, j) == false, depending on the version of mismatch invoked. In the first version comparisons are made with ==, and in the second version they are made with function object binary_pred.

20.7.3 Time Complexity

Linear. The number of comparisons done is the size of the range [first, i).

20.8   Equal

20.8.1   Prototypes

```
template <class InputIterator1, class InputIterator2>
bool equal(InputIterator1 first1, InputIterator1 last1,
           InputIterator2 first2);

template <class InputIterator1, class InputIterator2,
          class BinaryPredicate>
bool equal(InputIterator1 first1, InputIterator1 last1,
           InputIterator2 first2,
           BinaryPredicate binary_pred)
```

20.8.2   Description

equal returns true if the range [first1, last1) and the range of size last1 - first1 beginning at first2 contain the same elements in the same order, false otherwise. In the first version comparisons are made with ==, and in the second version they are made with function object binary_pred.

20.8.3   Time Complexity

Linear. The number of comparisons is the size of the range [first1, last1) if the result is true; otherwise it is the size of [first1, i), where i is the iterator referring to the first element in the range [first1, last1) that does not match the corresponding element in the range beginning at first2.

20.9   Search

20.9.1   Prototypes

```
template <class ForwardIterator1, class ForwardIterator2>
ForwardIterator1
    search(ForwardIterator1 first1, ForwardIterator1 last1,
           ForwardIterator2 first2, ForwardIterator2 last2);

template <class ForwardIterator1, class ForwardIterator2,
          class BinaryPredicate>
ForwardIterator1
    search(ForwardIterator1 first1, ForwardIterator1 last1,
           ForwardIterator2 first2, ForwardIterator2 last2,
           BinaryPredicate binary_pred);
```

20.9.2   Description

search checks whether the sequence in the second range [first2, last2) is a subsequence of the first range [first1, last1). If so, the iterator i in [first1, last1) that represents the start of the subsequence is returned. Otherwise, last1 is returned.

In the first version of the algorithm, comparisons are made with ==, while in the second they are made with function object binary_pred.

20.9.3   Time Complexity

Time complexity is quadratic. If N is the size of the range [first1, last1) and M is the size of the range [first2, last2), then the number of applications of

== or binary_pred is $(N - M)M$, which is less than or equal to $N^2/4$. The implementation does not use the Knuth-Morris-Pratt algorithm, which guarantees linear time, but tends to be slower in most practical cases than the naive algorithm with worst-case quadratic behavior. The worst case is extremely unlikely.

20.10 Mutating Sequence Algorithm Overview

Mutating sequence algorithms typically modify the containers on which they operate. There are 12 subcategories of algorithms in this category:

- copy copies elements to another (possibly overlapping) sequence;

- swap exchanges the elements of one sequence with those of another;

- transform replaces each element with the value returned by applying a given function to the element;

- replace replaces each element equal to a given value with a copy of another given value;

- fill replaces each element with copies of a given value;

- generate replaces each element with the value returned by calling a function;

- remove eliminates elements equal to a given value;

- unique eliminates consecutive equal elements;

- reverse reverses the relative order of the elements;

- `rotate` does a circular shift of the elements;

- `random_shuffle` reorders the elements pseudo-randomly;

- `partition` reorders the elements so that elements satisfying a given predicate precede those that don't.

Of these, `replace`, `remove`, and `unique` have both a version that uses `==` for comparisons and a version that uses a given predicate object. See Section 20.2 on page 325 regarding semantic requirements on the predicate object. The `partition` algorithm has a second version that is stable (i.e., preserves the relative order of the elements in each group).

20.11 Copy

20.11.1 Prototypes

```
template<class InputIterator, class OutputIterator>
OutputIterator copy(InputIterator first1,
                    InputIterator last1, OutputIterator first2);

template <class BidirectionalIterator1,
          class BidirectionalIterator2>
BidirectionalIterator2
    copy_backward(BidirectionalIterator1 first1,
                  BidirectionalIterator1 last1,
                  BidirectionalIterator2 last2);
```

20.11.2 Description

These algorithms copy elements from one range to another. `copy` copies [`first1`, `last1`) to [`first2`, `last2`), where `last2 == first2 + (last1 - first1)`, and returns `last2`. The algorithm proceeds forward, copying source elements in the order `first1`, `first1 + 1,...`, `last1 - 1`, with the consequence that the destination range can overlap with the source range provided it doesn't contain `first2`. Thus, for example, `copy` can be used to shift a range one position to the left but not to the right.

The opposite is true of `copy_backward`, which copies [`first1`, `last1`) to [`first2`, `last2`), where `first2 == last2 - (last1 - first1)`, and returns `first2`. It proceeds backward, copying source elements in the order `last1 - 1`, `last1 - 2,...`, `first1`. The copying thus works properly as long as the source range doesn't contain `last2`.

20.11.3 Time Complexity

Linear for both copy algorithms. At most N assignments are performed, where N is the size of the range [first1, last1).

20.12 *Swap*

20.12.1 Prototypes

```
template <class T>
void swap(T& x, T& y);

template <class ForwardIterator1, class ForwardIterator2>
ForwardIterator2 swap_ranges(ForwardIterator1 first1,
                             ForwardIterator1 last1,
                             ForwardIterator2 first2);
```

20.12.2 Description

swap exchanges the values stored in locations x and y. swap_ranges exchanges the elements in the range [first1, last2) with those in the range of size N = last1 - first1 beginning at first2. swap_ranges returns the past-the-end iterator, first2 + N.

20.12.3 Time Complexity

Constant for swap; linear for swap_ranges, which performs N element exchanges.

20.13 *Transform*

20.13.1 Prototypes

```
template <class InputIterator, class OutputIterator,
          class UnaryOperation>
OutputIterator transform(InputIterator first,
                         InputIterator last,
                         OutputIterator result,
                         UnaryOperation unary_op);

template <class InputIterator1, class InputIterator2,
          class OutputIterator, class BinaryOperation>
```

```
OutputIterator transform(InputIterator1 first1,
                         InputIterator1 last1,
                         InputIterator2 first2,
                         OutputIterator result,
                         BinaryOperation binary_op);
```

20.13.2 Description

The first version of transform generates a sequence of elements by applying a unary function unary_op to each element of the range [first, last).

The second version of transform accepts a range [first1, last1) and a range of length $N = $ last1 - first1 starting at first2 and generates a range by applying a binary function binary_op to each corresponding pair of elements from the ranges.

For both versions of transform, the resulting sequence is placed starting at the position result, and the past-the-end iterator, result + N, is returned.

result may be equal to first in the case of unary transform, or to first1 or first2 in the case of binary transform.

unary_op and binary_op must not have any side effects.

20.13.3 Time Complexity

Linear. The number of applications of unary_op is the size of the range [first, last) and the number of applications of binary_op is the size of the range [first1, last1).

20.14 Replace

20.14.1 Prototypes

```
template <class ForwardIterator, class T>
void replace(ForwardIterator first, ForwardIterator last,
             const T& old_value, const T& new_value);

template <class ForwardIterator, class Predicate, class T>
void replace_if(ForwardIterator first, ForwardIterator last,
                Predicate pred, const T& new_value);

template <class InputIterator, class OutputIterator,
          class T>
OutputIterator
  replace_copy(InputIterator first, InputIterator last,
               OutputIterator result,
               const T& old_value, const T& new_value);
```

```
template <class InputIterator, class OutputIterator,
          class Predicate, class T>
OutputIterator
  replace_copy_if(InputIterator first, InputIterator last,
                  OutputIterator result,
                  Predicate pred, const T& new_value):
```

20.14.2 Description

The `replace` algorithm modifies the range [first, last) so that all elements equal to `old_value` are replaced by `new_value`, while other elements remain unchanged.

`replace_if` modifies the range [first, last) so that all elements that satisfy the predicate `pred` are replaced by `new_value`, while other elements remain unchanged.

`replace_copy` and `replace_copy_if` are similar to `replace` and `replace_if`, except that the original sequence is not modified. Rather, the altered sequence is placed in the range of size N = last - first beginning at `result`. The past-the-end iterator, `result` + N, is returned.

`result` must not be in the range [first, last).

20.14.3 Time Complexity

Linear. The number of == operations performed, or of applications of the predicate `pred`, is N.

20.15 Fill

20.15.1 Prototypes

```
template <class ForwardIterator, class T>
void fill(ForwardIterator first, ForwardIterator last,
          const T& value);

template <class ForwardIterator, class Size, class T>
void fill_n(ForwardIterator first, Size n, const T& value);
```

20.15.2 Description

`fill` places `value` in all positions in the range [first, last).

`fill_n` places `value` in all positions in the range [first, first + n).

20.15.3 Time Complexity

Linear. The number of assignments for both versions of the algorithm is the size of the range [first, last).

20.16 Generate

20.16.1 Prototypes

```
template <class ForwardIterator, class Generator>
void generate(ForwardIterator first, ForwardIterator last,
              Generator gen);

template <class ForwardIterator, class Size,
          class Generator>
void generate_n(ForwardIterator first, Size n,
                Generator gen);
```

20.16.2 Description

generate fills the range [first, last) with the sequence generated by last - first successive calls of the function object gen.

generate_n fills the range of size n beginning at first with the sequence generated by n successive calls of gen.

20.16.3 Time Complexity

Linear. The number of assignments and calls of gen for generate is the size of the range [first, last), while for generate_n the number of assignments is n.

20.17 Remove

20.17.1 Prototypes

```
template <class ForwardIterator, class T>
ForwardIterator
  remove(ForwardIterator first, ForwardIterator last,
         const T& value);

template <class ForwardIterator, class Predicate>
ForwardIterator
  remove_if(ForwardIterator first, ForwardIterator last,
```

```
                     Predicate pred);

    template <class InputIterator, class OutputIterator,
             class T>
    OutputIterator
      remove_copy(InputIterator first, InputIterator last,
                 OutputIterator result, const T& value);

    template <class InputIterator, class OutputIterator,
         class Predicate>
    OutputIterator
      remove_copy_if(InputIterator first, InputIterator last,
                    OutputIterator result, Predicate pred);
```

20.17.2 Description

The function `remove` removes those elements from the range `[first, last)` that are equal to `value` and returns the location i that is the past-the-end iterator for the resulting range of values that are not equal to `value`.

The function `remove_if` removes those elements from the range `[first, last)` which satisfy the predicate `pred`, and it returns the location i that is the past-the-end iterator for the resulting range of values that do not satisfy `pred`.

It is important to note that neither `remove` nor `remove_if` alters the size of the original container: the algorithms operate by *copying* (with assignments) into the range `[first, i)`. No calls are made to the `insert` or `erase` member functions of the containers on which the algorithms operate.

`remove_copy` and `remove_copy_if` are similar to `remove` and `remove_if`, respectively, except that the resulting sequences are copied into the range beginning at `result`.

All versions of remove are *stable*; that is, the relative order of the elements that are not removed is the same as their relative order in the original range.

20.17.3 Time Complexity

Linear. The number of assignments is the number of elements *not* removed, at most the size of the range `[first, last)`, and the number of applications of `==` or `pred` is exactly `[first, last)`.

20.18 *Unique*

20.18.1 Prototypes

```
template <class ForwardIterator>
ForwardIterator
  unique(ForwardIterator first, ForwardIterator last);

template <class ForwardIterator, class BinaryPredicate>
ForwardIterator
  unique(Forwarditerator first, ForwardIterator last,
         BinaryPredicate binary_pred);

template <class inputIterator, class OutputIterator>
OutputIterator
  unique_copy(InputIterator first, InputIterator last,
              OutputIterator result);

template <class ForwardIterator, class BinaryPredicate>
OutputIterator
  unique_copy(InputIterator first, InputIterator last,
              OutputIterator result,
              BinaryPredicate binary_pred);
```

20.18.2 Description

unique eliminates consecutive duplicates from the range [first, last). An element is considered to be a consecutive duplicate if it is equal to an element in the location to its immediate right in the range.

In the first version of unique, checks for equality are made using operator==, while in the second they are made with the function object binary_pred.

unique_copy is similar to unique, except that the resulting sequence is copied into the range starting at result, leaving the original sequence unmodified.

All versions of unique return the end of the resulting range.

The unique algorithms are typically applied to a sorted range, since in this case all duplicates are consecutive duplicates.

20.18.3 Time Complexity

Linear. Exactly last - first applications of the corresponding predicates are done.

20.19 Reverse

20.19.1 Prototypes

```
template <class BidirectionalIterator>
void reverse(BidirectionalIterator first,
             BidirectionalIterator last);

template <class BidirectionalIterator, class OutputIterator>
OutputIterator
  reverse_copy(BidirectionalIterator first,
               BidirectionalIterator last,
               OutputIterator result);
```

20.19.2 Description

The `reverse` algorithm reverses the relative order of elements in the range `[first, last)`.

The `reverse_copy` algorithm places the reverse of the range `[first, last)` into the range beginning `result`, leaving `[first, last)` unmodified. It returns the past-the-end iterator `result + last - first`.

20.19.3 Time Complexity

Linear. For `reverse`, approximately $N/2$ element exchanges are performed, where N is the size of `[first, last)`. For `reverse_copy`, exactly N assignments are done.

20.20 Rotate

20.20.1 Prototypes

```
template <class ForwardIterator>
void rotate(ForwardIterator first, ForwardIterator middle,
            ForwardIterator last);

template <class ForwardIterator, class OutputIterator>
void
  rotate_copy(ForwardIterator first, ForwardIterator middle,
              ForwardIterator last, OutputIterator result);
```

20.20.2 Description

The `rotate` algorithm shifts elements in a sequence leftward as follows: for $N =$ `last - first`, $M =$ `middle - first`, and each nonnegative integer $i < N$, `rotate` places the element from the position `first` + i into the position

$$\text{first} + (i + M) \text{ \% } N.$$

`rotate_copy` is similar to `rotate`, except that it places the elements of the resulting sequence into the range [`result`, `result` + N), leaving [`first`, `last`) unmodified.

20.20.3 Time Complexity

Linear. `rotate` performs at most N swaps; `rotate_copy` performs exactly N assignments.

20.21 Random Shuffle

20.21.1 Prototypes

```
template <class RandomAccessIterator>
void random_shuffle(RandomAccessIterator first,
                    RandomAccessIterator last);


template <class RandomAccessIterator,
         class RandomNumberGenerator>
void random_shuffle(RandomAccessIterator first,
                    RandomAccessIterator last,
                    RandomNumberGenerator& rand);
```

20.21.2 Description

`random_shuffle` randomly reorders the elements in the range [`first`, `last`), using a pseudo-random number-generating function. The permutations produced by `random_shuffle` are approximately uniformly distributed; i.e., the probability of each of the $N!$ permutations of a range of size N is approximately $1/N!$. The second version takes a particular random number-generating function object `rand` such that each call to `rand()` returns a pseudo-randomly chosen `double` in the interval [0, 1).

20.21.3 Time Complexity

Linear. Performs exactly (`last - first`) - 1 swaps.

20.22 *Partition*

20.22.1 Prototypes

```
template <class BidirectionalIterator, class Predicate>
BidirectionalIterator
    partition(BidirectionalIterator first,
                BidirectionalIterator last, Predicate pred);

template <class BidirectionalIterator, class Predicate>
BidirectionalIterator
    stable_partition(BidirectionalIterator first,
                      BidirectionalIterator last,
                      Predicate pred);
```

20.22.2 Description

The `partition` algorithm places all elements in the range `[first, last)` that satisfy `pred` before all elements that do not satisfy it.

Both algorithms return an iterator i such that for any iterator j in the range `[first, i)`, `pred(*j) == true`, and for any iterator k in the range `[i, last)`, `pred(*k) == false`.

With `stable_partition`, the relative positions of the elements in both groups are preserved. `partition` does not guarantee this stability property.

20.22.3 Time Complexity

Linear for `partition`; linear or $O(N \log N)$ for `stable_partition`, depending on whether extra memory is available for a workspace.

`partition` performs approximately $N/2$ element exchanges, where N is the size of `[first, last)`, and exactly N applications of `pred`.

If extra memory for N elements is available, `stable_partition` performs $2N$ assignments. If not, it does at most $N \log N$ swaps. In either case, it does exactly N applications of `pred`.

20.23 *Sorting-Related Algorithms Overview*

There are nine subcategories of algorithms related in some way to sorting:

- `sort`, `stable_sort`, and `partial_sort` permute the elements of a sequence into ascending order.

- `nth_element` finds the nth smallest element of a sequence.

- `binary_search`, `lower_bound`, `upper_bound`, and `equal_range` search a sorted sequence using repeated bisection.

- `merge` merges two sorted sequences into one.

- `includes`, `set_union`, `set_intersection`, `set_difference`, and `set_symmetric_difference` are set operations on sorted structures.

- `push_heap`, `pop_heap`, `make_heap`, and `sort_heap` perform ordering operations on a sequence organized as a heap (providing priority queues, among other uses).

- `min`, `max`, `min_element`, and `max_element` find the minimum or maximum of a pair or sequence of elements.

- `lexicographical_compare` compares two sequences lexicographically.

- `next_permutation` and `prev_permutation` generate permutations of a sequence, based on lexicographical ordering of the set of all permutations.

All of the above algorithms have two versions: one that uses < for comparisons and another that uses a function object `comp` of type `Compare`.

`Compare comp` must be a function object that accepts two arguments, returns `true` if the first argument is less than the second, and returns `false` otherwise. `Compare comp` is used throughout for algorithms assuming an ordering relation. It is assumed that `comp` will not apply any nonconstant function through the dereferenced iterator.

For all algorithms that take `Compare`, there is a version that uses < instead. That is, `comp(*i, *j) == true` defaults to `*i < *j == true`.

Any *strict weak ordering* may be used for `comp`. "Strict" means an irreflexive relation, so, for example, we may use < or > on type `int` (or any built-in numeric type), but not <= or >=. "Weak" refers to requirements that are weaker than a total ordering (but stronger than a partial ordering). The exact requirements (Ref. 11, p. 33) for a relation R to be a strict weak ordering are as follows:

1. R must be a *partial ordering*:

   a. (Transitive) For all x, y, z, if $x\,R\,y$ and $y\,R\,z$, then $x\,R\,z$.

   b. (Irreflexive) For all x, $x\,R\,x$ is false.

2. The relation E defined by "$x\,E\,y$ if and only if both $x\,R\,y$ and $y\,R\,x$ are false" must be transitive.

When these requirements are met, E is in fact an *equivalence relation*:

   a. (Transitive) For all x, y, z, if $x\,E\,y$ and $y\,E\,z$, then $x\,E\,z$.

b. (Symmetric) For all x, y, if $x E y$, then $y E x$.

c. (Reflexive) For all x, $x E x$.

It can be shown that R induces a well-defined comparison relation R/E on the equivalence classes defined by E, such that R/E *is a total ordering*. Thus R itself is not required to be a total ordering, but R/E is.

Stated directly in terms of comp, the definition of the equivalence relation E is

$$x E y \text{ if and only if } !(\texttt{comp}(\texttt{x, y}) \text{ \&\& } !(\texttt{comp}(\texttt{y, x}).$$

The equivalence relation E is used not only in stating the requirements on comp, but also in stating other requirements on the sorting-related algorithms. For example, we define stability of a sorting algorithm as the property that the relative order of equivalent elements is preserved. The equivalence referred to is the relation E.

A sequence is *sorted with respect to a comparison function* comp if for any iterator i pointing into the sequence and any nonnegative integer n such that i + n is a valid iterator pointing to an element of the sequence,

$$\texttt{comp}(*(i + n), *i) == \texttt{false}.$$

20.24 Sort

20.24.1 Prototypes

```
template <class RandomAccessIterator>
void sort(RandomAccessIterator first,
         RandomAccessIterator last);

template <class RandomAccessIterator, class Compare>
void sort(RandomAccessIterator first,
         RandomAccessIterator last, Compare comp);

template <class RandomAccessIterator>
void stable_sort(RandomAccessIterator first,
                RandomAccessIterator last);

template <class RandomAccessIterator, class Compare>
void stable_sort(RandomAccessIterator first,
                RandomAccessIterator last, Compare comp);
```

```
template <class RandomAccessIterator>
void partial_sort(RandomAccessIterator first,
                  RandomAccessIterator middle,
                  RandomAccessIterator last);

template <class RandomAccessIterator, class Compare>
void partial_sort(RandomAccessIterator first,
                  RandomAccessIterator middle,
                  RandomAccessIterator last, Compare comp);

template <class InputIterator, class RandomAcessIterator>
RandomAccessIterator
  partial_sort_copy(InputIterator first, InputIterator last,
                    RandomAccessIterator result_first,
                    RandomAccessIterator result_last);

template <class InputIterator, class RandomAccessIterator,
          class Compare>
RandomAccessIterator
  partial_sort_copy(InputIterator first, InputIterator last,
                    RandomAccessIterator result_first,
                    RandomAccessIterator result_last,
                    Compare comp);
```

20.24.2 Description

For sorting, there are three principal algorithms: sort, stable_sort, and partial_sort. A copying version of partial_sort is also provided.

sort sorts the elements in the range [first, last).

stable_sort sorts the elements in the range [first, last) and ensures that the relative order of the equivalent elements is preserved.

For partial_sort, middle should point into the range [first, last). If $M = $ middle - first, the algorithm places in [first, middle) the M elements that would appear there if the entire range [first, last) were sorted. The order in which it leaves the rest of the elements (i.e., those in the range [middle, last)) is undefined.

For partial_sort_copy, let $N = $ last - first and $R = $ result_last - result_first. There are two cases:

1. If $R < N$, partial_sort_copy places in [result_first, result_last) the R elements that would appear in [first, first + R) if the entire range [first, last) were sorted. The range [first, last) is not modified. result_last is returned.

2. Otherwise, it places in [result_first, result_first + N) the elements from [first, last) in sorted order. The ranges [first, last) and [result_first + N, result_last) are not modified. result_first + N is returned.

20.24.3 Time Complexity

The sort algorithm sorts a sequence of length N using $O(N \log N)$ comparisons and assignments on the average. However, there are a few input sequences that cause it to blow up to quadratic time.

For *guaranteed* $O(N \log N)$ behavior, one can use partial_sort with middle == last. In general, if M = middle - first, partial_sort takes $O(N \log M)$ time.

The time for partial_sort_copy is $O(N \log K)$, where $K = \min(N, R)$.

The time for stable_sort is $O(N \log N)$ or $O(N(\log N)^2)$, depending on whether extra memory is available for a workspace. If extra memory for at least $N/2$ elements is available, the time is $O(N \log N)$.

20.25 Nth Element

20.25.1 Prototypes

```
template <class RandomAccessIterator>
void nth_element(RandomAccessIterator first,
                 RandomAccessIterator position,
                 RandomAccessIterator last);

template <class RandomAccessIterator, class Compare>
void nth_element(RandomAccessIterator first,
                 RandomAccessIterator position,
                 RandomAccessIterator last, Compare comp);
```

20.25.2 Description

The nth_element algorithm places an element of a sequence in the location where it would be if the sequence were sorted.

In the first version of the algorithm, element comparisons are done using <, while in the second version they are done using the function object comp.

After a call to nth_element, the element placed in position is the nth smallest element of the range, where n = position - first. Furthermore, for any iterator i in the range [first, position) and any iterator j in the range [position, last), either !(*j < *i) (in case of the first version) or !comp(*j, *i) (in case of the second version). That is, the algorithm partitions the elements of the sequence according to size: elements to the left of position are all less than or equal to those to its right. The order in which the elements appear in each partition is undefined.

20.25.3 Time Complexity

Linear on the average, quadratic in the worst case.

20.26 Binary Search

All of the algorithms in this section are versions of binary search.

Although binary search is typically efficient (i.e., performs in logarithmic time) only for random access sequences (such as vectors, deques, or arrays), the algorithms here have been written to work even on nonrandom access sequences (such as lists). For nonrandom access sequences, the total time taken is linear in the size of the container, but the number of comparisons is still only logarithmic.

20.26.1 Prototypes

```
template <class ForwardIterator, class T>
bool binary_search(ForwardIterator first,
                   ForwardIterator last, const T& value);

template <class ForwardIterator, class T, class Compare>
bool binary_search(ForwardIterator first,
                   ForwardIterator last, const T& value,
                   Compare comp);

template <class ForwardIterator, class T>
ForwardIterator
   lower_bound(ForwardIterator first, ForwardIterator last,
               const T& value);

template <class ForwardIterator, class T, class Compare>
ForwardIterator
   lower_bound(ForwardIterator first, ForwardIterator last,
               const T& value, Compare comp);

template <class ForwardIterator, class T>
ForwardIterator
   upper_bound(ForwardIterator first, ForwardIterator last,
               const T& value);
```

```
template <class ForwardIterator, class T, class Compare>
ForwardIterator
  upper_bound(ForwardIterator first, ForwardIterator last,
              const T& value, Compare comp);


template <class ForwardIterator, class T>
pair<ForwardIterator, ForwardIterator>
  equal_range(ForwardIterator first, ForwardIterator last,
              const T& value);


template <class ForwardIterator, class T>
pair<ForwardIterator, ForwardIterator>
  equal_range(ForwardIterator first, ForwardIterator last,
              const T& value, Compare comp);
```

20.26.2 Description

For each of these algorithms, the range [first, last) must be sorted according to <, or according to comp in the case of those that take a Compare argument.

The binary_search algorithms returns true if value is in the range [first, last), and false otherwise.

The lower_bound algorithms return an iterator referring to the *first* position in [first, last) into which value may be inserted while maintaining the sorted ordering.

The upper_bound algorithms return an iterator referring to the *last* position [first, last) into which value may be inserted while maintaining the sorted ordering.

The equal_range functions return a pair of iterators, those that would be returned by lower_bound and upper_bound.

20.26.3 Time Complexity

Logarithmic for random access sequences, linear otherwise. The number of comparison operations is only logarithmic in either case. For nonrandom access sequences, the number of traversal operations (++) is linear, making the total time linear.

For binary_search, lower_bound and upper_bound, the number of comparisons is at most $\log N + 1$, and for equal_range it is at most $2 \log N + 1$, where N is the size of the range [first, last).

20.27 Merge

20.27.1 Prototypes

```
template <class InputIterator1, class InputIterator2,
        class OutputIterator>
OutputIterator
  merge(InputIterator1 first1, InputIterator1 last1,
        InputIterator2 first2, InputIterator2 last2,
        OutputIterator result);

template <class InputIterator1, class InputIterator2,
        class OutputIterator, class Compare>
OutputIterator
  merge(InputIterator1 first1, InputIterator1 last1,
        InputIterator2 first2, InputIterator2 last2,
        OutputIterator result, Compare comp);

template <class BidirectionalIterator>
void inplace_merge(BidirectionalIterator first,
                   BidirectionalIterator middle,
                   BidirectionalIterator last);

template <class BidirectionalIterator, class Compare>
void inplace_merge(BidirectionalIterator first,
                   BidirectionalIterator middle,
                   BidirectionalIterator last,
                   Compare comp);
```

20.27.2 Description

merge merges two sorted ranges [first1, last1) and [first2, last2) into the range [result, result + N), where N = N1 + N2, N1 = last1 - first1, and N2 = last2 - first2. The merge is stable; that is, for equivalent elements in the two ranges, the elements from the first range always precede the elements from the second. merge returns result + N. The result of merge is undefined if the resulting range overlaps with either of the original ranges.

inplace_merge merges two sorted consecutive ranges [first, middle) and [middle, last), putting the result into the range [first, last). The merge is stable.

20.27.3 Time Complexity

Linear in the case of `merge`. With `in_place` merge, the time complexity depends on whether there is extra memory available for a workspace. If extra memory for $N =$ `last - first` elements is available, the time taken is $O(N)$; otherwise it is $O(N \log N)$.

With both algorithms the number of comparisons is at most N.

20.28 Set Operations on Sorted Structures

The library provides five algorithms for set operations: `includes`, `set_union`, `set_intersection`, `set_difference`, and `set_symmetric_difference`. These operations work on sorted structures, including STL sorted associative containers.

The algorithms even work with *multisets* containing multiple equivalent elements. The semantics of the operations have been generalized to multisets in the standard way, by defining union to contain the maximum number of occurrences of an element, intersection to contain the minimum number of occurrences, and so on.

20.28.1 Prototypes

```
template <class InputIterator1, class InputIterator2>
bool includes(InputIterator1 first1, InputIterator1 last1,
            InputIterator2 first2, InputIterator2 last2);

template <class InputIterator1, class InputIterator2,
          class Compare>
bool includes(InputIterator1 first1, InputIterator1 last1,
            InputIterator2 first2, InputIterator2 last2,
            Compare comp)

template <class InputIterator1, class InputIterator2,
          class OutputIterator>
OutputIterator
  set_union(InputIterator1 first1, InputIterator1 last1,
            InputIterator2 first2, InputIterator2 last2,
            OutputIterator result);
```

```
template <class InputIterator1, class InputIterator2,
          class OutputIterator, class Compare>
OutputIterator
  set_union(InputIterator1 first1, InputIterator1 last1,
            InputIterator2 first2, InputIterator2 last2,
            OutputIterator result, Compare comp)

template <class InputIterator1, class InputIterator2,
          class OutputIterator>
OutputIterator
  set_intersection(InputIterator1 first1,
                   InputIterator1 last1,
                   InputIterator2 first2,
                   InputIterator2 last2,
                   OutputIterator result);

template <class InputIterator1, class InputIterator2,
          class OutputIterator, class Compare>
OutputIterator
  set_intersection(InputIterator1 first1,
                   InputIterator1 last1,
                   InputIterator2 first2,
                   InputIterator2 last2,
                   OutputIterator result, Compare comp)

template <class InputIterator1, class InputIterator2,
          class OutputIterator>
OutputIterator
  set_difference(InputIterator1 first1,
                 InputIterator1 last1,
                 InputIterator2 first2,
                 InputIterator2 last2,
                 OutputIterator result);

template <class InputIterator1, class InputIterator2,
          class OutputIterator, class Compare>
OutputIterator
  set_difference(InputIterator1 first1,
                 InputIterator1 last1,
                 InputIterator2 first2,
                 InputIterator2 last2,
                 OutputIterator result,
                 Compare comp);
```

```
template <class InputIterator1, class InputIterator2,
         class OutputIterator>
OutputIterator
  set_symmetric_difference(InputIterator1 first1,
                           InputIterator1 last1,
                           InputIterator2 first2,
                           InputIterator2 last2,
                           OutputIterator result);

template <class InputIterator1, class InputIterator2,
         class OutputIterator>
OutputIterator
  set_symmetric_difference(InputIterator1 first1,
                           InputIterator1 last1,
                           InputIterator2 first2,
                           InputIterator2 last2,
                           OutputIterator result,
                           Compare comp)
```

20.28.2 Description

`includes` returns `true` if every element in the `[first2, last2)` is contained in `[first1, last1)`, `false` otherwise.

Each of the remaining algorithms places its result in the range beginning at `result` and returns the past-the-end iterator.

`set_union` constructs a sorted union of the elements from the two ranges. `set_union` is stable; that is, if an element in the first range is equivalent to one in the second range, the one from the first range is copied.

`set_intersection` constructs a sorted intersection of the elements from the two ranges. `set_intersection` is guaranteed to be stable.

`set_difference` constructs a sorted difference of the elements from the two ranges. This difference contains elements that are present in the first set but not in the second.

`set_symmetric_difference` constructs a sorted symmetric difference of the elements from the two ranges, which means all elements that are in the first range but not in the second and all that are in the second but not in the first.

The result of each of these algorithms is undefined if the resulting range overlaps with either of the original ranges.

20.28.3 Time Complexity

Linear. In all cases, at most $2 (N1 + N2) - 1$ comparisons are performed, where $N1 = $ `last1 - first1` and $N2 = $ `last2 - first2`.

20.29 *Heap Operations*

A "heap," in the context of sorting, is a particular organization of a sequence that allows certain selection and sorting operations to be done in logarithmic time. Given a range [first, last), where first and last are random access iterators, we say that the range is a *heap* if two key properties are satisfied:

- the value to which the iterator first points is the largest element in the range;

- the value to which the iterator first points may be removed by pop_heap, or a new element added by push_heap, in logarithmic time, and in both cases the resulting range is a heap.

These properties allow heaps to be used as priority queues.

In addition to pop_heap and push_heap, there are two more heap algorithms: make_heap, for creating a heap out of an arbitrary range, and sort_heap, for putting a heap into sorted order.

20.29.1 Prototypes

```
template <class RandomAccessIterator>
void push_heap(RandomAccessIterator first,
               RandomAccessIterator last);

template <class RandomAccessIterator, class Compare>
void push_heap(RandomAccessIterator first,
               RandomAccessIterator last, Compare comp);

template <class RandomAccessIterator>
void pop_heap(RandomAccessIterator first,
              RandomAccessIterator last);

template <class RandomAccessIterator, class Compare>
void pop_heap(RandomAccessIterator first,
              RandomAccessIterator last, Compare comp);

template <class RandomAccessIterator>
void make_heap(RandomAccessIterator first,
               RandomAccessIterator last);

template <class RandomAccessIterator, class Compare>
void make_heap(RandomAccessIterator first,
               RandomAccessIterator last, Compare comp);
```

```
template <class RandomAccessIterator>
void sort_heap(RandomAccessIterator first,
               RandomAccessIterator last);

template <class RandomAccessIterator, class Compare>
void sort_heap(RandomAccessIterator first,
               RandomAccessIterator last, Compare comp);
```

20.29.2 Description

If the range [first1, last - 1) is a heap, push_heap permutes the elements in [first, last) into a heap. We say that the element at last - 1 is "pushed into the heap."

If the range [first, last) is a heap, pop_heap swaps the value in the location first with the value in the location last - 1 and permutes the range [first, last - 1) into a heap.

make_heap rearranges the elements in the range [first, last) into a heap.

sort_heap sorts the elements in the heap in the range [first, last).

20.29.3 Time Complexity

Let N be the size of the range [first, last).

push_heap and pop_heap take logarithmic time. push_heap performs at most log N comparisons, and pop_heap at most 2 log N comparisons.

make_heap takes linear time and does at most 3 N comparisons.

sort_heap takes O(N log N) time and does at most N log N comparisons.

20.30 Min and Max

20.30.1 Prototypes

```
template <class T>
const T& min(const T& a, const T& b);

template <class T, class Compare>
const T& min(const T& a, const T& b, Compare comp);

template <class T>
const T& max(const T& a, const T& b);

template <class T, class Compare>
const T& max(const T& a, const T& b, Compare comp);
```

```
template <class ForwardIterator>
ForwardIterator
  min_element(ForwardIterator first, ForwardIterator last);

template <class ForwardIterator, class Compare>
ForwardIterator
  min_element(ForwardIterator first, ForwardIterator last,
              Compare comp);
template <class ForwardIterator>
ForwardIterator
  max_element(ForwardIterator first, ForwardIterator last);

template <class ForwardIterator, class Compare>
ForwardIterator
  max_element(ForwardIterator first, ForwardIterator last,
              Compare comp);
```

20.30.2 Description

min returns the smaller of its two arguments, while max returns the larger. If the two arguments are equivalent, the first is returned.

min_element returns the first iterator referring to a minimal element in the range [first, last).

max_element returns the first iterator referring to a maximal element in the range [first, last).

20.30.3 Time Complexity

Constant for min or max, linear for min_element or max_element.

The number of element comparisons for min_element or max_element is exactly $\max(N - 1, 0)$, where N = last - first.

20.31 Lexicographical Comparison

20.31.1 Prototypes

```
template <class InputIterator1, class InputIterator2>
bool lexicographical_compare(InputIterator1 first1,
                             InputIterator1 last1,
                             InputIterator2 first2,
                             InputIterator2 last2);
```

```
template <class InputIterator1, class InputIterator2,
          class Compare>
bool lexicographical_compare(InputIterator1 first1,
                             InputIterator1 last1,
                             InputIterator2 first2,
                             InputIterator2 last2,
                             Compare comp)
```

20.31.2 Description

The lexicographical comparison of two sequences [first1, last1) and [first2, last2) is defined as follows: traverse the sequences, comparing corresponding pairs of elements e1 and e2:

if e1 < e2, stop and return true;

if e2 < e1, stop and return false;

otherwise, continue to the next corresponding pair of elements. If the first sequence is exhausted but the second is not, then return true, otherwise return false.

20.31.3 Time Complexity

Linear. The number of comparisons done is at most i, where first + i is the first position at which a disagreement occurs.

20.32 *Permutation Generators*

The library provides two permutation generation algorithms: next_permutation and prev_permutation. Each takes a sequence and produces a distinct permutation of it, in such a way that $N!$ successive applications yield all permutations of N elements. A strict weak ordering on the elements, given by < or comp, is required. Using such an ordering, let the permutations of a sequence be ordered lexicographically. In this ordering of the permutations, the first (smallest) permutation is the one in which elements are in ascending order and the last (largest) permutation is the one in which elements are in descending order. next_permutation permutes a sequence into its successor in this lexicographical ordering of permutations, and prev_permutation permutes it into its predecessor.

20.32.1 Prototypes

```
template <class BidirectionalIterator>
bool next_permutation(BidirectionalIterator first,
                      BidirectionalIterator last);
```

```
template <class BidirectionalIterator, class Compare>
bool next_permutation(BidirectionalIterator first,
                      BidirectionalIterator last,
                      Compare comp);

template <class BidirectionalIterator>
bool prev_permutation(BidirectionalIterator first,
                      BidirectionalIterator last);

template <class BidirectionalIterator, class Compare>
bool prev_permutation(BidirectionalIterator first,
                      BidirectionalIterator last,
                      Compare comp);
```

20.32.2 Description

next_permutation permutes the sequence in [first, last) into its successor in the lexicographical ordering of all permutations. If such a permutation exists, the algorithm returns true. Otherwise, it transforms the sequence into the smallest permutation (i.e., the one in ascending order) and returns false.

prev_permutation permutes the sequence in [first, last) into its predecessor in the lexicographical ordering of all permutations. If such a permutation exists, it returns true. Otherwise, it transforms the sequence into the largest permutation (i.e., the the one in descending order) and returns false.

20.32.3 Time Complexity

Linear. At most $N/2$ swaps and $N/2$ comparisons are done, where $N =$ last - first.

20.33 Generalized Numeric Algorithms Overview

The library provides four subcategories of algorithms for numeric processing:

- accumulate computes the sum of the elements in a sequence;

- inner_product computes the sum of the products of corresponding elements in two sequences;

- partial_sum computes the partial sums of the elements of a sequence and stores them in another (or the same) sequence;

- adjacent_difference computes the differences of adjacent elements and stores them in another (or the same) sequence.

In each case, a second version is provided that allows using other binary operators instead of the usual operators. For example, one can compute the product of the integers in a sequence by calling `accumulate` with the `times<int>` function object, so that it uses * instead of +.

As the category name "*generalized* numeric algorithms" suggests, the elements and operators are not necessarily numeric. For example, `accumulate` could be used to merge all the lists in a vector of lists, by passing it a function object that encapsulates the list `merge` member function.

20.34 *Accumulate*

20.34.1 Prototypes

```
template <class InputIterator, class T>
T accumulate(InputIterator first, InputIterator last,
             T initial_value);

template <class InputIterator, class T,
          class BinaryOperation>
T accumulate(InputIterator first, InputIterator last,
             T initial_value, BinaryOperation binary_op);
```

20.34.2 Description

The first version of `accumulate` initializes a variable (call it `accumulator`) with `initial_value`, modifies it with

```
accumulator = accumulator + *i
```

for every iterator `i` in the range [`first, last`) in order, and returns `accumulator`.

The second version is the same except that `binary_op` is used instead of +, as follows:

```
accumulator = binary_op(accumulator, *i).
```

`binary_op` is assumed not to cause any side effects.

20.34.3 Time Complexity

Linear. The number of applications of + or `binary_op` is the size of the range [`first, last`).

20.35 Inner Product

20.35.1 Prototypes

```
template <class InputIterator1, class InputIterator2,
        class T>
T inner_product(InputIterator1 first1, InputIterator1 last1,
            InputIterator2 first2, T initial_value);


template <class InputIterator1, class InputIterator2,
        class T, class BinaryOperation1,
        class BinaryOperation2>
T inner_product(InputIterator1 first1, InputIterator1 last1,
            InputIterator2 first2, T initial_value,
            BinaryOperation1 binary_op1,
            BinaryOperation2 binary_op2);
```

20.35.2 Description

The first version of `inner_product` initializes a variable (call it `accumulator`) with `initial_value`, modifies it with

```
accumulator = accumulator + (*i1) * (*i2)
```

for every iterator `i1` in the range `[first1, last2)` and every iterator `i1` in the range `[first2, first2 + (last1 - first2))` in order, and returns `accumulator`.

The second version is the same except that `binary_op1` is used instead of `+` and `binary_op2` is used instead of `*`, as follows:

```
accumulator =
    binary_op1(accumulator, binary_op2(*i1, *i2)).
```

`binary_op1` and `binary_op2` are assumed to cause no side effects.

20.35.3 Time Complexity

Linear. The number of applications of `+` or `binary_op1`, and the number of applications of `*` or `binary_op2`, is the size of the range `[first, last)`.

20.36 *Partial Sum*

20.36.1 Prototypes

```
template <class InputIterator, class OutputIterator>
OutputIterator
   partial_sum(InputIterator first, InputIterator last,
               OutputIterator result);

template <class InputIterator, class OutputIterator,
          class BinaryOperation>
OutputIterator
   partial_sum(InputIterator first, InputIterator last,
               OutputIterator result,
               BinaryOperation binary_op);
```

20.36.2 Description

Let x_k = *(first + k), for $k = 0, 1, \ldots, N - 1$, where N = last - first. Then the kth *partial sum* of the elements in the range [first, last) is defined as

$$s_k = (\ldots((x_0 + x_1) + x_2) + \ldots) + x_k.$$

The first version of partial_sum places s_k in result + k, for $k = 0, 1, \ldots, N - 1$. The second version does the same thing, except that it computes the kth partial "sum" with binary_op:

$$s_k = \text{binary\_op}(\ldots \text{binary\_op}(\text{binary\_op}(x_0, x_1), x_2), \ldots, x_k).$$

binary_op is expected not to have any side effects.

In both cases, partial_sum returns result + N.

Note that result may be equal to first; i.e., it is possible for the algorithm to work "in place," meaning that the algorithm can generate the partial sums and replace the original sequence with them.

20.36.3 Time Complexity

Linear. The number of applications of + or binary_op is exactly $N - 1$.

20.37 Adjacent Difference

20.37.1 Prototypes

```
template <class InputIterator, class OutputIterator>
OutputIterator
  adjacent_difference(InputIterator first,
                      InputIterator last,
                      OutputIterator result);


template <class InputIterator, class OutputIterator
          class BinaryOperation>
OutputIterator
  adjacent_difference(InputIterator first,
                      InputIterator last,
                      OutputIterator result,
                      BinaryOperation binary_op);
```

20.37.2 Description

Let $x_k = \verb|*(first + k)|$, for $k = 0, 1, \ldots, N - 1$, where $N = $ `last - first`. Then the kth *adjacent difference*, for $k = 1, \ldots, N - 1$, of the elements in the range [`first`, `last`) is defined as

$$d_k = x_k - x_{k-1}.$$

The first version of `adjacent_difference` places d_k in `result + k`, for $k = 1, \ldots, N - 1$. The second version does the same thing, except that it computes the kth adjacent "difference" with `binary_op`:

$$d_k = \verb|binary_op|(x_k, x_{k-1}).$$

In both cases, `adjacent_difference` places `*first` in `*result` and returns `result + N`.

`result` may be equal to `first`; i.e., the algorithm can work "in place."

20.37.3 Time Complexity

Linear. The number of applications of – or `binary_op` is exactly $N - 1$.

CHAPTER 21

Function Object and Function Adaptor Reference Guide

21.1 Requirements

21.1.1 Function Objects

A function object encapsulates a function in an object for use by other components. This is done by overloading the function call operator, `operator()`, of the corresponding class.

Passing a function object to an algorithm is similar to passing a pointer to a function, with one important difference. Function objects are classes that have `operator()` overloaded, which makes it possible to

- pass function objects to algorithms *at compile time*, and

- increase *efficiency*, by inlining the corresponding call.

These factors make a difference when the functions involved are very simple ones, such as integer additions or comparisons.

21.1.2 Function Adaptors

Function adaptors are STL classes that allow users to construct a wider variety of function objects. Using function adaptors is often easier than directly constructing a new function object type with a struct or class definition. There are three subcategories of function adaptors:

1. *Binders* are function adapters that convert binary function objects into unary function objects by binding an argument to some particular value.

2. *Negators* are function objects that reverse the sense of predicate function objects.

3. *Adaptors for pointers to functions* allow pointers to (unary and binary) functions to work with function adaptors the library provides.

21.2 *Arithmetic Operations*

21.2.1 Files

```
#include <function.h>
```

21.2.2 Defined Function Object Classes

STL provides basic function object classes for all of the arithmetic operators in the language. The functionality of the operators is described below.

```
template <class T> struct plus<T>
```

The `plus` function object accepts two operands of type `T` and returns their sum.

```
template <class T> struct minus<T>
```

The `minus` function object accepts two operands of type `T` and returns the result of subtracting the second operand from the first.

```
template <class T> struct times<T>
```

The `times` function object accepts two operands of type `T` and returns their product.

```
template <class T> struct divides<T>
```

The `divides` function object accepts two operands of type `T` and returns the result of dividing the first operand by the second.

```
template <class T> struct modulus<T>
```

The `modulus` function object accepts two operands, `x` and `y`, of type `T` and returns the result of the computation `x % y`.

```
template <class T> struct negate<T>
```

`negate` is a unary function object that accepts a single operand of type `T` and returns its negated value.

21.3 *Comparison Operations*

21.3.1 Files

```
#include <function.h>
```

21.3.2 Defined Function Object Classes

STL provides basic function object classes for all of the comparison operators in the language. The basic functionality of the comparison objects is described below.

```
template <class T> struct equal_to<T>
```

An object of this type accepts two parameters, x and y, of type T and returns true if x == y, false otherwise.

```
template <class T> struct not_equal_to<T>
```

An object of this type accepts two parameters, x and y, of type T and returns true if x != y, false otherwise.

```
template <class T> struct greater<T>
```

An object of this type accepts two parameters, x and y, of type T and returns true if x > y, false otherwise.

```
template <class T> struct less<T>
```

An object of this type accepts two parameters, x and y, of type T and returns true if x < y, false otherwise.

```
template <class T> struct greater_equal<T>
```

An object of this type accepts two parameters, x and y, of type T and returns true if x >= y, false otherwise.

```
template <class T> struct less_equal<T>
```

An object of this type accepts two parameters, x and y, of type T and returns true if x <= y, false otherwise.

21.4 Logical Operations

21.4.1 Files

```
#include <function.h>
```

21.4.2 Defined Function Object Classes

STL provides basic function object classes for the following logical operators in the language: and, or, not. The basic functionality of the logical operators is described below.

```
template <class T> struct logical_and<T>
```

An object of this type accepts two parameters, x and y, of type T and returns the boolean result of the logical "and" operation: x && y.

```
template <class T> struct logical_or<T>
```

An object of this type accepts two parameters, x and y, of type T and returns the boolean result of the logical "or" operation: x || y.

```
template <class T> struct logical_not<T>
```

An object of this type accepts a single parameter, x, of type T and returns the boolean result of the logical "not" operation: !x.

21.5 *Negator Adaptors*

Negators are function adaptors that take a predicate and return its complement. STL provides the negators not1 and not2, which take a unary and binary predicate respectively, and return their complements.

21.5.1 Files

```
#include <function.h>
```

21.5.2 Function Adaptors

```
template <class Predicate>
unary_negate<Predicate> not1(const predicate& x)
```

This function accepts a *unary* predicate x as input and returns its complement, !x.

```
template <class Predicate>
binary_negate<Predicate> not2(const predicate& x)
```

This function accepts a *binary* predicate x as input and returns its complement, !x.

21.6 *Binder Adaptors*

Binders are function adaptors that convert binary function objects into unary function objects by binding an argument to some particular value. STL provides two binders, bind1st and bind2nd, which are described below.

21.6.1 Files

```
#include <function.h>
```

21.6.2 Function Adaptors

```
template <class Operation, class T>
binder1st<Operation>
  bind1st(const Operation& op, const T& x)
```

> This adapter accepts a function object op of two arguments and a value x, of type T. It returns a function object of one argument, constructed out of op with the *first* argument bound to x.

```
template <class Operation, class T>
binder2nd<Operation>
  bind2nd(const Operation& op, const T& x)
```

> This adapter accepts a function object op of two arguments and a value x, of type T. It returns a function object of one argument, constructed out of op with the *second* argument bound to x .

21.7 Adaptors for Pointers to Functions

Adaptors for pointers to functions are provided to allow pointers to unary and binary functions to work with the function adaptors provided in the library. They also can help avoid the "code bloat" problem arising from multiple template instances in the same program (see Section 11.3 on page 187).

21.7.1 Files

```
#include <function.h>
```

21.7.2 Description

```
template <class Arg, class Result>
ptr_fun(Result (*x) (Arg))
```

> This function adapter accepts a pointer to a unary function that takes an argument of type Arg and returns a result of type Result. A function object of type pointer_to_unary_function<Arg, Result> is constructed out of this argument and then returned.

```
template <class Arg1, class Arg2, class Result>
ptr_fun(Result (*x) (Arg1, Arg2))
```

This function adapter accepts a pointer to a binary function that takes arguments of type `Arg1` and `Arg2` and returns a result of type `Result`. A function object of type `pointer_to_binary_function<Arg1, Arg2, Result>` is constructed out of this argument and then returned.

CHAPTER 22   *Allocator Reference Guide*

22.1 *Introduction*

Every STL container class uses an `Allocator` class to encapsulate information about the memory model the program is using.

Different memory models have different requirements for pointers, references, integer sizes, and so forth. The `Allocator` class encapsulates information about pointers, constant pointers, references, constant references, sizes of objects, difference types between pointers, allocation and deallocation functions, and some other functions. The exact set of types and functions defined within the allocator is explained in Section 22.2, *The Default Allocator Interface*, later in this chapter.

Since memory model information can be encapsulated in an allocator, STL containers can work with different memory models simply by providing different allocators. All allocator operations are expected to take amortized constant time.

22.1.1 Passing Allocators to STL Containers

Once an allocator class for a particular memory model has been written, it must be passed on to the STL container for that container to work properly in the concerned memory model. This is done by passing the allocator to the STL container as a template parameter.

For example, the `vector` container has the following interface:

```
template <class T, class Allocator = allocator>
class vector;
```

Here the `Allocator` parameter defaults to `allocator`. Since some compilers do not yet support default template parameters, STL versions for these compilers may supply `Allocator` by other means, such as with preprocessor commands.

22.1.2 Extracting Information from an Allocator Object

Once an allocator has been passed to a container, the container must somehow extract the memory model information from the `Allocator` class. This information is extracted simply by accessing the typedefs and member functions of the

`Allocator` class. For example, the public interface of the vector class mentioned above contains the following typedefs to extract information about references and pointers from the `Allocator` class:

```
typedef   typename Allocator::types<T>::reference
          reference;

typedef   typename Allocator::types<T>::const_reference
          const_reference;

typedef   typename Allocator::types<T>::pointer
          iterator;

typedef   typename Allocator::types<T>::const_pointer
          const_iterator;
```

22.2 *The Default Allocator Interface*

The interface of the default allocator is as follows:

```
class allocator {
 public:
   typedef size_t     size_type;
   typedef ptrdiff_t difference_type;

   template <class T>
   class types {
     typedef T*          pointer;
     typedef const T*   const_pointer;
     typedef T&          reference;
     typedef const T&   const_reference;
     typedef T           value_type;
   };

   allocator();
   ~allocator();

   template<class T>
     typename types<T>::pointer
         address(types<T>::reference x) const;
```

```
template<class T>
  typename types<T>::const_pointer
      address(types<T>::const_reference x) const;
template<class T, class U>
  typename types<T>::pointer
      allocate(size_type, types<U>::const_pointer hint);
template<class T>
  void deallocate(types<T>::pointer p);
      size_type max_size() const;
};

class allocator::types<void> {  // specialization
 public:
   typedef void* pointer;
   typedef const void* const_pointer;
   typedef void  value_type;
};

void* operator new(size_t N, allocator& a);
};
```

In the allocator interface it can be seen that the type information is encapsulated in the nested template class `types`.

22.2.1   Nested Template Class Types

The nested template class `types` has the following members, which are all dependent on its template argument, T:

```
typedef T* pointer
```

The type of a pointer in the memory model.

```
typedef const T* const_pointer
```

The type of a constant pointer in the memory model.

```
typedef T& reference
```

The type of a reference in the memory model.

```
typedef const T& const_reference
```

The type of a constant reference in the memory model.

```
typedef T value_type
```

`value_type` refers to the type of the objects in the container. By default, containers contain objects of the type with which they are instantiated. For example, `vector<int *>` is a declaration of a vector of pointers to integers.

22.2.2 Other Members of Class `allocator`

The class `allocator` has the following other members:

```
typedef size_t size_type
```

`size_type` is the type that can represent the size of the largest object in the memory model.

```
typedef ptrdiff_t difference_type
```

This is the type that can represent the difference between any two pointers in the memory model.

```
allocator()
```

Constructs an allocator object.

```
~allocator()
```

Destroys an allocator object.

```
template <class T>
  typename types<T>::pointer
    address(types<T>::reference x)
```

Returns a pointer to the referenced object x.

```
template <class T>
  typename types<T>::const_pointer
    const_address(types<T>::const_reference x)
```

Returns a constant pointer to the referenced object x.

```
template <class T, class U>
  typename types<T>::pointer
    allocate(size_type n, types<U>::const_pointer hint)
```

This member function allocates memory for n objects of type `size_type` but the objects are not constructed. It uses the global `new` operator. Note that different memory models require different `allocate` functions (which is why the function has been encapsulated in the memory allocator class). `allocate` may raise an appropriate exception. The pointer `hint` can be used as an aid for locality of reference. In a container member function, the self-reference pointer `this` is usually a good choice to use for `hint`. Since the function is a template member, it can be specialized for particular types in custom allocators.

```
template <class T>
  void deallocate(types<T>::pointer p)
```

Deallocates all of the storage pointed to by the pointer p using the global `delete` operator. All objects in the area pointed to by p should be destroyed before the call of `deallocate`. Since the function is a template member, it can be specialized for particular types in custom allocators.

```
size_type max_size()
```

Returns the largest positive value of `difference_type`. This is the same as the largest number of elements that the container can hold in the given memory model.

22.3 *Custom Allocators*

In this section we look at customized allocators. A common case of allocators occurs in the use of different memory models in DOS/Windows systems, where we have *far* pointers as well as *huge* pointers. In this case the data types representing pointers (`size_type`) as well as the difference between two pointers (`difference_type`) differ across memory models. Thus, we could have two different kinds of allocators, which can be used with the large and huge memory models on DOS/Windows systems:

- `far_allocator`, for use with the large memory model. This allocator allows the user to work with 32-bit far pointers, with a 16-bit segment address and a 16-bit segment offset.

- `huge_allocator`, for use with the huge memory model. This also uses far pointers.

Thus, we could have vectors of varying sizes using one of these allocators depending on the memory model used.

```
vector<int> vec_default(100);
// A vector of 100 integers using the default allocator.

vector<int, far_allocator> vec_large(1000);
// A vector of 1,000 integers using the large memory model.
```

```
vector<int, huge_allocator> vec_huge(100000);
// A vector of 100,000 integers using the huge allocator.
```

Code for the far allocator follows. In this case, since the addressable range is 64 K, the `size_type` is a 32-bit value and `difference_type` is a 16-bit value.

```
class far_allocator {
public:
    typedef unsigned long    size_type;
    typedef ptrdiff_t difference_type;

    template <class T>
    class types {
     public:
        typedef T value_type;
        typedef T __far * pointer;
        typedef const T __far * const_pointer;
        typedef T __far & reference;
        typedef const T __far & const_reference;
    };

    allocator();
    ~allocator();

    template<class T>
     typename types<T>::pointer
      address(types<T>::reference x) const;

    template<class T>
     typename types<T>::const_pointer
      address(types<T>::const_reference x) const;

    template<class T, class U>
     typename types<T>::pointer
      allocate(size_type, types<U>::const_pointer hint);

    template<class T>
     void deallocate(types<T>::pointer p);

    size_type max_size() const;
};
```

```
class far_allocator<void> {
 public:
  typedef void __far * pointer;
  typedef const void __far * const_pointer;
  typedef void value_type;
};
```

Non-STL Include Files Used in Example Programs

A.1 *File Used in "Anagram Finding" Examples in Chapters 13 and 14*

The file ps.h defines a class PS and two binary predicate objects firstLess and firstEqual, used in the anagram finding example programs discussed in Chapters 13 and 14. See Section 13.2 (on page 203) and Section 13.3 (on page 203) for explanations of these definitions.

ps.h.
```
struct PS : pair<vector<char>, string> {
  PS() : pair<vector<char>,string>(vector<char>(), string())
    { }

  PS(const string& s) : pair<vector<char>, string>(s, s) {
    sort(first.begin(), first.end());
  }

  operator string() const { return second; }
};


struct FirstLess : binary_function<PS, PS, bool> {
  bool operator()(const PS& p, const PS& q) const
  {
    return p.first < q.first;
  }
} firstLess;


struct FirstEqual : binary_function<PS, PS, bool> {
  bool operator()(const PS& p, const PS& q) const
  {
```

```
        return p.first == q.first;
    }
} firstEqual;
```

A.2 Files Used in "Shape Example" in Chapter 17

These files are replicated directly from Section 6.4 of Stroustrup (Ref. 14).

screen.h.
```cpp
const int XMAX=40;
const int YMAX=24;
struct point {
    int x,y;
    point() {}
    point(int a, int b) { x=a; y=b; }
};
extern void put_point(int a, int b);
inline void put_point(point p) { put_point(p.x, p.y); }
extern void put_line(int, int, int, int);
inline void put_line(point a, point b)
    { put_line(a.x, a.y, b.x, b.y); }
extern void screen_init();
extern void screen_destroy();
extern void screen_refresh();
extern void screen_clear();
```

screen.cpp.
```cpp
#include "screen.h"
#include <iostream.h>
enum color { black='*', white=' ' };
char screen[XMAX][YMAX];
void screen_init()
{
    for (int y=0; y<YMAX; y++)
        for (int x=0; x<XMAX; x++)
            screen[x][y] = white;
}
void screen_destroy() {}
inline int on_screen(int a, int b)    // clipping
{
    return 0<=a && a<XMAX && 0<=b && b<YMAX;
}
```

```
void put_point(int a, int b)
{
    if (on_screen(a, b)) screen[a][b] = black;
}
void put_line(int x0, int y0, int x1, int y1)
/*
   Plot the line (x0, y0) to (x1, y1).
   The line being plotted is b(x-x0) +a(y-y0) = 0.
   Minimize abs(eps) where eps = 2*(b(x-x0) + a(y-y0).
   See Newman and Sproull:
   ``Principles of Interactive Computer Graphics''
   McGraw-Hill, New York, 1979, pp. 33-44.
*/
{
    register int dx = 1;
    int a = x1 - x0;
    if (a < 0) dx = -1, a = -a;
    register int dy = 1;
    int b = y1 - y0;
    if (b < 0) dy = -1, b = -b;
    int two_a = 2*a;
    int two_b = 2*b;
    int xcrit = -b + two_a;
    register int eps = 0;
    for(;;) {
        put_point(x0,y0);
        if (x0==x1 && y0 == y1) break;
        if (eps <= xcrit) x0 += dx, eps += two_b;
        if (eps>=a || a<=b) y0 += dy, eps -= two_a;
    }
}

void screen_clear() { screen_init(); }

void screen_refresh()
{
    for (int y=YMAX-1; 0<=y; y--) {       // top to bottom
        for (int x=0; x<XMAX; x++)            // left to right
            cout << screen[x][y];
        cout << '\n';
    }
}
```

shape.h.
```
#include "screen.cpp"

inline int max(int a, int b) { return a<b ? b : a; }
inline int min(int a, int b) { return a<b ? a : b; }

struct shape {
  static shape* list;
  shape* next;
  shape() { next = list; list = this; }

  virtual point north() const = 0;
  virtual point south() const = 0;
  virtual point east() const = 0;
  virtual point west() const = 0;
  virtual point neast() const = 0;
  virtual point seast() const = 0;
  virtual point nwest() const = 0;
  virtual point swest() const = 0;
  virtual void draw() = 0;
  virtual void move(int, int) = 0;
};

class line : public shape {
/*
    The line from "w" to "e".
    north() is defined as ``above the center,
    as far north as the northernmost point.''
*/
  point w, e;
 public:
  point north() const
    { return point((w.x+e.x)/2, max(e.y,w.y)); }
  point south() const
    { return point((w.x+e.x)/2, min(e.y,w.y)); }
  point east() const
    { return point(max(e.x, w.x), (w.y+e.y)/2); }
  point west() const
    { return point(min(e.x, w.x), (w.y+e.y)/2); }
  point neast() const
    { return point(max(e.x, w.x), max(e.y, w.y)); }
  point seast() const
    { return point(max(e.x, w.x), min(e.y, w.y)); }
```

```
   point nwest() const
      { return point(min(e.x, w.x), max(e.y, w.y)); }
   point swest() const
      { return point(min(e.x, w.x), min(e.y, w.y)); }
   void move(int a, int b)
      { w.x += a; w.y += b; e.x += a; e.y += b; }
   void draw() { put_line(w,e); }
   line(point a, point b) { w = a; e = b; }
   line(point a, int len)
      { w = point(a.x + len - 1, a.y); e = a; }
};

class rectangle : public shape {
/*
   nw ---- n ---- ne
   |              |
   w       c      e
   |              |
   sw ---- s ---- se
*/
    point sw, ne;
 public:
  point north() const
     { return point((sw.x+ne.x)/2, ne.y); }
  point south() const
     { return point((sw.x+ne.x)/2, sw.y); }
  point east() const
     { return point(ne.x, (ne.y+sw.y)/2); }
  point west() const
     { return point(sw.x, (ne.y+sw.y)/2); }
  point neast() const { return ne; }
  point seast() const { return point(ne.x, sw.y); }
  point nwest() const { return point(sw.x, ne.y); }
  point swest() const { return sw; }
  void move(int a, int b)
     { sw.x += a; sw.y += b; ne.x += a; ne.y += b; }
  void draw();
  rectangle(point, point);
};

void shape_refresh();        // draw all shapes
void stack(shape* p, const shape* q); // put p on top of q
```

shape.cpp.

```cpp
#include "shape.h"

rectangle::rectangle(point a, point b)
{
    if (a.x <= b.x) {
        if (a.y <= b.y) {
            sw = a;
            ne = b;
        }
        else {
            sw = point(a.x, b.y);
            ne = point(b.x, a.y);
        }
    }
    else {
        if (a.y <= b.y) {
            sw = point(b.x, a.y);
            ne = point(a.x, b.y);
        }
        else {
            sw = b;
            ne = a;
        }
    }
}

void rectangle::draw()
{
    point nw(sw.x, ne.y);
    point se(ne.x, sw.y);
    put_line(nw,ne);
    put_line(ne,se);
    put_line(se,sw);
    put_line(sw,nw);
}

void shape_refresh()
{
    screen_clear();
    for (shape* p = shape::list; p; p=p->next) p->draw();
    screen_refresh();
}
```

```
void stack(shape* p, const shape* q)   // put p on top of q
{
    point n = q->north();
    point s = p->south();
    p->move(n.x-s.x, n.y-s.y+1);
}

shape* shape::list = 0;
```

APPENDIX B   *STL Resources*

B.1 *Internet Addresses for*
HP Reference Implementation of STL

At the time of publication, the Hewlett-Packard Reference Implementation of STL was available on the Internet via anonymous FTP at the following sites

> *butler.hpl.hp.com/stl*   (Hewlett Packard)
> *ftp.cs.rpi.edu/pub/stl*   (Rensselaer Polytechnic Institute)

The version at the HP site is the final version released by HP, dated October 31, 1995. The version at the RPI site is a minor modification of the final HP release that makes it compatible with several compilers. It also corrects a few bugs. See the Section B.3 and the README file at the RPI site for further information.

B.2 *World Wide Web Address for*
Source Code for Examples in this Book

Files and information related to this book are available at Addison-Wesley's World Wide Web Site on the Internet, at

> *http://www.aw.com/cp/musser-saini.html*

The files available at this site include

- Source files for all example programs in this book.

- The dictionary file used as input to the example programs in Part II.

- bstring.h, the source file for the string class used with many of the example programs (donated by Modena Software Inc.). This class satisfies most of the requirements for the string class specified by the ANSI/ISO Draft Standard for C++, but it is not completely up to date with more recent changes in the Draft Standard.

B.3 STL-Compatible Compilers

The book's examples, bstring.h, and STL source code (the modified version available at the RPI site, see Section B.1), have all been tested successfully with the following compilers:

Apogee, version 3.0 (SUN Unix),
Borland C++, version 4.5 (DOS/Windows),
IBM xlC (AIX),
IBM CSet++ (OS/2),
Microsoft Visual C++, version 4.0 (DOS/Windows).

The examples and bstring.h have also been tested with the Free Software Foundation's compiler,

GNU C++, version 2.7.2,

which is available on many platforms and comes with its own adaptation of HP STL. All of the example programs compile and execute properly with this version except Examples 5-9, 6-9, 13-1, 14-1, and 16-1. For information on obtaining this free compiler, see

http://www.gnu.ai.mit.edu

Other compilers that have been reported to be able to compile STL include DEC C++ 5.0, EDG C++ front-end 2.29 (several compilers based on it), IBM VisualAge C++ 3.0, Kuck and Associates' Photon C++, Metrowerk's Codewarrior 7, Rational Apex C/C++ 2.0.6 , SGI C++ 4.0, Sun C++ 4.1, Symantec C++ 7.2, Watcom C++ 10.5. For further information on STL-compatibility of these and other compilers, see Warren Young's Web site at

http://www.cyberport.com/~tangent/programming/stlres.html

B.4 *Other Related STL and C++ Documents*

ANSI/ISO C++ Draft Standard
> *ftp://research.att.com/dist/c++std/WP/*

B.5 *Generic Programming and STL Discussion List*

To join an on-going technical discussion of generic programming and STL, send e-mail to:

> *genstl-request@graphics.stanford.edu*

Specify `subscribe` in the subject and the body of your message. An archive of the traffic on this mailing list is available at

> *ftp://ftp-graphics.stanford.edu/pub/genstl-archive/*

References

1. Accredited Standards Committee X3 (American National Standards Institute), Information Processing Systems, *Working Paper for Draft Proposed International Standard for Information Systems—Programming Language C++*. Doc No. X3J16/95-0185, WG21/N0785.

2. M. Ellis and B. Stroustrup, *The Annotated C++ Reference Manual*, Addison-Wesley, Reading, MA, 1990.

3. M. Jazayeri, "Component Programming—A Fresh Look at Software Components," *Proc. 5th European Software Engineering Conference*, Sitges, Spain, September 25–28, 1995.

4. D. Kapur, D. R. Musser, and A. A. Stepanov, "Operators and Algebraic Structures," *Proc. of Conference on Functional Programming Languages and Computer Architecture*, Portsmouth, NH, October 1981.

5. D. Kapur, D. R. Musser, and A. A. Stepanov, "Tecton, a Language for Manipulating Generic Objects," *Proc. of Workshop on Program Specification*, Aarhus, Denmark, August 1981, *Lecture Notes in Computer Science*, Springer-Verlag, New York, Vol. 134, 1982.

6. D. McIlroy, "Mass-Produced Software Components," Petrocelli/Charter, 1976.

7. D. R. Musser and A. A. Stepanov, "Generic Programming," *ISSAC '88 Symbolic and Algebraic Computation Proceedings*, P. Gianni, ed., *Lecture Notes in Computer Science*, Springer-Verlag, New York, Vol. 358.

8. D. R. Musser and A. A. Stepanov, *The Ada Generic Library: Linear List Processing Packages*, Springer-Verlag, New York, 1989.

9. D. R. Musser and A. A. Stepanov, "Algorithm-Oriented Generic Libraries," *Software Practice and Experience*, Vol. 24(7), July 1994.

10. P. J. Plauger, A. A. Stepanov, M. Lee, and D. R. Musser, *STL Libraries*, Prentice-Hall, Englewood Ciffs, NJ, to appear.

11. F. S. Roberts, *Measurement Theory*, Gian-Carlo Rota, ed., *Encyclopedia of Mathematics and Its Applications*, Vol. 7, Addison-Wesley, Reading, MA, 1979.

12. A. A. Stepanov and M. Lee, *The Standard Template Library*, Technical Report HPL-94-34, April 1994, revised July 7, 1995.

13. B. Stroustrup, "Making a `vector` Fit for a Standard," *The C++ Report*, October 1994.

14. B. Stroustrup, *The C++ Programming Language*, Second Edition, Addison-Wesley, Reading, MA, 1991.

15. B. Stroustrup, *The Design and Evolution of C++*, Addison-Wesley, Reading, MA, 1994.

Index

A

W